Lecture Notes
in Business Information Processing

525

Series Editors

Wil van der Aalst, *RWTH Aachen University, Aachen, Germany*
Sudha Ram, *University of Arizona, Tucson, AZ, USA*
Michael Rosemann, *Queensland University of Technology, Brisbane, QLD, Australia*
Clemens Szyperski, *Microsoft Research, Redmond, WA, USA*
Giancarlo Guizzardi, *University of Twente, Enschede, The Netherlands*

LNBIP reports state-of-the-art results in areas related to business information systems and industrial application software development – timely, at a high level, and in both printed and electronic form.

The type of material published includes

- Proceedings (published in time for the respective event)
- Postproceedings (consisting of thoroughly revised and/or extended final papers)
- Other edited monographs (such as, for example, project reports or invited volumes)
- Tutorials (coherently integrated collections of lectures given at advanced courses, seminars, schools, etc.)
- Award-winning or exceptional theses

LNBIP is abstracted/indexed in DBLP, EI and Scopus. LNBIP volumes are also submitted for the inclusion in ISI Proceedings.

Abhishek Kathuria · Prasanna P. Karhade ·
Bin Zhu · Ria Sonpatki
Editors

Generative AI in e-Business

22nd Workshop on e-Business, WeB 2023
Hyderabad, India, December 9, 2023
Revised Selected Papers

 Springer

Editors
Abhishek Kathuria ⓘD
Indian School of Business
Hyderabad, Telangana, India

Prasanna P. Karhade ⓘD
The Chinese University of Hong Kong
Shatin, Hong Kong

Bin Zhu
Oregon State University
Corvallis, OR, USA

Ria Sonpatki ⓘD
Indian School of Business
Hyderabad, Telangana, India

ISSN 1865-1348   ISSN 1865-1356 (electronic)
Lecture Notes in Business Information Processing
ISBN 978-3-031-74436-5   ISBN 978-3-031-74437-2 (eBook)
https://doi.org/10.1007/978-3-031-74437-2

© The Editor(s) (if applicable) and The Author(s), under exclusive license
to Springer Nature Switzerland AG 2025

This work is subject to copyright. All rights are solely and exclusively licensed by the Publisher, whether
the whole or part of the material is concerned, specifically the rights of translation, reprinting, reuse of
illustrations, recitation, broadcasting, reproduction on microfilms or in any other physical way, and transmission
or information storage and retrieval, electronic adaptation, computer software, or by similar or dissimilar
methodology now known or hereafter developed.
The use of general descriptive names, registered names, trademarks, service marks, etc. in this publication
does not imply, even in the absence of a specific statement, that such names are exempt from the relevant
protective laws and regulations and therefore free for general use.
The publisher, the authors and the editors are safe to assume that the advice and information in this book
are believed to be true and accurate at the date of publication. Neither the publisher nor the authors or the
editors give a warranty, expressed or implied, with respect to the material contained herein or for any errors
or omissions that may have been made. The publisher remains neutral with regard to jurisdictional claims in
published maps and institutional affiliations.

This Springer imprint is published by the registered company Springer Nature Switzerland AG
The registered company address is: Gewerbestrasse 11, 6330 Cham, Switzerland

If disposing of this product, please recycle the paper.

Preface

The Workshop on e-Business (WeB) is a premier annual conference on electronic business. The purpose of WeB is to provide an open forum for e-Business researchers and practitioners worldwide to share topical research findings, explore novel ideas, discuss success stories and lessons learned, map out major challenges, and collectively chart future directions for e-Business. Since 2000, WeB has attracted valuable, novel research that addresses both the technical and organizational aspects of e-business. The 22nd Annual Workshop on e-Business (WeB 2023) was held in a hybrid format, partially virtually and partially at the Novotel Hyderabad Convention Centre, Hyderabad, India, on December 9, 2023. This book constitutes revised selected papers from this conference.

The WeB 2023 theme was "Generative AI in e-Business." Generative AI, with its ability to create new content, automate tasks, and personalize experiences, presents unprecedented opportunities for businesses navigating the evolving digital world. It is a technology poised to redefine the digital landscape. The past decade has witnessed a dramatic shift towards digital and e-business solutions, accelerated by the COVID-19 pandemic. As we emerge from these global disruptions, businesses must harness the power of generative AI to thrive in this new reality. This technology can revolutionize e-commerce by generating personalized product recommendations, creating engaging marketing content, and even automating customer service interactions. Beyond customer-facing applications, generative AI can optimize supply chains, personalize learning experiences, and even drive innovation in product development. However, with this immense potential come critical considerations around ethics, bias, and responsible implementation. WeB 2023 explored both the transformative potential and the challenges of integrating generative AI into e-business models, paving the way for a future where AI empowers businesses and enriches lives.

WeB 2023 allowed academic scholars and practitioners worldwide to exchange ideas and share research findings that explored the issues, opportunities, and solutions related to e-business, digital transformation, and advancements in the age of AI. The articles presented at the workshop covered a broad range of issues from multiple perspectives. They employed various business research methods such as surveys, analytical modeling, experiments, computational models, data science, and design science.

The thirteen edited papers included in this LNBIP volume underwent a double-blind review process with an average of two reviewers and were carefully selected from more than 50 submissions. We are grateful to the reviewers and editors for providing insightful feedback and to the authors for their contributions.

August 2024

Abhishek Kathuria
Prasanna P. Karhade
Bin Zhu
Ria Sonpatki

Organization

Honorary Chairs

Hsinchun Chen	University of Arizona, USA
Michael J. Shaw	University of Illinois at Urbana-Champaign, USA
Andrew B. Whinston	University of Texas at Austin, USA
Benn R. Konsynski	Emory University, USA

Conference Co-chairs

Sam Seongmin Jeon	Gachon University, South Korea
Prasanna Karhade	Chinese University of Hong Kong, China
Abhishek Kathuria	Indian School of Business, India
Jooho Kim	City University of New York, USA
Bin Zhu	Oregon State University, USA

Advisory Committee

Kenny Cheng	University of Florida, USA
Ming Fan	University of Washington, USA
Karl Lang	City University of New York, USA
Jennifer Xu	Bentley University, USA
Han Zhang	Georgia Institute of Technology, USA
Bin Zhu	Oregon State University, USA

Program Committee

Arthur Goncalves De Carvalho	Miami University, USA
Hsin-Lu Chang	National Chengchi University, Taiwan
Xiaohui Chang	Oregon State University, USA
Michael Chau	University of Hong Kong, China
Cheng Chen	University of Illinois at Chicago, USA
Ching-Chin Chern	National Taiwan University, Taiwan
Su Dong	Elon University, USA
Aidan Duane	South East Technological University, Ireland

Giang Hoang   National University of Singapore, Singapore
Yuheng Hu   University of Illinois at Chicago, USA
Seongmin Jeon   Gachon University, South Korea
Chunghan Kang   Georgia Institute of Technology, USA
Timothy Kaskela   Oregon State University, USA
Sarah Khan   North Carolina State University, USA
Kelvin King   Syracuse University, USA
Anthony Lee   National Taiwan University, Taiwan
Sam Lee   Texas State University, USA
Chenwei Li   University of Hong Kong, China
Hongxiu Li   Tampere University, Finland
Shengli Li   Peking University, China
Xitong Li   HEC Paris, France
Jifeng Luo   Shanghai Jiaotong University, China
Xin Luo   University of New Mexico, USA
Selwyn Piramuthu   University of Florida, USA
Liangfei Qiu   University of Florida, USA
Yufei Shen   HEC Paris, France
Vijayan Sugumaran   Oakland University, USA
Kai Wang   National University of Kaohsiung, Taiwan
Jason Xiong   Appalachian State University, USA
Ling Xue   Georgia State University, USA
Dezhi Yin   University of South Florida, USA
Adeel Zaffar   Lahore University of Mgt. Sciences, Pakistan
Peiqin Zhang   Texas State University, USA
Wei Zhou   ESCP Europe, France
Wenqi Zhou   Duquesne University, USA

Contents

Is Software Customization an Impediment or Enabler for Digital Transformation in the Era of Large Language Models

Govindarajan Narayanan[✉], Rahul Kharat, and Abhishek Kathuria

Indian School of Business, Hyderabad, India
{govind_n,rahul_kharat,abhishek_kathuria}@isb.edu

Abstract. This research-in-progress paper investigates the impact of Large Language Models (LLMs) on Digital Transformation (DT) across various industries, highlighting a paradigm shift in software customization and integration. Utilizing a mixed-methods approach, the study combines qualitative case studies and Qualitative Comparative Analysis (QCA) to explore the transformative effects of LLMs in business environments. Key findings reveal that LLMs significantly enhance customization capabilities, streamline data integration, and promote agile decision-making processes. This transition marks a critical evolution in DT strategies, offering new opportunities for operational efficiency and competitive advantage. The paper contributes vital insights to both academic discourse in technology management and practical business strategy, emphasizing the increasingly central role of LLMs in the digital-first business landscape.

Keywords: Digital Transformation · Large Language Models · Software Customization · Mixed-Methods Research Design · Qualitative Case Studies · Qualitative Comparative Analysis · Research in Progress

1 Introduction

Digital Transformation (DT) has become an essential aspect of the modern business landscape, signifying a profound shift in how organizations operate, compete, and deliver value to customers. This transformation transcends mere technological integration. It involves reimagining an organization's core functions and customer interactions through digital technology [1, 2]. Digital Transformation is not just about adopting new technologies but about reinventing the organizational DNA to flourish in the digital age. In a comprehensive study by Deloitte [3], which analyzed over 4,650 financial disclosures from global organizations, the critical role of aligning strategy with execution in digital transformation efforts was underscored. Deloitte's research suggests that effectively coordinated digital transformation strategies can unlock up to US$1.25 trillion in new value. However, improperly executed strategies carry substantial risks, potentially leading to a value erosion of more than US$1.5 trillion. This analysis reveals that achieving successful digital transformation extends beyond mere ambition and substantial investments. It requires strategically integrating these initiatives with the organization's overall business objectives [3].

© The Author(s), under exclusive license to Springer Nature Switzerland AG 2025
A. Kathuria et al. (Eds.): WeB 2023, LNBIP 525, pp. 1–14, 2025.
https://doi.org/10.1007/978-3-031-74437-2_1

Research indicates that transformation success rates are generally low, with only about 30% succeeding. Specifically, digital transformations are even more challenging, and only 16% of them achieve long-term performance improvements, with success rates varying significantly by industry and company size. Notably, industries such as high-tech report success rates of up to 26%, whereas traditional sectors like oil and gas show success rates as low as 4% [4]. Furthermore, smaller organizations (fewer than 100 employees) are 2.7 times more likely to experience successful digital transformations than larger organizations with over 50,000 employees [4]. These disparities underscore the complexities of implementing digital transformations across different organizational scales and sectors.

Historically, software customization was a focal point in technology adaptation. This approach aimed to mold technology to meet specific organizational needs and simplify processes. Customization was seen as a means to empower organizations, tailoring functionalities to streamline operations most effectively. This was especially true with software products, where the primary motivation for customization often stemmed from user familiarity and preferences.

In the era preceding large language models (LLMs), customization in software like Enterprise Resource Planning (ERP) systems was the norm. ERP providers typically collaborate with implementation partners to fulfill these custom requirements. Past experiences and comfort levels of users drove much of this customization. According to [5], offering robust, accessible, and cost-effective customization options is a strategic advantage for SaaS vendors, especially for attracting customers in niche markets.

Academic research has delved deeply into ERP customization. Rothenberger and Srite [6] in 2009 provided a comprehensive analysis, identifying key factors influencing customization levels and organizing existing knowledge into a coherent framework. Uppström, Lönn [7] 2015 highlighted the evolution of customization in cloud ERP systems, advocating for new customization options and comparative analysis with traditional models.

Despite its benefits, customization has challenges, such as cost overruns, implementation hurdles, and sometimes ineffectual outcomes. Parthasarathy and Sharma [8] 2017 found that modifications in ERP systems' modules do not significantly impact quality, but alterations to the database and source code do. This insight is crucial for companies utilizing customized ERP systems.

However, machine learning and natural language processing have revolutionized this paradigm. Modern LLMs like GPT-3 or GPT-4 offer advanced customization capabilities, allowing users to tailor models to specific industries, jargon, or conversational styles. This shift has transformed customization from a barrier to an enabler, opening new avenues for application across various sectors.

The evolution of LLMs exemplifies this transition, where customization has shifted from being a constraint to a facilitator. This change is particularly significant as LLMs become more integrated into various industries. Initially, limited customization options in LLMs restricted their effectiveness in specific domains. However, technological advancements and methodological innovations have now made customization a key feature, enhancing the adaptability and utility of these models. This reflects a more significant trend in AI development, where user-centric design and flexibility are increasingly vital.

In summary, Digital Transformation in the contemporary business world is more than just adopting new technologies. It represents a holistic shift in how businesses operate, engage with customers, and make decisions. The role of customization, especially in the context of LLMs, has evolved significantly, highlighting the transformative impact of AI and natural language processing in enhancing business processes and decision-making [9].

2 Research Objectives

The primary objective of this research is to examine the evolving role of Digital Transformation (DT) in modern businesses, with a particular focus on the impact of Large Language Models (LLMs) in transforming software customization practices. The study aims to:

1. Understand the Transformational Role of DT: Investigate how DT, primarily through the integration of LLMs, is redefining business operations, customer engagement, and decision-making processes.
2. Explore the Shift in Customization Paradigms: Assess the transition from traditional software customization to the advanced customization capabilities LLMs offer.
3. Evaluate the Business Implications: Analyze the practical implications of LLMs in various business sectors in digital transformation.

3 Research Design

3.1 Conceptual Framework

The study is framed within a comprehensive, mixed-methods research design, intricately combining qualitative case studies with a methodical Qualitative Comparative Analysis (QCA). This design is deliberately chosen to delve deeply into the multifaceted nature of digital transformation, particularly in the context of the burgeoning influence of Large Language Models (LLMs) on business operations and strategy.

The qualitative aspect of the research design is rooted in a series of meticulously chosen case studies. These cases are selected to represent a diverse spectrum of industries, including manufacturing, IT consultancy, banking, policy management, and financial training. The richness of these cases provides a fertile ground for exploring the application, challenges, and implications of digital transformation and LLM integration in different business contexts.

QCA, a methodological innovation in comparative research, forms the backbone of the analytical approach [10]. By employing QCA, this research aims to systematically compare different instances of digital transformation, identifying patterns and conditions that lead to successful outcomes. Through the lens of chosen case studies, this analysis will specifically focus on key factors, such as the degree of customization required and the complexity of data integration concerning requirements across different functions and industries.

3.2 Methodological Approach

The QCA component of the study involves a detailed, evidence-based coding process. This process is critical for ensuring the robustness and credibility of the comparative analysis. Each case is assessed based on binary codings (1 for high/present, 0 for low/absent) across key conditions and outcomes. This approach, grounded in empirical evidence, provides a nuanced understanding of the complex dynamics influencing digital transformation initiatives.

The study utilizes a truth table, a key tool in QCA, to record the presence or absence of each condition across the cases and the corresponding outcomes. This method is instrumental in identifying causal configurations and understanding the intricate interplay of various factors in digital transformation success [10, 11].

The analysis distinguishes between necessary and sufficient conditions for successful digital transformation. This distinction is vital to understanding which factors must be present for success and which can guarantee success. The ERP, CRM, and AML cases from the traditional and LLM-driven paradigms offer rich insights into these dynamics.

The research design aims to contribute theoretically to the fields of digital transformation and business strategy. By integrating LLMs' advanced capabilities into the traditional digital transformation narrative, the study seeks to redefine the understanding of customization, integration, and operational efficiency in business processes.

The expected outcome of this research is a comprehensive, empirically grounded understanding of how digital transformation, especially in the context of LLMs, is redefining business strategy and operations. The study aims to offer actionable insights for businesses and contribute to academic discourse on digital transformation and technology management.

4 Case Studies

4.1 Case 1: ERP System at an Industrial Equipment Manufacturer

At an industrial equipment manufacturer, the ERP system's integration with custom workflows presented significant challenges. While managing the production of their best-selling heat exchanger, the need for a customized Bill of Materials (BOM) and ad hoc reporting processes led to bottlenecks and inefficiencies. The case highlights the complexities of aligning standard ERP processes with custom requirements across different departments. For detailed comparative aspects, refer to the Cross-Case Analysis Tables 1 and 2.

4.2 Case 2: CRM at an IT Consultancy

In the IT consultancy firm, the standard CRM platform needed to be revised to cater to the diverse needs of various client profiles. The firm had to create custom dashboards to accommodate different sales cycles and client industries, leading to inefficiencies in sales tracking and client relationship management. This case underscores the challenges in balancing standardized CRM functionalities with the need for customization to address client diversity. For further insights, see the Cross-Case Analysis Tables 1 and 2.

4.3 Case 3: Digital Operations in Banking Risk Management

The banking institution's anti-money laundering (AML) system struggled with a high rate of false positives in transaction monitoring. This necessitated a labor-intensive manual review process and complex data integration from various databases. The case illustrates the inefficiencies in fraud detection processes and the implications of fragmented data analysis. Additional details are available in the Cross-Case Analysis Tables 1 and 2.

4.4 Case 4: Streamlining Policy Management via an In-House Language Model

This case demonstrates a revolutionary shift in handling complex policy management through an in-house LLM. The LLM's advanced capabilities eliminated the traditional customization challenges, enabling seamless integration of policies with diverse data sources. This was pivotal in providing stakeholders with clear, actionable insights while maintaining strict data privacy and operational efficiency.

Table 1. Cross Case Analysis (a)

Aspect	ERP at Industrial Equipment Manufacturer	CRM at IT Consultancy	Digital Operations in Banking (AML Workflow)	Streamlining Policy Management via an In-House LLM	Hybrid LLM Deployment in Financial Company
Industry	Manufacturing	IT Consultancy	Banking	Varied Industries (Policy Management)	Financial Services
System Used	ERP (Enterprise Resource Planning)	CRM (Customer Relationship Management)	AML (Anti-Money Laundering) Detection Systems	In-House Language Learning Model (LLM)	Hybrid (In-House and SaaS-based) LLMs
Primary Challenge	Integration of custom workflows with standard ERP processes	Balancing standard CRM functions with custom requirements for diverse client profiles	Managing high false positives in fraud detection and integrating data from multiple databases	Simplifying complex policy clauses and ensuring operational efficiency in policy management	Balancing proprietary knowledge security with the need for expansive domain-specific training content
Customization Need	Custom BOM (Bill of Materials) for different departments; ad-hoc reporting	Custom dashboards for different sales stages, client industries, and geographical regions	Custom data extraction and analysis methods for different types of transactions and customer profiles	Tailoring the LLM to specific policy language and structure, integrating with various data sources	Customization of in-house LLM for company-specific training; leveraging SaaS-based LLM for broader financial knowledge
Impact on Workflow	Complex inter-departmental coordination leading to bottlenecks	Inefficient sales tracking due to varying client requirements and operational costs	Time-consuming manual review process due to high false positives and diverse data sources	Streamlined policy understanding and decision-making; reduced need for complex policy language interpretation	Efficient creation and management of training materials; seamless integration of internal and external content

Table 2. Cross Case Analysis (b)

Aspect	ERP at Industrial Equipment Manufacturer	CRM at IT Consultancy	Digital Operations in Banking (AML Workflow)	Streamlining Policy Management via an In-House LLM	Hybrid LLM Deployment in Financial Company
Data Handling	Separate viewing and processing requirements for engineering and planning departments	Different sales and operational metrics for varying customer accounts	Integration of customer, transaction, and product data for accurate fraud detection	Merging policy data with other datasets for comprehensive insights; maintaining data privacy	Secure handling of sensitive internal data; accessing external data for domain-specific training
Reporting and Insights	Difficulty in obtaining comprehensive insights due to non-standard, ad-hoc reporting	Challenges in gaining accurate sales insights due to multiple custom dashboards	Inefficiencies in generating accurate suspicious activity reports (SAR) due to fragmented data analysis	Enhanced decision-making through integrated business intelligence; standardized policy documentation	Comprehensive training coverage, incorporating a wide spectrum of financial topics without data security compromise
Cross-Functional Impact	Inefficiencies in order processing and production logistics	Inconsistencies in sales management and client relationship tracking	Operational delays in fraud detection and regulatory compliance	Improved policy clarity and accessibility for business stakeholders; consistent documentation across the organization	Enhanced training materials, balancing in-depth proprietary knowledge with external information for employee education
Potential Improvement	Streamlining ERP workflows with standardized yet flexible BOM structures and reporting systems	Developing a more adaptive CRM system that can cater to diverse client needs while maintaining standard sales process stages	Implementing advanced analytics to reduce false positives and integrating databases for streamlined data access and analysis	Deploying LLM solutions to address specific business needs within constraints of data privacy and computational resources	Leveraging the strengths of both in-house and external SaaS-based LLMs to enhance training content while maintaining data integrity

Implementation Strategy: Utilizing the LLM's adaptability, the organization implemented a system facilitating real-time user interactions and an offline approach for comprehensive data processing. The in-house model, finely tuned to the company's requirements, was trained on relevant corporate policies and legal texts, ensuring high accuracy and relevance.

Outcomes: The LLM's robustness led to simplified, standardized policy clauses and an enhanced decision-making framework, integrating business intelligence without the typical bottlenecks associated with customization.

4.5 Case 5: Hybrid LLM Deployment for Domain-Specific Training Content in a Financial Company

In this case, the financial company's hybrid LLM deployment eradicates previous customization and integration challenges. The dual framework, combining in-house and SaaS-based LLMs, efficiently managed and generated domain-specific training content, leveraging the expansive capabilities of LLMs for a nuanced content management strategy.

Implementation Strategy: The in-house LLM catered to internal training needs, while the SaaS-based LLM filled knowledge gaps in external domains. This symbiotic relationship, facilitated by the LLMs' advanced capabilities, ensured a smooth transition and integration of content.

Outcomes: The deployment resulted in a comprehensive training suite, balancing proprietary knowledge security with access to a wide range of financial topics, a feat previously challenged by customization and data integration limitations.

Each case study provides a unique perspective on the challenges of digital transformation, particularly in terms of software customization and its impact on cross-functional efficiency. The accompanying table offers a more granular comparison across these diverse industries.

5   Defining Outcomes and Conditions for QCA

5.1 Outcome Definition

Efficiency and Effectiveness in Digital Transformation Initiatives: This study's outcome of interest is the degree of efficiency and effectiveness achieved in digital transformation initiatives within diverse organizational contexts. This encompasses aligning digital systems with operational objectives, seamless data integration, and improved decision-making processes.

5.2 Conditions Definition

For the QCA, we identify several key conditions hypothesized to influence this outcome:

- Degree of Customization Required (Customization): This condition evaluates how digital systems require modifications or bespoke solutions to meet specific operational needs.
- Complexity of Data Integration (Data Integration): This assesses the challenges encountered in integrating and harmonizing data from multiple sources within the organization.
- Diversity of Client or Product Profiles (Client/Product Diversity): This condition reflects the variety of client needs or product offerings the digital systems are expected to accommodate.
- Adaptability of Standard Software Systems (Software Adaptability): This evaluates the flexibility of standard digital systems in accommodating diverse and evolving business requirements.

5.3   Application to the Cases

The identified conditions are applied to each case to assess their influence on the outcome:

- *ERP at Industrial Equipment Manufacturers*: High customization, medium data integration complexity, low client/product diversity, low software adaptability.
- *CRM at IT Consultancy*: High customization, medium to low data integration complexity, high client/product diversity, medium software adaptability.
- *Digital Operations in Banking (AML Workflow)*: Medium to high customization, high data integration complexity, low client/product diversity, medium software adaptability.

6   Substantiation of Coding in QCA

This section provides detailed evidence for the binary codings used in the Qualitative Comparative Analysis of our case studies. These codings (1 for high/present, 0 for low/absent) represent assessments of key conditions and outcomes in each case.

6.1   Customization

- *ERP at Industrial Equipment Manufacturer*: High (1). The significant customization for a specific Bill of Materials (BOM) and ad-hoc reporting aligns with Botta-Genoulaz and Millet (2005), who discuss the complexities and necessities of ERP customization in manufacturing industries.
- *CRM at IT Consultancy*: High (1). Custom dashboards for various client profiles match observations by Payne and Frow (2005) regarding CRM systems' need for customization to enhance client relationship management.
- *Digital Operations in Banking*: High (1). Customization of the anti-money laundering system reflects findings by Canhoto and Clear (2020) on the necessity of tailored solutions in banking for effective fraud detection.
- *Policy Management via In-House LLM*: High (1). The customization of the LLM for policy management can be substantiated by the works of Susskind and Susskind (2015), who highlight the growing importance of tailored AI solutions in legal and policy frameworks.
- *Hybrid LLM in Financial Company*: High (1). The bespoke LLM solution for training reflects the discussion by Arner et al. (2015) on the customization of fintech solutions to cater to specific financial training needs.

6.2   Data Integration

- ERP at Industrial Equipment Manufacturer: Low (0). The focus on internal workflow integration rather than external data is consistent with the challenges described in the ERP literature (Moon, 2007).
- CRM at IT Consultancy: High (1). The integration of diverse client data into CRM systems aligns with Goodhue, Wixom and Watson [12] 2002 insights on the critical role of data integration in CRM effectiveness.

– Digital Operations in Banking: Coded as High (1). The complex data integration required in banking AML systems, especially for consolidating data from multiple sources for effective fraud analysis, aligns with insights from Arner, Barberis and Buckley [13] 2016. They discuss the challenges and intricacies of integrating various data types and sources in financial institutions, emphasizing how this complexity is critical to effective digital operations in the financial sector.
– Policy Management via In-House LLM: High (1). Bughin, Hazan [14] 2018 discussion of AI's role in enhancing data integration in complex environments supports advanced data integration capabilities.
– Hybrid LLM in Financial Company: High (1). Philippon [15] 2016 discusses the integration of in-house and external data sources as reflecting the trends in AI-driven data management in finance.

6.3 Client/Product Diversity

– ERP at Industrial Equipment Manufacturer: Low (0). The limited product variation aligns with Davenport [16] in 1998 arguments notes that, ERP systems often cater to standardized processes rather than diverse product lines.
– CRM at IT Consultancy: High (1). This aligns with Payne and Frow [17] 2005 observations on the need for CRM systems to adapt to diverse client profiles.
– Digital Operations in Banking: Low (0). The focused nature of AML systems in banking, as discussed by Canhoto and Clear [18] 2020, often leads to limited client/product diversity.
– Policy Management via In-House LLM: High (1). The variety of policy areas covered by the LLM reflects Susskind and Susskind [19] 2015 perspectives on the diverse applications of AI in legal frameworks.
– Hybrid LLM in Financial Company: High (1). The diversity in training content resonates with Arner, Barberis and Buckley [13] 2016 discussion on the broad applicability of fintech solutions.

6.4 Software Adaptability

– ERP at Industrial Equipment Manufacturer: Low (0). The challenges in ERP adaptability are consistent with Davenport [16] 1998 critique of the rigidity of traditional ERP systems.
– CRM at IT Consultancy: High (1). As discussed by Payne and Frow [17] 2005, CRM systems' adaptability is essential for managing varied client relationships effectively.
– Digital Operations in Banking: Coded as High (1). Banking software's adaptability, especially for fraud detection in AML systems, is crucial. This aligns with the discussions by He, Leckow [20] in 2017, who emphasize the importance of adaptable software systems in financial institutions for effective risk management and fraud detection. These systems must be flexible enough to respond to evolving fraudulent tactics and integrate new regulatory requirements.
– Policy Management via In-House LLM: High (1). Bughin, Hazan [14] 2018 insights into the adaptability of AI in complex decision-making environments support the flexibility of LLM for various policy scenarios.

– Hybrid LLM in Financial Company: High (1). The adaptability of the hybrid LLM model for training in finance aligns with the trends identified by Philippon [15] 2016 in the evolution of financial technology.

Each coding in the QCA table is grounded in specific examples and analyses drawn from the case studies, ensuring a robust and credible foundation for the subsequent comparative analysis. This approach allows for a nuanced understanding of the complex dynamics influencing digital transformation initiatives in varied organizational contexts. This framework sets the stage for an in-depth QCA, using these conditions to examine and compare the cases systematically.

7 Truth Table and Analysis of Necessary and Sufficient Conditions in QCA

7.1 Truth Table Construction:

Table 3 represents the Truth Table. The truth table in QCA records the presence or absence of each condition across cases and notes whether the outcome of interest is achieved. This method helps identify causal configurations. The conditions are Degree of Customization (C), Complexity of Data Integration (DI), Diversity of Client/Product Profiles (CPD), and Adaptability of Standard Software Systems (SAS).

Table 3. Truth Table

Case ID	C	DI	CPD	SAS	EEDT
ERP_Manufacturer	1	0	0	0	0
CRM_IT_Consultancy	1	1	1	1	1
Banking_Risk_Management	1	1	0	1	0
Policy_Management_LLM	1	1	1	1	1
Financial_Training_LLM	1	1	1	1	1

7.2 Analysis of Necessary and Sufficient Conditions

The analysis focuses on identifying conditions that are either necessary or sufficient for the desired outcome.

- Necessary Conditions: A condition is necessary if it must be present for the outcome to occur. Its presence in all cases with a positive outcome suggests its necessity.
- Sufficient Conditions: A condition is sufficient if its presence ensures the outcome. If the outcome consistently occurs with the presence of a condition, it is considered sufficient.

Application to the Cases

- The ERP case shows high customization without a positive outcome, indicating that customization alone is insufficient.
- The CRM case, with all favorable conditions, suggests that a combination of these factors may be necessary for success.
- The banking case does not achieve the outcome despite high customization and data integration, indicating that these alone are not sufficient for success.

This analysis reveals the intricate dynamics of various conditions in digital transformation. The combination of conditions, rather than any single factor, determines the outcome. For instance, the interplay of high customization, diverse client profiles, and adaptable software is crucial in the CRM case at the IT consultancy.

8 Findings and Conceptual Framework

Incorporating LLMs in these cases signifies a paradigm shift in the digital transformation landscape. The findings highlight:

1. Elimination of Customization Barriers: LLMs' advanced capabilities have virtually eliminated the challenges of software customization, enabling more agile and adaptable digital solutions.
2. Seamless Data Integration: LLMs facilitate the integration of diverse data sources, simplifying previously complex and time-consuming processes.
3. Hybrid Models as a New Standard: The use of hybrid LLM systems reflects a new standard in operational efficiency, blending in-house precision with the expansive knowledge of SaaS-based models.

The conceptual framework developed from these cases illustrates a transition from conventional digital transformation challenges to a new era where LLMs drive efficiency, effectiveness, and adaptability. This evolution marks a significant leap in how organizations approach digital initiatives, harnessing the power of LLMs to overcome previous limitations in customization and data integration.

9 Business Implications

Our findings have several significant implications for businesses engaged in or contemplating digital transformation:

1. Redefining Customization: LLMs offer a level of customization previously unattainable with traditional software systems, allowing businesses to tailor digital solutions precisely to their specific needs.
2. Enhancing Data Integration: LLMs' advanced capabilities simplify the integration of diverse data sources, a process once a major challenge in digital systems.
3. Promoting Hybrid Models: The emergence of hybrid LLM systems, combining in-house precision with SaaS-based models, sets a new standard for operational efficiency and security.

4. Facilitating Agile Decision-Making: LLMs' agility and adaptability enable faster and more informed decision-making processes, which are crucial in the fast-paced business world.
5. Transforming Business Processes: Integrating LLMs into various business processes marks a significant leap in how organizations approach digital initiatives, leading to improved efficiency and effectiveness.

10   Future Research

Future research stemming from this study should expand the scope and depth of analysis in the realm of LLMs in business. A key area is broadening case studies, incorporating a more diverse set of industries and geographical regions to enrich the dataset for Qualitative Comparative Analysis (QCA). This expansion will allow for a more comprehensive understanding of LLM applications and validate the findings more robustly. Longitudinal studies could further illuminate the long-term impacts and sustainability of LLM integration in various business operations. Additionally, incorporating empirical validation of the QCA findings and integrating quantitative methods could offer a richer, multi-dimensional understanding of LLM impacts, revealing patterns and correlations that might be overlooked in a purely qualitative approach.

Technological advancements in LLMs necessitate continuous research to stay abreast of evolving capabilities and implications. Future studies should also delve into the ethical, societal, and regulatory aspects of LLM deployment in businesses, addressing concerns like data privacy, algorithmic bias, and employment impacts. Interdisciplinary research, combining technology, sociology, psychology, and economics insights, could provide a holistic view of how LLMs are reshaping business landscapes. Collaborations with practitioners will ground this research in practical realities, ensuring that academic explorations align with real-world challenges and opportunities in digital transformation.

More broadly, LLMs are merely a precursor to the age of AI. As more advanced AI systems become prevalent, future visions of business value from AI [21, 22] will become prescient. However, AI-based DT will be a core prerequisite to reap the promised benefits – and this study will inform future work that will enable this transition. Current research of IT business value will have to be revisited, renewed and refreshed. From pathways [23–26] to contingencies [27–29] to types of value of AI based DT [e.g., innovation, and other outcomes] [30, 31], will all be promising avenues of future research.

11   Conclusion

The study conclusively highlights that the advent of LLMs has brought about a fundamental shift in digital transformation strategies. This shift transcends traditional approaches, offering unprecedented customization and integration capabilities that redefine how businesses operate and compete. As organizations adapt to this new era, the role of LLMs in enhancing business processes, decision-making, and customer engagement becomes increasingly vital. Therefore, the future of digital transformation lies in leveraging the power of advanced technologies like LLMs to overcome previous limitations and drive business success in an ever-evolving digital landscape.

References

1. Sampson, S.E., Chase, R.B.: Customer contact in a digital world. J. Serv. Manag. **31**(6), 1061–1069 (2020)
2. Saldanha, T.J., Kathuria, A., Khuntia, J., Konsynski, B.R.: Ghosts in the machine. how marketing and human capital investments enhance customer growth when innovative services leverage self-service technologies. Inf. Syst. Res. **33**(1), 76–109 (2022)
3. Deloitte: New Deloitte report finds digital transformation can open up US$1.25 trillion in additional market capitalization. Deloitte (2023)
4. Company, M.: Unlocking success in digital transformations. Mckinsey & Company (2018)
5. Sun, W., Zhang, X., Guo, C.J., Sun, P., Su, H.: Software as a service: Configuration and customization perspectives. in 2008 ieee congress on services part ii (services-2 2008). IEEE (2008)
6. Rothenberger, M.A., Srite, M.: An investigation of customization in ERP system implementations. IEEE Trans. Eng. Manage. **56**(4), 663–676 (2009)
7. Uppström, E., Lönn, C.-M., Hoffsten, M., Thorström, J.: New implications for customization of ERP systems. In: 2015 48th Hawaii International Conference on System Sciences. IEEE (2015)
8. Parthasarathy, S., Sharma, S.: Impact of customization over software quality in ERP projects: an empirical study. Software Qual. J. **25**, 581–598 (2017)
9. Sinha, A., Pedada, K., Purkayastha, A., Srivastava, R., Balani, S.: Digital transformation as disruptive strategy: using data and AI to unlock growth, build resilience and create shareholder value. California Management Review (2022)
10. Ragin, C.C.: The comparative method: Moving beyond qualitative and quantitative strategies. Univ. of California Press (2014)
11. Schneider, C.Q., Wagemann, C.: Set-theoretic methods for the social sciences: A guide to qualitative comparative analysis. Cambridge University Press (2012)
12. Goodhue, D., Wixom, B.H., Watson, H.J.: Realizing business benefits through CRM: Hitting the right target in the right way. MIS Q. Executive **1**(2), 4 (2002)
13. Arner, D.W., Barberis, J., Buckley, R.P.: The evolution of Fintech: A new post-crisis paradigm. Geo. J. Int'l L. **47**, 1271 (2015)
14. Bughin, J., Hazan, E., Sree Ramaswamy, P., DC, W., Chu, M.: Artificial intelligence the next digital frontier (2017)
15. Philippon, T.: The fintech opportunity. National Bureau of Economic Research (2016)
16. Davenport, T.H.: Putting the enterprise into the enterprise system. Harv. Bus. Rev. **76**(4), 121–131 (1998)
17. Payne, A., Frow, P.: A strategic framework for customer relationship management. J. Mark. **69**(4), 167–176 (2005)
18. Canhoto, A.I., Clear, F.: Artificial intelligence and machine learning as business tools: A framework for diagnosing value destruction potential. Bus. Horiz. **63**(2), 183–193 (2020)
19. Susskind, R.E., Susskind, D.: The future of the professions: How technology will transform the work of human experts. Oxford University Press (2015)
20. He, M.D., et al.: Fintech and financial services: Initial considerations. International Monetary Fund (2017)
21. Konsynski, B.R., Kathuria, A., Karhade, P.P.: Cognitive Reapportionment and the Art of Letting Go: A Theoretical Framework for the Allocation of Decision Rights. J. Manag. Inf. Syst. **41**(2), 328–340 (2024)
22. Ning, X., Khuntia, J., Kathuria, A., Konsynski, B.R.: Artificial Intelligence (AI) and cognitive apportionment for service flexibility. In: Xu, J., Zhu, B., Liu, X., Shaw, M.J., Zhang, H., Fan, M. (eds.) The Ecosystem of e-Business: Technologies, Stakeholders, and Connections. WEB 2018. Lecture Notes in Business Information Processing, pp. 182–189. Springer, Cham (2019)

23. Jha, S., Chaturvedi, D.: Systematic literature review of cloud computing research between 2010 and 2023. In: Kathuria, A., Karhade, P., Zhao, K., Chaturvedi, D. (eds.) Digital Transformation in the Viral Age. WEB 2022. Lecture Notes in Business Information Processing, pp. 99–118. Springer, Cham (2022)

24. Sachdeva, A., Kathuria, A., Karhade, P., Ray, S.: How Do Family Businesses Embark on Digital Transformation? A Call for Future IS Research. In: Kathuria, A., Karhade, P., Zhao, K., Chaturvedi, D. (eds.) Digital Transformation in the Viral Age. WEB 2022. Lecture Notes in Business Information Processing, pp. 99–118. Springer, Cham (2022)

25. Cho, W., Malik, O., Karhade, P., Kathuria, A.: Need for Speed in the Sharing Economy: How IT capability drives Innovation Speed? In: Proceedings of the Hawaii International Conference on System Sciences (HICCS). 2022. Maui (2022)

26. Khuntia, J., Saldanha, T., Kathuria, A., Tanniru, M.R.: Digital service flexibility: a conceptual framework and roadmap for digital business transformation. Eur. J. Inf. Syst. **33**(1), 61–79 (2024)

27. Karhade, P., Kathuria, A.: Missing impact of ratings on platform participation in India: a call for research in GREAT domains. Commun. Assoc. Inf. Syst. **47**(1), 19 (2020)

28. Karhade, P., Kathuria, A., Dasgupta, A., Malik, O., Konsynski, B.R.: Decolonization of digital platforms: a research agenda for GREAT domains. In: Garimella, A., Karhade, P., Kathuria, A., Liu, X., Xu, J., Zhao, K. (eds.) The Role of e-Business During the Time of Grand Challenges. WEB 2020. Lecture Notes in Business Information Processing, pp. 51–58. Springer, Cham (2021)

29. Dasgupta, A., Karhade, P., Kathuria, A., Konsynski, B.: Holding space for voices that do not speak: design reform of rating systems for platforms in GREAT economies. In: Proceedings of the Hawaii International Conference on System Sciences (HICCS). Virtual (2021)

30. Andrade-Rojas, M.G., Saldanha, T.J., Kathuria, A., Khuntia, J., Boh, W.: How Information Technology Overcomes Deficiencies for Innovation in Small and Medium-Sized Enterprises: Closed Innovation vs. Open Innovation. Information Systems Research (2024)

31. Andrade, M., Saldanha, T., Khuntia, J., Kathuria, A., Boh, W.: Overcoming Deficiencies for Innovation in SMEs: IT for Closed Innovation versus IT for Open Innovation. In: Proceedings of the International Conference on Information Systems (ICIS). Virtual (2020)

The Determinants of Digital Government Transformation Through Collaborative Governance

Aris Suhada Mian$^{(\boxtimes)}$ ⓘ, Jun Shen ⓘ, and Elena Vlahu-Gjorgievska ⓘ

University of Wollongong, Wollongong 2522, New South Wales, Australia
asm549@uowmail.edu.au, {jshen,elenavg}@uow.edu.au

Abstract. The aim of this paper is to address the contribution of collaborative governance to digital government performance by adequately assessing the determinants of collaboration from the perspective of organisation capability in managing excessive innovation problems. Transformation is complex, requires a long change process and has specific implications for how governments collaborate and innovate to improve the quality of work performance and the value of public service. The central hypothesis of this work is that collaborative governance could improve performance and promote collaborative digital innovation in a government context. This paper explores the multiple influencing factors including the competency of an institution, innovation through dynamic capability, collaborative leadership, co-creation strategy and digital platform capability. Thus, bringing forward organisation adaptation and IT management perspectives on the relationship between collaborative governance and digital government performance.

Keywords: Digital Government · Collaborative Governance · Digital Platform Capability · Collaborative Leadership

1 Introduction

Public sector organisations are now expected to cooperate with organisations that offer similar services rather than to compete for public customers. If neglected, competition is assumed to lead to duplication of services with undesirable consequences in the public sector [1], therefore the government requires collaboration between policy and public service delivery systems [2]. In the context of collaborative governance theory, people are concerned with how multiple organisations work together to address complex social challenges [3]. The success rate of collaboration is hindered by barriers that impede progress, such as communication, cognition and power [4]. However, changes in value creation could have positive impacts and be populated as parameters to measure the effectiveness of strategy performance: operational efficiency, organisational performance, and improvement [5].

Some believe that calculations of self-interest and value maximisation outweigh the benefit of social relations when creating a network. For example, the system is centralised for small agencies seeking support from the Webmaster and decentralised for

© The Author(s), under exclusive license to Springer Nature Switzerland AG 2025
A. Kathuria et al. (Eds.): WeB 2023, LNBIP 525, pp. 15–24, 2025.
https://doi.org/10.1007/978-3-031-74437-2_2

larger agencies with their own resources for web development [6]. Network complexity, power imbalances, and increased risks can make implementation difficult [7]. Another key challenge in managing collaborative innovation with multiple partners is that each partner has a well-established innovation process [8]. Maintaining collaboration is also challenging due to its informal nature, suggesting that formalisation could undermine the dynamism and collective purpose and weaken organisational memory due to burnout and staff turnover [9]. This indicates a need to take action in order to improve connectivity and align problem-solving efforts to stimulate technological innovation, which significantly impacts the digital transformation process [10]. This is particularly useful for ascertaining whether a small institution with lack of resources or larger one run for complex project [11].

The collaboration shares a common purpose and maintains individual goals, and usually all activities and important decisions are coordinated by one of the members, which act as the lead organisation. This lead organisation manages the network of collaborators and supports member organisations in reaching network's goals that may be difficult to accept, as their role will shift from planning to orchestrating [12]. Furthermore, the success of collaboration not only depends on one certain aspect. To explore those aspects and influencing factors, different collaborative governance frameworks can be used [6], which can lead towards better understanding and exploration of the complex interactive relationships between information technologies, organisations and institutions [13].

This study aims to determine organisations' effectiveness in implementing digital transformation strategies in collaborative government, focusing on the following objectives:

a. To identify the key success factors of implementation of digital government through collaborative governance.
b. To find the effectiveness of collaboration competencies on institutional arrangement, and innovation through dynamic capability.
c. To understand the effect of value co-creation strategy and the IT support of digital platform capability.
d. To explain how managerial view the challenges of collaborative digital government by moderating using collaborative leadership.

2   Conceptual Framework and Hypothesis Development

2.1   Theoretical Background

For this research few theories can be employed. The Technology Enactment Theory specifies two organisational forms for public sector organisations: bureaucratic and networks that are effected by institutional arrangement [14]. While the Dynamic Capability Theory define institutional arrangement as: "the ability of an organisation to integrate, construct and reconfigure internal and external resources to cope with a rapidly changing environment" [15]. Teece [16] reveals that dynamic capabilities are comprised of three main constructs: (1) sensing opportunities and threats, (2) seizing opportunities, and (3) transforming the organisation's business model and broader resource base. These dynamic capabilities [16] can be mapped with the digital government performance outcomes (as shown in Table 1), which can be referred to as business resilience or anti-fragility [10].

Table 1. Dynamic capability mapped into resilience or anti-fragility.

Dynamic Capability Theory	Resilience/anti-fragile
Sensing Capability	Agility, Efficiency, Security compliance, Cognitive ability, Visibility
Seizing Capability	Redundancy, Flexibility, Self-properties
Transforming Capability	Adaptability, Fault tolerance

On the other side, the Diffusion of Innovations Theory aims to explain how, why and at what speed new ideas and technology spread [17] based on five perceived attributes: (1) relative advantage, (2) compatibility, (3) complexity, (4) trialability, and (5) observability. Furthermore, the constructs of Boundary Resources Theory refer to [18] including but not limited to platform interoperability (compatibility), allowing for new modules to be added (reconfiguration and integration), and safe connectivity (security).

2.2 Institutional Arrangement Competency and Digital Government Performance

Institutional arrangements of public sector for continues transformation model comprises of, cultural, structural and legal formal which refers to the technology enactment theory [14, 19]. Legal Framework Sufficiency qualitatively emphasize that the maturity of public organisation to shape digital transformation depends on appropriateness of their broader political and normative context [20]. For example, positive legislation and a strong willingness to participate may either set up obstacles or support collaboration. Orchestration Capability on ecosystem is quite challenging as it involves non-hierarchical co-ordination. Therefore orchestration should be the responsibility of the top managers of the sector, who should understand and recognise the dynamics of collaborative ecosystems [12]. Kristoffersen, Mikalef [21] stated that resources orchestration capability has an important role to play in organisation performance. Absorptive Capacity is valuable to enable a firm to generate innovation from outside information [22]. Liu, Zhao and Zhao [23] states that as a firm's absorptive capacity increases, its ability to innovate also increases business performance.

A higher resource Integration Capability could speed up the knowledge collaboration and innovation [24]. The resource integration such as workflow integration, allows leading departments to perform the collaboration, information sharing, and business integration between departments [22]. Accordingly, the integration of information across organisational boundaries is necessary.

Therefore, participation from policy makers and other stakeholders is needed to re-design the institutional environment and make it more adaptable for collaborative governance and cross-boundary information integration. Thus, we present the following hypothesis (Fig. 1):

Hypothesis 1. *Institutional arrangement competency significantly and positively affects digital government performance.*

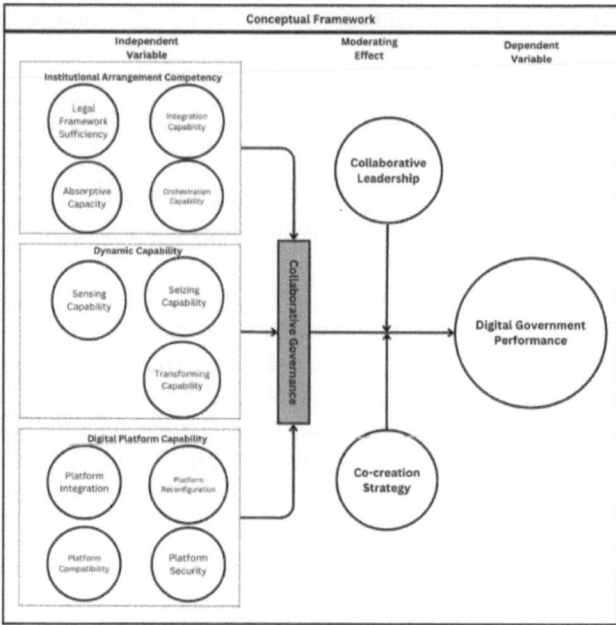

Fig. 1. Research Framework

2.3 Dynamic Capability and Digital Government Performance

Nayal, Raut [25] found that collaborative advantages positively affected sustainable business performance, but they argued that there isn't correlation between digital transformation and collaborative advantages. Our study hypothesizes that dynamic capabilities and innovation are functional capabilities that impact a government's superior performance in digital transformation. Sensing Capability refers to the government's ability to perceive opportunities and threats while Seizing Capability could be understood as an organisation's ability to grab opportunities or respond to threats [16]. Transforming Capability refers to reconfiguring the capacity to carry out transformations, e.g., improving competitiveness through the reconfiguration of organisational asset [16]. Also, Pundziene and Geryba [26] stated that dynamic capabilities have a significantly positive impact on collaborative innovation (partnership network and relational collaboration). This relationship has not been tested in term of perception of making digital innovation through dynamic capability and its impact on digital government performance. The hypothesis claims that high-functioning dynamic capabilities generate superior digital government performance. To test this theory, we hypothesize below.

Hypothesis 2. *Dynamic capability significantly and positively affects digital government performance.*

2.4 Digital Platform Capability and Digital Government Performance

The theory of innovation diffusion and boundary resources are the underlying of this construct relations. Study have shown that an improvement in innovation performance can be achieved by contribution of digital platform capabilities [27]. Cenamor, Parida and Wincent [28] found in their study that digital platform is essential for activating innovativeness as it facilitates rapid flow of knowledge between internal and external sources. Consequently, digital collaboration needs proper governance systems, including relational and contractual mechanisms, to tackle coordination and knowledge sharing issues [29]. The capabilities of platform to reconfiguration and to integrate could improve relational skills and partner knowledge [27, 28] which drive cross sector collaboration [4]. Integrate several different information system is not easy, that way platform compatibility has positive influence on the degree of information sharing [30]. As platforms become more widely shared, the risks associated with their use increase, making trust a critical factor. The implementation of digital government and collaborative governance involved challenges on platform security such as data privacy and digital literacy among officials and citizens. Indeed, one could hypothesise below.

Hypothesis 3. *Digital platform capability significantly and positively affects digital government performance.*

2.5 Collaborative Leadership and Digital Government Performance

In contrast to the classic idea of a hierarchical leader who imposes the view on his/her followers, the literature on collaborative leadership makes a distinction between four facilitating roles of collaborative leaders: the roles of convener (or steward), mediator, catalyst [31] and bridge-builder [32]. A report published in [33] suggest that transformational leadership significantly and positively affects firm innovative performance. In addition, Fan, Zhang and Yen [30] stated that top management support has a positive influence on the degree of G2G information sharing. It could be hypothesized as:

Hypothesis 4. *Collaborative leadership significantly and positively affects digital government performance.*

Breaugh, Rackwitz and Hammerschmid [34] focused on leadership and institutional design in collaborative government digitalisation, but they suggested further research on non-leadership agents and end-user platforms for understanding the ecosystem. The role of government is to facilitate collaborative relationships, where public managers, as leaders in the public sector, should explicitly address democratic norms and the role of citizens in both formulating and realizing shared goals. Ting, Sui [33] stated that transformational leadership also moderates knowledge management and firm innovative performance, but lack of research investigates the collaborative leadership as a moderator variable. To test this theory, we hypothesised the following:

Hypothesis 5. *Collaborative leadership significantly moderates the relationship between institutional arrangement competency and digital government performance.*

Hypothesis 6. *Collaborative leadership significantly moderates the relationship between dynamic capability and digital government performance.*

2.6 Innovation Using Dynamic Capability, Co-Creation Strategy and Digital Government Performance.

Institution continuously communicates with end users such as consumers, citizens, stakeholders or public through the process of value co-creation and develop products and services by collaborating with different departments to increase their target [10]. Although co-creation improves governance processes and outcomes by involving more stakeholders in decision-making and problem solving [35], co-creation has not yet become a common way of thinking due to the strong belief in bureaucratic expertise among administrative authorities. Proposition on organisational maturity for co-creation proposed by [36] concerns the impact on collaboration in the context of digitalisation. The effect of digitalisation through dynamic capability on government performance is affected by the mediating variable of government partnering agility [37]. Furthermore, Hsu [38] found that cocreation strategies including opinion, intellectual capital, participation and rapid respond are significantly correlate with new product development performance. Accordingly, we propose the following hypothesis.

Hypothesis 7. *Dynamic Capability significantly and positively affects co-creation strategy.*

Hypothesis 8. *Co-creation strategy significantly and positively affects digital government performance.*

3 Research Methodology

This study involves the collection and analysis of data using both qualitative and quantitative methods, in which the data are collected sequentially [39]. The use of qualitative prior to quantitative is to establish contextual background and to better understand the research problem [40]. We will use thematic analysis of NVivo software to analyse data collected from semi-structured interviews conducted in three government institutions with participants involved in collaborative digital government. The partial least squares structural equation modelling (PLS-SEM) method will be used in handling numerous dependent and independent variables while controlling for multicollinearity. This method is robust and accurate in predicting latent variables based on response variables as well as works well with reflective and formative latent variables for small sample sizes [41].

The data will be gathered from potential respondents with following criteria: (1) their organisation has at least one collaborative digital transformation project, (2) each organisation has at least two partners involved. To be considered as a selected project the project must have a duration of three years or longer [42] and meet the complexity criteria [11]. Key informants for this study will include senior, project and top managers who control comprehensive knowledge regarding their organisation's partnerships and innovation process with major stakeholders. The unit of analysis in this study is the project unit.

Two limitations of the paper should be taken into consideration. Firstly, it is important to note that similar to prior papers in previous compendium [43], the paper only presents hypotheses. It is still part of ongoing research without providing empirical data to support these hypotheses, which can hinder the credibility and robustness of the study's findings. The theoretical constructs proposed remain speculative and lack substantiation through real-world observations. This limitation underscores the preliminary nature of the research presented, highlighting the need for future studies to test and validate the hypotheses put forth empirically. By addressing this limitation through empirical data collection and analysis, researchers can strengthen the validity and reliability of their research outcomes, ensuring a more comprehensive and evidence-based contribution to the field.

Secondly, the data collection has limitations from the general research perspective. The restriction of data collection, which will be gathered from a single country at a time, may limit the generalizability of the findings beyond that specific context [43–47]. However, the use of mixed methods contributes to a novelty that could impact the broader applicability of the research outcomes and may allow the ability to draw universal conclusions. Furthermore, an approach will involve using multiple data sources (case studies from several units), known as data triangulation, to enhance the internal validity of the study.

4   Conclusion

In conclusion, we have shown the conceptual frameworks of the determinants of digital government performance through collaborative governance. The results are interesting and help to justify the advantages of collaboration. Based on theories and literature, there are certain key factors that still require further investigation. We recognise limitation of this study is that we do not consider the partnership type with vendor or provider. In this study, we focus on within intra and inter government organisational collaboration and citizen involvement, which cover four important element of organisational adaptation in (structure, people, process, and technology) [48]. The expected outcome of this transformation study will result in applying it to new collaboration government service or channels, impacting on improvement its performance.

Acknowledgments. This study was funded by the Indonesia Endowment Fund for Education (LPDP) Ministry of Finance Republic Indonesia.

References

1. Nutt, P.C.: Comparing public and private sector decision-making practices. J. Pub. Administ. Res. Theory **16**(2), 289–318 (2006)
2. Osborne, S.P.: Public service logic : creating value for public service users, citizens, and society through public service delivery. Routledge critical studies in public management. Taylor & Francis Group, New York, Routledge (2021)
3. Ansell, C., Gash, A.: Collaborative governance in theory and practice. J. Pub. Administ. Res. Theory **18**(4), 543–571 (2008)
4. Rouzbehani, K.R.: Time to Track Cross-Sector Collaboration: Digital Prescriptions for Governing Fragmented Governments. in HCI in Business, Government and Organizations. Information Systems and Analytics. Springer International Publishing (2019)

5. Vial, G.: Understanding digital transformation: A review and a research agenda. J. Strateg. Inf. Syst. **28**(2), 118–144 (2019)
6. Gasco-Hernandez, M., Gil-Garcia, J.R., Luna-Reyes, L.F.: Unpacking the role of technology, leadership, governance and collaborative capacities in inter-agency collaborations. Government Information Quarterly **39**(3) (2022)
7. Torfing, J.: Collaborative innovation in the public sector: the argument. Public Manag. Rev. **21**(1), 1–11 (2019)
8. Bai, O., Wei, J., Yang, X., Chen, R.: Third-party relational governance and collaborative innovation performance: The role of IPR protection. Int. J. Innov. Stud. **4**(1), 1–15 (2020)
9. Butcher, J.R., Gilchrist, D.J., Phillimore, J., Wanna, J.: Attributes of effective collaboration: insights from five case studies in Australia and New Zealand. Policy Design and Practice **2**(1), 75–89 (2019)
10. Camarinha-Matos, L.M., Fornasiero, R., Ramezani, J., Ferrada, F.: Collaborative networks: a pillar of digital transformation. Appl. Sci. **9**(24), 5431 (2019)
11. Weinzimer, P.: Strategic IT Governance 2.0: How CIOs Succeed at Digital Innovation. CRC Press (2022)
12. Bygstad, B., Iden, J., Øvrelid, E.: The emergence of a national collaborative digital ecosystem. A study of one-citizen-one-health-record in Norway. In: Norsk IKT-konferanse for forskning og utdanning (2022)
13. Luna-Reyes, L.F., Gil-Garcia, J.R.: Digital government transformation and internet portals: The co-evolution of technology, organizations, and institutions. Gov. Inf. Q. **31**(4), 545–555 (2014)
14. Fountain, J.E.: Building the Virtual State Information Technology and Institutional Change. Brookings Institution Press, Washington, District of Columbia (2001)
15. Teece, D.J., Pisano, G., Shuen, A.: Dynamic capabilities and strategic management. Strateg. Manag. J. **18**(7), 509–533 (1997)
16. Teece, D.J.: Explicating dynamic capabilities: the nature and microfoundations of (sustainable) enterprise performance. Strateg. Manag. J. **28**(13), 1319–1350 (2007)
17. Rogers, E.M.: Diffusion of innovations. 5th ed., Free P, New York, N.Y (2003)
18. Ghazawneh, A., Henfridsson, O.: Balancing platform control and external contribution in third-party development: the boundary resources model. Info. Sys. J. (Oxford, England) **23**(2), 173–192 (2013)
19. Faro, B., Abedin, B., Kozanoglu, D.C.: Continuous transformation of public–sector organisations in the digital era. In: 25th Americas Conference on Information Systems, AMCIS 2019 (2019)
20. Jukić, T., Pluchinotta, I., Hržica, R., Vrbek, S.: Organizational maturity for co-creation: Towards a multi-attribute decision support model for public organizations. Gov. Inf. Q. **39**(1), 101623 (2022)
21. Kristoffersen, E., Mikalef, P., Blomsma, F., Li, J.: The effects of business analytics capability on circular economy implementation, resource orchestration capability, and firm performance. Int. J. Prod. Econ. **239**, 108205 (2021)
22. Fan, B., Liu, R., Huang, K., Zhu, Y.: Embeddedness in cross-agency collaboration and emergency management capability: Evidence from Shanghai's urban contingency plans. Gov. Inf. Q. **36**(4), 101395 (2019)
23. Liu, X., Zhao, H., Zhao, X.: Absorptive capacity and business performance. Ind. Manag. Data Syst. **118**(9), 1787–1803 (2018)
24. Zhang, Y., Wang, D., Xiao, X.: Network Characteristics of Innovation Ecosystem: Knowledge Collaboration and Enterprise Innovation, p. 09717218231161216. Technology and Society, Science (2023)

25. Nayal, K., Raut, R.D., Yadav, V.S., Priyadarshinee, P., Narkhede, B.E.: The impact of sustainable development strategy on sustainable supply chain firm performance in the digital transformation era. Bus. Strateg. Environ. **31**(3), 845–859 (2022)
26. Pundziene, A., Geryba, I.: Managing Technological Innovation: Dynamic Capabilities, Collaborative Innovation, and Born-Digital SMEs' Performance. IEEE Transactions on Engineering Management, 1–14 (2023)
27. Sarwar, Z., Gao, J., Khan, A.: Nexus of digital platforms, innovation capability, and strategic alignment to enhance innovation performance in the Asia Pacific region: a dynamic capability perspective. Asia Pacific Journal of Management (2023)
28. Cenamor, J., Parida, V., Wincent, J.: How entrepreneurial SMEs compete through digital platforms: the roles of digital platform capability, network capability and ambidexterity. J. Bus. Res. **100**, 196–206 (2019)
29. Wang, F., Zhao, J., Chi, M., Li, Y.: Collaborative innovation capability in IT-enabled inter-firm collaboration. Ind. Manag. Data Syst. **117**(10), 2364–2380 (2017)
30. Fan, J., Zhang, P., Yen, D.C.: G2G information sharing among government agencies. Information & Management **51**(1), 120–128 (2014)
31. Ansell, C., Gash, A.: Stewards, mediators, and catalysts: Toward a model of collaborative leadership. The Innovation Journal, suppl. Special Issue: Collaborative Innovation in the Public Sector **17**(1), 2–21 (2012)
32. Hovik, S., Hanssen, G.S.: The impact of network management and complexity on multi-level coordination. Public Administration **93**(2), 506–523 (2015)
33. Ting, I.W.K., Sui, H.J., Kweh, Q.L., Nawanir, G.: Knowledge management and firm innovative performance with the moderating role of transformational leadership. J. Knowl. Manag. **25**(8), 2115–2140 (2021)
34. Breaugh, J., Rackwitz, M., Hammerschmid, G.: Leadership and institutional design in collaborative government digitalisation: Evidence from Belgium, Denmark, Estonia, Germany, and the UK. Gov. Inf. Q. **40**(2), 101788 (2023)
35. Torfing, J., Ansell, C.: Co-Creation: The New Kid on the Block in Public Governance. Policy & Politics (2021)
36. Weißmüller, K.S., Ritz, A., Yerramsetti, S.: Collaborating and co-creating the digital transformation: Empirical evidence on the crucial role of stakeholder demand from Swiss municipalities. Public Policy and Administration, 09520767231170100 (2023)
37. Xiao, J., Zhang, H., Han, L.: How digital transformation improve government performance: the mediating role of partnering agility. IEEE Access **11**, 59274–59285 (2023)
38. Hsu, Y.: A value cocreation strategy model for improving product development performance. J. Bus. Ind. Mark. **31**(5), 695–715 (2016)
39. Creswell, J.W., Clar, V.L.P.: Designing and Conducting Mixed Methods Research. 3 ed. Core textbook. SAGE Publications, Thousand Oaks (2017)
40. Saunders, M.N.K., Lewis, P., Thornhill, A.: Research methods for business students. 8th edition. Pearson, Harlow, United Kingdom (2019)
41. Hair, J.F., Hult, G.T.M., Ringle, C.M., Sarstedt, M., A primer on partial least squares structural equation modeling (PLS-SEM). Third edition. (eds.): Thousand Oaks. SAGE Publications Inc., California (2022)
42. Karasti, H., Baker, K.S., Millerand, F.: Infrastructure Time: Long-term Matters in Collaborative Development. Comp. Supp. Cooperat. Work (CSCW) **19**(3), 377–415 (2010)
43. Jaiswal, A., Kathuria, A., Karhade, P.P.: Benefits of Business Intelligence Systems and Multiple National Cultures During Covid-19. In: From Grand Challenges to Great Solutions: Digital Transformation in the Age of COVID-19. WEB 2021. Lecture Notes in Business Information Processing, pp. 15–29. Springer, Cham (2021)

44. Karhade, P., Kathuria, A., Dasgupta, A., Malik, O., Konsynski, B.R.: Decolonization of digital platforms: a research agenda for GREAT domains. In: Garimella, A., Karhade, P., Kathuria, A., Liu, X., Xu, J., Zhao, K. (eds.) The Role of e-Business During the Time of Grand Challenges. WEB 2020. Lecture Notes in Business Information Processing, pp. 51–58. Springer, Cham (2021)
45. Dasgupta, A., Karhade, P., Kathuria, A., Konsynski, B.: Holding space for voices that do not speak: design reform of rating systems for platforms in GREAT economies. In: Proceedings of the Hawaii International Conference on System Sciences (HICCS). Virtual (2021)
46. Karhade, P., Kathuria, A.: Missing impact of ratings on platform participation in India: a call for research in GREAT domains. Commun. Assoc. Inf. Syst. **47**(1), 19 (2020)
47. Sonpatki, R., Kathuria, A., Sethi, S.: Earnings Call Transcripts as a Source and Resource for Information Systems Research. In: Kathuria, A., Karhade, P., Zhao, K., Chaturvedi, D. (eds.) Digital Transformation in the Viral Age. WEB 2022. Lecture Notes in Business Information Processing, 38–63. Springer, Cham (2024)
48. Gong, Y., Yang, J., Shi, X.: Towards a comprehensive understanding of digital transformation in government: analysis of flexibility and enterprise architecture. Gov. Inf. Q. **37**(3), 101487 (2020)

The Impact of Online Health Misinformation on the Public

Chung-Fu Chen[1], Cheuk Hang Au[2]($\boxtimes$) , and Kevin K. W. Ho[3]

[1] Department of Information Management, National Chung Cheng University, Chiayi, Taiwan
[2] School of Business and Law, Edith Cowan University, Perth, Australia
c.au@ecu.edu.au
[3] Institute of Business Sciences, University of Tsukuba, Tokyo, Japan

Abstract. Online health misinformation has become a more significant concern in recent years, especially since the COVID-19 pandemic. This has led to a pressing need to reduce its negative impact, such as decreasing trust and readership on online media and increased likelihood of social instability during the pandemic. Focusing on healthcare misinformation, we propose a theoretical model that explains the internal and external factors that influence the ability to distinguish healthcare misinformation. This model will be tested in future research, and it is hoped that we can advance theoretical understanding of misinformation and provide practical implications for both online media outlets and governments.

Keywords: Misinformation · Social media · Fake news · Information overload · Self-thinking

1 Introduction

The Internet offers quick and easy information access, increasing users' reliance on online sources for politics, healthcare, and more. Revenue in the Digital Newspapers & Magazines market is projected to reach US$43.0 billion in 2027 [1]. This convenience, however, has also led to the proliferation of false content [2]. During the COVID-19 pandemic, social media became hotspots for misinformation [3]. Over 25% of the top-viewed YouTube videos about COVID-19 contained misleading details, affecting millions of viewers [4]. Readers may be aware of the misinformation problems, but they struggle to discern the authenticity, particularly when overloaded with both information and misinformation. Consequently, misinformation fuels their general distrust of news sources, while authentic news outlets may see reduced readership, even if they consistently provide accurate information. To maintain corporate responsibility and their survival, news outlets, and online platforms must understand and educate readers with information literacy to distinguish misinformation.

Regarding health misinformation, it promotes unscientific methods to handle the virus [5], escalating health risks and hindering public health measures [6]. Amid its vast volume, the ability to discern health information (or "health literacy") is crucial. Health literacy encompasses an individual's knowledge, motivation, and capacity to

© The Author(s), under exclusive license to Springer Nature Switzerland AG 2025
A. Kathuria et al. (Eds.): WeB 2023, LNBIP 525, pp. 25–32, 2025.
https://doi.org/10.1007/978-3-031-74437-2_3

access, understand, evaluate, and utilize health information to make healthcare-related decisions [7, 8].

This study aims to pinpoint critical factors affecting readers' ability to discern health misinformation. It is hoped that our results could assist both governments and media outlets in equipping readers with skills to distinguish between real and fake health information. In turn, media outlets, especially those whose journalists have invested effort in delivering authentic news and information, can regain readers' trust. At the same time, social panic is less likely to be induced by misinformation. Accordingly, our research question is: "How do different external and internal factors impact individuals' ability to discern real from fake news?".

2 Literature Review on Health Misinformation

Misinformation can be understood as any incorrect information which may be disseminated by politicians, interest groups, and media [9, 10]. Misinformation may not necessarily involve deceptive intent, but may be disseminated due to unintentional mistakes, negligence, or unconscious bias [9]. On the other hand, disinformation refers to misinformation with the intention of deception and causing harm [11]. Also, fake news refers to intentionally and verifiably false and misleading information packaged as news media articles and disseminated. We can further categorize fake news into six different modes of existence: satire, parody, fabrication, manipulation, propaganda, and advertising [12, 13].

Nowadays, social media, such as Facebook and Twitter, have transformed news seeking, dissemination, and presentations. The discussion of misinformation and fake news is closely linked to the widespread use of social media [12]. Some scholars argued that the proliferation of the Internet has made the boundary line between online news and information, regardless of authenticity, more blurred than before [10]. In this paper, we collectively refer them as online "information" (or "misinformation" in case of wrong information).

Economic motives and ideological motives primarily drive the generation of online misinformation. They may spread like a virus, providing content creators with clickbait that can be converted into ad revenue [14]. In recent years, misinformation and fake news on the Internet have received increasing attention because they have the potential to change people's perceptions of significant social issues [15], decrease public trust in news outlets, and even pose national security threats [16].

More specifically, in the healthcare context, health misinformation can be defined as fact-based claims related to health that may lack scientific evidence. Similar to other forms of misinformation, they are commonly disseminated on social media, given people are increasingly adopting social media for seeking medical advice or other forms of health information [17]. In a given piece of health misinformation, one may claim the ineffectiveness or exaggerate the side effects of some well-established medical solutions, such as vaccination [18]. Some of them may also be mixed advertisements of products and services offered by the sources of health misinformation. As a result of health misinformation, unnecessary medical expenses may be incurred, while diagnosis and patient treatment may be delayed. Worse still, many health misinformation appeal to anti-vaccination claims, which may increase the risk of global epidemics [19].

·The proliferation of health misinformation has become a more serious concern during the COVID-19 pandemic [20]. On social media, misinformation related to COVID-19 has created fear among the public and shifted the focus of decision-makers, impeding the work of the World Health Organization and public health officials around the globe [18, 21]. Worst still, the proliferation of false or misleading information regarding the COVID-19 pandemic, mixed in with accurate or genuine information, has significantly increased the cognitive cost of determining the accuracy of the information. This led to cognitive fatigue, reduced motivation, and anxiety among the public when dealing with a large volume of news information, ultimately decreasing their ability to assess the truthfulness of information [22].

3 Theoretical Framework

In response to our research question, we assume that one will self-reflect upon encountering a piece of information, in order to determine its authenticity. More specifically, self-reflection means self-observation and report of one's thoughts and feelings. It is a conscious mental process relying on past experiences to think, reason, and examine self-awareness [23, 24]. Factors influencing people's ability to discern health misinformation may be classified as internal or external. Examples of external factors include (1) the information overload effect and (2) the echo chamber effect [25, 26]. Information overload, also termed infobesity [27–30], occurs when individuals receive an overwhelming amount of information that surpasses their capacity to process it [31].

The abundance of health information on social media can contribute to information overload, particularly when combined with people's limited attention spans. This overload might hinder their comprehensive assessment of information on social media, increasing the risk of encountering misinformation [32]. The echo chamber effect refers to personalized information environments that revolve around users' interests, potentially creating a secluded space [32]. There are signs indicating a connection between the echo chamber and the dissemination of misinformation since individuals who reinforce their existing beliefs would inadvertently foster an environment conducive to the emergence of rumors and misinformation [33]. Therefore, we hypothesize:

H1: *Information overload is negatively correlated to one's self-reflection.*

H2: *Echo chamber effect is negatively correlated to one's self-reflection.*

For internal factors, self-confidence is another essential indicator. Here, we should mention the third-person effect, which describes how people tend to believe that persuasive content in the media affects others more significantly than themselves [34, 35]. This suggests that individuals think that others are more susceptible to the influence of health fake news on social media than they are, reflecting a level of self-confidence. Additionally, when individuals encounter media content with adverse social implications, the third-person effect becomes more pronounced [36]. It is because people often perceive themselves as more intelligent, more knowledgeable, and less susceptible to harm than others, making them less vulnerable to the influence of adverse media [37]. Moreover, self-enhancement refers to the psychological process in which people feel good about themselves and enhance their self-esteem. To maintain and boost self-esteem, individuals believe that they have more potent cognitive abilities than others and are, therefore, better equipped to counteract the influence of the media [38]. Therefore, we hypothesize:

H3: *Self-Confidence is positively correlated to one's self-reflection*

Moreover, while Au, Họ and Chiu [39] found a significant negative impact of media reputation on identifying incorrect information in a previous study on political news, we believe this effect was due to the differing political stances in political news that influenced the results. Since the field of health news does not have this issue, we conjecture the importance of media reputation will be relevant in the context of health fake news. Furthermore, scholars have found that a higher awareness of incorrect information leads to better identification of false content in their research. Therefore, we propose the following hypotheses:

H4: *The importance placed on media reputation is positively correlated to one's self-reflection.*

H5: *The willingness to self-monitor is positively correlated to one's self-reflection.*

Also, Himma-Kadakas [40] showed that the current news media workflow creates a favorable environment for the dissemination of deceptive and false information, leading to the proliferation of fake news. It is because journalists might be constrained in a way that forces them to skip traditional information processing stages, such as consideration and verification, resulting in the publication of unverified news content. Therefore, we believe that in the context of fake health news, the abundance of health information may lead the public to skip some stages of processing health news. This leads to reduce ability to discern fake news, which, in turn, affects the process of self-reflection. So, we propose the hypothesis:

H6: *Self-reflection is positively correlated to the ability to discern misinformation.*

Combining the above hypotheses, we have arrived at the following theoretical model presented in Fig. 1.

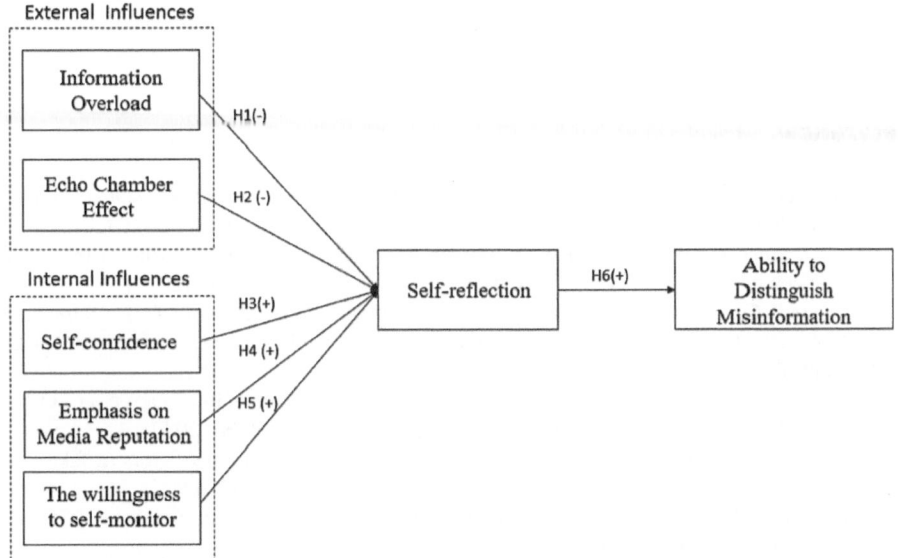

Fig. 1. Our research model on the impact of Health fake news on the public in social media.

4 Future Works and Concluding Remarks

Our study is not without limitations. First, prior research has found differences between Western and non-Western contexts [28, 30, 41–43]. While our model-building efforts were based on a wide range of literature – i.e., both Western and non-Western contexts (WEIRD and GREAT) [41, 44], it will still be desirable to test the model concerning the boundary conditions of cultural contexts. Second, in response to our research question, future research may also consider other methods such as qualitative methods and systematic literature review to identify other factors that may also play a role on readers' self-reflection.

In this research-in-progress paper, we focused on health misinformation and have proposed the impact of several external and internal factors that may drive readers' self-thinking in information consumption contexts, which in turn drive their ability to distinguish online misinformation. We will test the model using an online survey, with measurement items adopted from the literature. For the ability to distinguish misinformation, we will use a health information authenticity test to measure respondents' actual ability, which will provide them with real and fake news for testing.

We believe in the significance of addressing this topic, and we encourage other researchers to explore it in different directions, such as the influence of factors not included in our theoretical model. In the end, it is hoped that we can advance theoretical understanding of fake news and provide practical implications for both government and news outlets on how to educate news readers in distinguishing fake news. In turn, news outlets can regain their reputation, the lost trust and readership, while society is less likely to be destabilized due to health misinformation.

Disclosure of Interests. The authors have no competing interests to declare that are relevant to the content of this article.

References

1. Statista: Digital Newspapers & Magazines – Worldwide (2022). https://www.statista.com/out look/amo/media/newspapers-magazines/digital-newspapers-magazines/worldwide
2. Shu, K., Sliva, A., Wang, S., Tang, J., Liu, H.: Fake news detection on social media: a data mining perspective. ACM SIGKDD Explorations Newsl. **19**(1), 22–36 (2017)
3. Pennycook, G., McPhetres, J., Zhang, Y., Lu, J.G., Rand, D.G.: Fighting COVID-19 misinformation on social media: Experimental evidence for a scalable accuracy-nudge intervention. Psychol. Sci. **31**(7), 770–780 (2020)
4. Li, H.O.-Y., Bailey, A., Huynh, D., Chan, J.: YouTube as a source of information on COVID-19: a pandemic of misinformation? BMJ Glob. Health **5**(5), e002604 (2020)
5. Apuke, O.D., Omar, B.: Fake news and COVID-19: modelling the predictors of fake news sharing among social media users. Telematics Inform. **56**, 101475 (2021)
6. van Der Linden, S., Roozenbeek, J., Compton, J.: Inoculating against fake news about COVID-19. Front. Psychol. **11**, 566790 (2020)
7. Altin, S.V., Finke, I., Kautz-Freimuth, S., Stock, S.: The evolution of health literacy assessment tools: a systematic review. BMC Public Health **14**, 1–13 (2014)
8. Paakkari, L., Okan, O.: COVID-19: health literacy is an underestimated problem. The Lancet Public Health **5**(5), e249–e250 (2020)
9. Giglietto, F., Iannelli, L., Valeriani, A., Rossi, L.: 'Fake news' is the invention of a liar: How false information circulates within the hybrid news system. Curr. Sociol. **67**(4), 625–642 (2019)
10. Au, C.H., Ho, K.K., Chiu, D.K.: The role of online misinformation and fake news in ideological polarization: barriers, catalysts, and implications. Information Systems Frontiers, 1–24 (2022)
11. Freelon, D., Wells, C.: Disinformation as political communication, pp. 145–156. Taylor & Francis (2020)
12. Tandoc, Jr, E.C., Lim, Z.W., Ling, R.: Defining "fake news" A typology of scholarly definitions. Digital Journalism **6**(2), 137–153 (2018)
13. Lewandowsky, S., Ecker, U.K., Seifert, C.M., Schwarz, N., Cook, J.: Misinformation and its correction: continued influence and successful debiasing. Psychol. Sci. Pub. Inter. **13**(3), 106–131 (2012)
14. Allcott, H., Gentzkow, M.: Social media and fake news in the 2016 election. J. Eco. Perspect. **31**(2), 211–236 (2017)
15. Danzig, J.: How fake news caused Brexit. UACES (2017). https://europe.ideasoneurope.eu/2017/11/14/fake-news-caused-brexit/(датазвернення:09.04.2023)
16. Kwon, K.H., Rao, H.R.: Cyber-rumor sharing under a homeland security threat in the context of government Internet surveillance: The case of South-North Korea conflict. Gov. Inf. Q. **34**(2), 307–316 (2017)
17. Chou, W.-Y.S., Oh, A., Klein, W.M.: Addressing health-related misinformation on social media. JAMA **320**(23), 2417–2418 (2018)
18. Desai, A.N., Ruidera, D., Steinbrink, J.M., Granwehr, B., Lee, D.H.: Misinformation and disinformation: the potential disadvantages of social media in infectious disease and how to combat them. Clinical Infectious Diseases **74**(Supplement_3), e34–e39 (2022)
19. Broniatowski, D.A., et al.: Weaponized health communication: twitter bots and Russian trolls amplify the vaccine debate. Am. J. Public Health **108**(10), 1378–1384 (2018)

20. Cinelli, M., et al.: The COVID-19 social media infodemic. Sci. Rep. **10**(1), 1–10 (2020)
21. Director-General's: Novel Coronavirus Media Briefing on 2019 (2020)
22. Nisbet, E.C., Kamenchuk, O.: Russian news media, digital media, informational learned helplessness, and belief in COVID-19 misinformation. Int. J. Pub. Opin. Res. **33**(3), 571–590 (2021)
23. Gläser-Zikuda, M.: Self-reflecting methods of learning research. Encyclopedia of the Sciences of Learning, 3011–3015 (2012)
24. Tyler, J., Boldi, M.-O., Cherubini, M.: Contemporary self-reflective practices: A large-scale survey. Acta Physiol. (Oxf) **230**, 103768 (2022)
25. Bawden, D., Robinson, L.: Information overload: An introduction. In: Oxford research encyclopedia of politics (2020)
26. Rhodes, S.C.: Filter bubbles, echo chambers, and fake news: How social media conditions individuals to be less critical of political misinformation. Polit. Commun. **39**(1), 1–22 (2022)
27. Karhade, P., Kathuria, A., Malik, O., Konsynski, B.: Digital platforms and infobesity: a research agenda. In: Garimella, A., Karhade, P., Kathuria, A., Liu, X., Xu, J., Zhao, K. (eds.) The Role of e-Business During the Time of Grand Challenges. WEB 2020. Lecture Notes in Business Information Processing, pp. 67–74. Springer, Cham (2020)
28. Malik, O., Jaiswal, A., Kathuria, A., Karhade, P.: Leveraging BI systems to overcome infobesity: a comparative analysis of incumbent and new entrant firms. In: Proceedings of the Hawaii International Conference on System Sciences (HICCS). Maui (2022)
29. Malik, O., Karhade, P., Kathuria, A., Jaiswal, A., Yen, B.: Unravelling the origins of infobesity: the impact of frequency on intensity. In: Proceedings of the Hawaii International Conference on System Sciences (HICCS). Maui (2022)
30. Jaiswal, A., Malik, O., Karhade, P., Kathuria, A.: Too many cooks spoil the broth: infobesity in multicultural firms during Covid-19. In: Proceedings of the Hawaii International Conference on System Sciences (HICSS). Maui (2022)
31. Tandoc, Jr, E.C., Kim, H.K.: Avoiding real news, believing in fake news? Investigating pathways from information overload to misbelief. Journalism **24**(6), 1174–1192 (2023)
32. Lazer, D., et al.: Combating fake news: An agenda for research and action (2017)
33. Törnberg, P.: Echo chambers and viral misinformation: modeling fake news as complex contagion. PLoS ONE **13**(9), e0203958 (2018)
34. Davison, W.P.: The third-person effect in communication. Public Opin. Q. **47**(1), 1–15 (1983)
35. Jang, S.M., Kim, J.K.: Third person effects of fake news: fake news regulation and media literacy interventions. Comput. Hum. Behav. **80**, 295–302 (2018)
36. Tang, S., Willnat, L., Zhang, H.: Fake news, information overload, and the third-person effect in China. Global Media and China **6**(4), 492–507 (2021)
37. Gunther, A.C., Storey, J.D.: The influence of presumed influence. J. Commun. **53**(2), 199–215 (2003)
38. Boyle, M.P., McLeod, D.M., Rojas, H.: The role of ego enhancement and perceived message exposure in third-person judgments concerning violent video games. Am. Behav. Sci. **52**(2), 165–185 (2008)
39. Au, C.H., Ho, K.K., Chiu, D.K.: Does political extremity harm the ability to identify online information validity? testing the impact of polarisation through online experiments. Gov. Inf. Q. **38**(4), 101602 (2021)
40. Himma-Kadakas, M.: Alternative facts and fake news entering journalistic content production cycle. Cosmopolitan Civil Societies: An Interdisciplinary J. **9**(2), 25–41 (2017)
41. Karhade, P., Kathuria, A.: Missing impact of ratings on platform participation in India: a call for research in GREAT domains. Commun. Assoc. Inf. Syst. **47**(1), 19 (2020)
42. Karhade, P.P., Dong, J.Q.: Innovation outcomes of digitally enabled collaborative problemistic search capability. MIS Q. **45**(2), 693–717 (2021)

43. Dasgupta, A., Karhade, P., Kathuria, A., Konsynski, B.: Holding space for voices that do not speak: design reform of rating systems for platforms in GREAT economies. In: Proceedings of the Hawaii International Conference on System Sciences (HICCS). Virtual (2021)
44. Henrich, J., Heine, S.J., Norenzayan, A.: The weirdest people in the world? Behavioral and Brain Sciences **33**(2–3), 61–83 (2010)

The Cognition Cube: A Framework
for Organizing AI Systems Research

Abhishek Kathuria⬤ and Devina Chaturvedi$^{(\boxtimes)}$⬤

Indian School of Business, Hyderabad, India
{abhishek_kathuria,devina_chaturvedi}@isb.edu

Abstract. The past few years have witnessed a rapid evolution in artificial intelligence (AI), marking the advent of a new cognitive era. Concurrently, academic interest in the organizational adoption and impacts of AI has surged, reflected in a diverse array of research across management disciplines. This chapter presents the Cognition Cube, a theoretical framework designed to synthesize emerging thematic trends in literature concerning AI's firm-level impacts. Organized into temporal evaluations, foundational definitions of intelligent, agentic, and cognitive systems, and exemplar studies within the cube's dimensions of AI, Human, and Task, this framework categorizes existing research and guides future inquiries. Highlighting areas such as cognitive reapportionment, GREAT economies, and innovation, the chapter aims to stimulate further research, anticipating significant growth in the study of AI's organizational implications as we advance into the cognitive age.

Keywords: artificial intelligence · organizational impact · agentic systems · cognition · research framework

1 Introduction

The past few years have witnessed an increasing pace of innovation related to artificial intelligence (AI), heralding the oncoming age of cognition. Concurrent with advancements in AI technology and systems, the academic community's interest in the organizational adoption of AI and its impacts has also been increasing. This is reflected in an array of research papers published across a broad spectrum of management fields, including strategy [16, 34], organizational behavior [3, 7], operations management [19, 37], accounting [17, 18], marketing [35, 50], and information systems [14, 23, 25]. The purpose of this chapter is to provide a cohesive framework for synthesizing the emerging thematic trends from this burgeoning body of literature. In this chapter, we present to you the Cognition Cube – a theoretical artifact and framework to organize published and future research related to the firm-level impacts of AI.

The Cognition Cube is a versatile tool for categorizing literature on AI systems across three fundamental domains of interest – AI, Human, and Task. While these domains are predefined and serve as the core dimensions of the Cube, the categorization within each dimension is designed to evolve dynamically. In this chapter, we illustrate a 3 × 4 ×

© The Author(s), under exclusive license to Springer Nature Switzerland AG 2025
A. Kathuria et al. (Eds.): WeB 2023, LNBIP 525, pp. 33–45, 2025.
https://doi.org/10.1007/978-3-031-74437-2_4

4 cube that delineates foundational categories within each dimension based on existing literature. This current avatar of the cube depicts 48 cells within the cube, which can lead to $2^{48} \approx 2.8 \times 10^{14}$ possible combinations along the three dimensions for researchers to investigate. However, as new research identifies additional sub-dimensions or characteristics, the Cube is engineered to expand dynamically. For example, integrating gender as a characteristic within the Human dimension would transform the cube into a $3 \times 8 \times 4$ configuration with 96 cells and $2^{96} \approx 7.9 \times 10^{28}$ possible combinations. Further, adding a dimension such as urgency to the task dimension would expand the cube into a $3 \times 8 \times 8$ configuration with 192 cells and $2^{192} \approx 6.3 \times 10^{57}$ possible combinations. Finally, this extensibility applies to the domains of interest as well, whereby the Cube could be transformed into higher dimensional polytope, each dimension associated with a different domain of interest. For example, adding the scope of impact as a dimension with individuals, teams, organizations, ecosystems, and society as its sub-dimensions would give us the 'Cognition Polychoron'. Ergo, the Cube lends itself to a multitude of n-dimensional polytopes. This adaptability underscores the Cube's strength as a dynamically extensible tool to organize and drive AI systems research.

The rest of this chapter is organized as follows. First, we delineate the temporal focus of the research in terms of evaluating the impacts of AI systems on organizations. Second, we provide key foundational definitions related to the differences between intelligent systems, agentic systems, and cognitive systems. Third, we introduce the cognition cube by first unpacking its three dimensions – AI, Human, and Task. Fourth, we provide some exemplar studies and their location within this cube. Fifth, we illustrate the use of this cube as both an organizer of as well as a guidepost for research of organizational-level impacts of AI by providing examples from recent studies. Finally, we detail three specific areas of examination that proffer exciting avenues for future research within the contours of the cognition cube - Cognitive reapportionment, GREAT economies, and innovation.

2   Temporal Focus of Research Outputs

AI systems research outputs can be categorized into three distinct phases: pre-implementation studies, implementation studies, and post-implementation studies. These phases represent different stages in the lifecycle of AI projects. While an AI system progresses sequentially through these phases, research into all three phases has evolved concurrently.

Pre-implementation studies investigate how managers appraise different types of AI when considering AI investments and their potential to create business value [40]. This stream of research also explores socio-technical challenges and opportunities pertaining to AI [12]. While several calls have been made for research on such pre-implementation issues [1, 6, 11], literature in this phase is sparse [40].

Implementation studies focus on the actual deployment and integration of AI systems within business environments. This stream of research focuses on AI implementation related issues related to decision-making processes, decision rights allocation, and the overall management of AI projects. In particular, studies have explored managerial acceptance of AI advice for decision-making [17, 25], Human-AI collaboration [22], and the effect of explainability of AI predictions on human decision-making [10].

Post-implementation studies assess the consequences and benefits of AI use. This stream of research analyzes how AI systems perform in practice, evaluating their impact on organizational processes and outcomes. In particular, the effect of AI adoption on job performance [14], customer behavior [35, 41], and societal outcomes [38, 50] have been examined to determine the consequences of AI use.

The Cognition Cube could be applied to organize literature across all three temporal dimensions. Each of these temporal dimensions could be envisaged as the overlying temporal dimensionality of the cube. The cube can, thus, be used to organize thoughts, ideas, and published studies related to all pre-implementation decisions, during-implementation decisions, and post-implementation decisions.

3   Foundational Definitions

Understanding the distinctions between intelligent systems, agentic systems, and cognitive systems is crucial to clarify the evolving capabilities of artificial intelligence and delineate the levels of sophistication in computational systems. Below, we provide three foundational definitions that elucidate how systems progress from basic problem-solving capabilities to more advanced forms of autonomy and cognition. Further, we illustrate the differences between intelligent systems, agentic systems, and cognitive systems in Fig. 1.

Intelligent Systems are foundational systems utilizing computational tools such as learning algorithms and statistical models to derive knowledge for problem-solving and decision-making [14, 48].

Agentic Systems build upon this foundation by incorporating decision-making responsibility, allowing them the ability to perceive and act, such as take on specific rights for task execution and responsibilities based on pre-specified outcomes [8, 42].

Cognitive Systems represent the pinnacle, possessing the ability not only to learn and think but also understand information deeply. This distinction, highlighted by Herbert Simon, emphasizes the qualitative leap from mere intelligence to cognition, akin to the difference between "rote learning" and "meaningful understanding" [45]. Thus, cognition is the ability to *think* and *understand*. Cognitive systems, therefore, are intelligent systems equipped with the sophisticated capability to utilize knowledge as a cognitive tool, demonstrating a profound depth of understanding [33, 45].

4   Introducing the Cube

In this section, we introduce a three-dimensional framework designed to categorize AI systems literature based on the role of AI, the characteristics of human users, and the nature of tasks performed. We call this the Cognition Cube. The dimensions are AI, Human, and Task. Regardless of the temporal focus of research, all AI systems can be broadly classified within this framework, which can accommodate a wide range of studies. While we present a 3 × 4 × 4 cube, it can be further elaborated into a more complex structure with higher granularity as the field progresses. We simply provide initial categories for each dimension based on the current landscape of the literature. Nonetheless, it is essential to recognize that these categorizations can evolve as more research emerges and more sub-dimensions are identified, allowing the framework to expand iteratively.

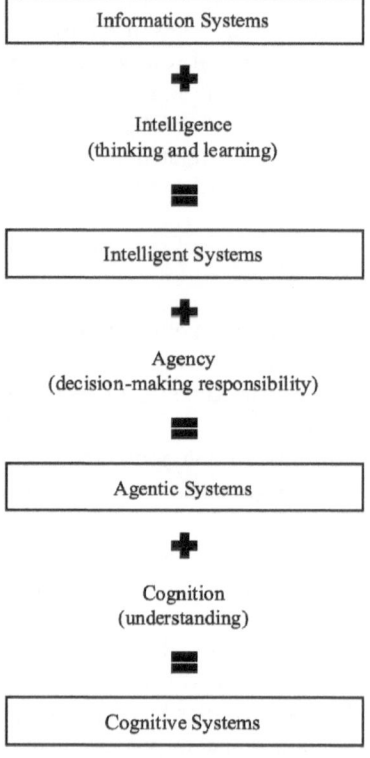

Fig. 1. AI System Definitions

4.1 AI Dimension: Assist, Augment, Automate

The first dimension categorizes AI systems based on their role in supporting human activities. Along this dimension, we categorize AI systems into three categories based on the level of human involvement in tasks along with AI use. The three categories are as follows:

- Assist: AI systems in this category provide support to human decision-making or actions without fully replacing human involvement. Examples include recommendation systems and diagnostic tools in healthcare. These systems enhance human efficiency by offering suggestions or identifying potential issues.
- Augment: AI systems that enhance human capabilities fall into this category. They go beyond simple assistance by adding significant value through insights or functionalities that humans alone could not easily achieve. This also includes systems that perform routine, repetitive tasks, but do not entirely replace human effort. Advanced data analytics platforms and hybrid chatbots are typical examples.

- Automate: These AI systems perform tasks autonomously, often replacing human effort entirely, especially in repetitive or procedural tasks. Examples include robotic process automation and workflow automation.

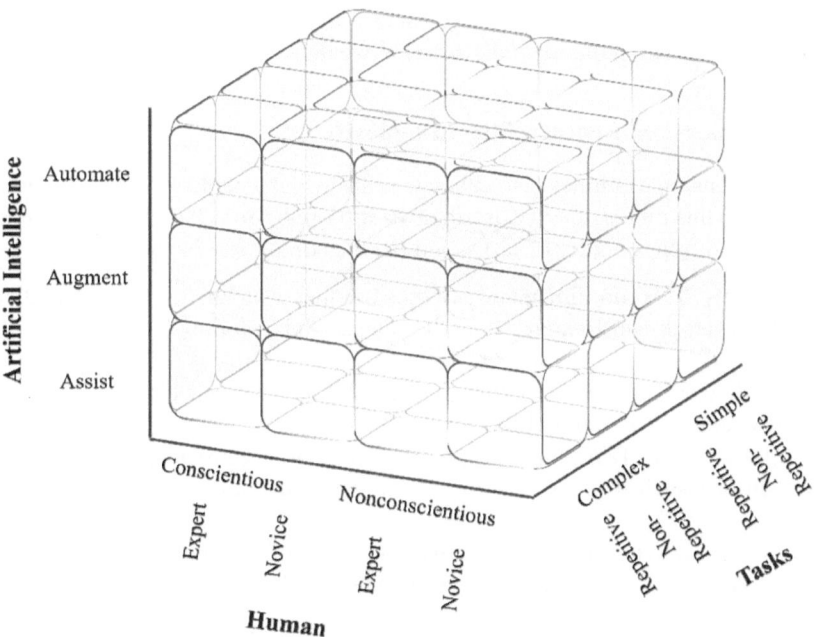

Fig. 2. The Cognition Cube

4.2   Human Dimension: Conscientiousness, Expertise

The second dimension examines the characteristics of human users interacting with AI systems. Along this dimension, we put forth two sub-dimensions:

- Conscientiousness: This sub-dimension differentiates users based on their attentiveness and deliberation in their core tasks. This dimension describes a human's "tendency to act in an organized or thoughtful way" [2]. Conscientiousness has long been debated to be "the most important" personality predictor of performance at work [9, 36]. Within the context of AI systems, Man Tang et al. (2022) [36] highlight that conscientiousness is a factor that could influence the optimality of employees' AI system utilization. Along this sub-dimension, humans may be categorized as follows:

    - Conscientious: Users who are careful, thoughtful, and precise in performing their core tasks, ensuring optimal decision-making.
    - Non-Conscientious: Users who may be less organized and thoughtful in performing their core tasks.

- Expertise Level: This sub-dimension distinguishes users based on their knowledge and experience. Several studies have demonstrated that the utilization of AI systems and their effect on performance improvements differ based on employees' expertise [3, 25, 49]. Along this sub-dimension, humans may be categorized as follows:

  - Novice: Users who are new to the task or domain
  - Expert: Experienced users with deep knowledge and skill

4.3 Task Dimension: Repeatability, Complexity

The third dimension examines task characteristics which enable or inhibit AI adoption by humans. To this dimension, we ascribe two sub-dimensions based on (i) the need for customization or repeatability of tasks, and (ii) the complexity of the tasks.

- Repeatability: This sub-dimension assesses whether tasks are routine and predictable. Along this sub-dimension, tasks may be categorized as follows:

  - Repetitive: Tasks that are routine, predictable, and involve well-defined steps, such as data entry or assembly line work.
  - Non-Repetitive: Tasks that vary in execution and require adaptation to changing conditions, such as creative writing or strategic planning.

- Complexity: This sub-dimension evaluates the level of difficulty or intricacy involved in tasks. Along this sub-dimension, tasks may be categorized as follows:

  - Simple: Tasks that are straightforward and require minimal cognitive effort, such as basic calculations or sorting.
  - Complex: Tasks that involve intricate decision-making, problem-solving, or handling uncertain or novel situations, such as scientific research or crisis management.

This framework, illustrated in Fig. 2, allows researchers and practitioners to categorize and analyze AI systems in a structured manner. By applying this three-dimensional framework, we can systematically explore the varied landscape of AI systems, identify gaps in the literature, and guide future research and development efforts in AI. This three-dimensional framework – comprising the AI, Human, and Task dimensions – offers a structured and flexible approach for categorizing and analyzing AI systems literature. While our initial 3 × 4 × 4 cube provides a foundational classification, it is essential to recognize that this framework is dynamic and can evolve with new research insights. As the field progresses, studies can either fit into one (or more) of these cubes or add to the richness of classification along these dimensions. For instance, gender could be added as a sub-dimension within the Human dimension, further refining the categorization of user characteristics. This adaptability ensures that the framework remains relevant, helping researchers systematically explore the diverse landscape of AI systems, identify gaps in the literature, and guide future research and development efforts effectively.

5 Application of the Cognition Cube

In this section, we illustrate the application of the cube through three recent papers. Given that much of the research is implementation and post-implementation, we illustrate the cube using examples from this stream of research.

The first paper we examine is by Gnewuch et al. (2023) [23], titled "More Than a Bot: The Impact of Disclosing Human Involvement on Customer Interactions with Hybrid Service Providers." The AI system discussed in this paper is designed to augment human service providers, working as "hybrid agents" to interact with customers rather than replacing human involvement. It provides automated responses and facilitates smoother communication, supporting a seamless integration of AI into the service process. Users, who are service providers, are characterized as conscientious due to their careful and deliberate use of the AI system to ensure optimal customer interactions. Furthermore, the paper explores how both novice and expert service providers interact with the AI system, which is designed to accommodate varying levels of expertise. Although customer service interactions involve complex tasks often involve handling a wide range of queries and issues, the bot is tailored to assist with repetitive interactions, which are comparatively simple in nature. Thus, this paper lies at the intersection of Augment, Conscientious (Novice and Expert), and Repetitive and Simple dimensions of AI-Human-Task respectively. This is illustrated in Fig. 3.

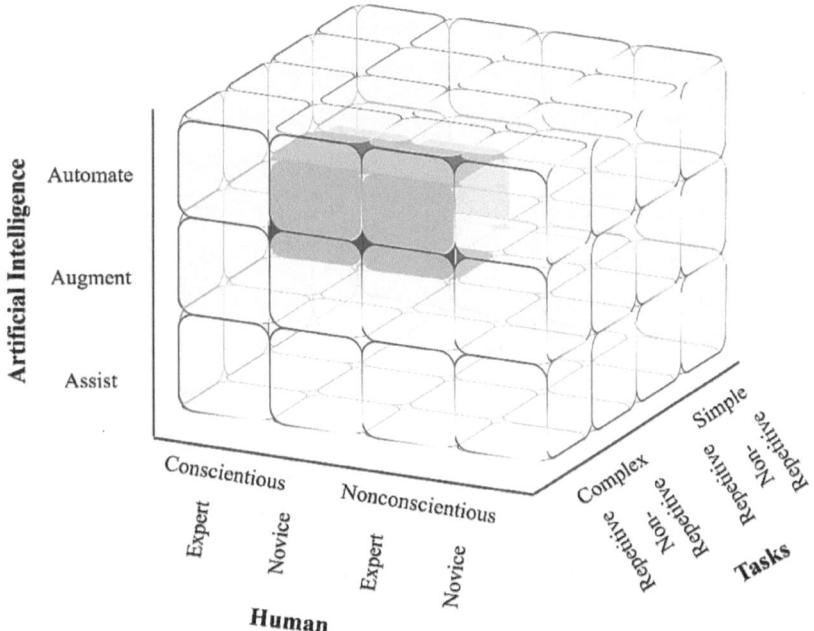

Fig. 3. Location of Gnewuch et al. (2023) within the Cognition Cube

The next paper we examine is by Chen et al. (2022) [14], titled "How Does Intelligent System Knowledge Empowerment Yield Payoffs? Uncovering the Adaptation

Mechanisms." This study explores how AI systems can significantly enhance human capabilities through augmentation. Unlike simple assistance, the AI system in this study provides advanced insights and functionalities that empower users to perform their tasks more effectively. Users in this research are described as conscientious, given their attentive and deliberate interaction with the AI system to fully leverage its capabilities. The study focuses on expert individuals with substantial domain knowledge, highlighting their ability to utilize advanced AI features effectively. Their tasks involve adapting to dynamic conditions and require personalized responses, which characterizes them as non-repeatable and complex. Thus, this paper lies at the intersection of Augment, Conscientious and Expert, and Non-repetitive and Complex dimensions of AI-Human-Task, respectively. This is illustrated in Fig. 4.

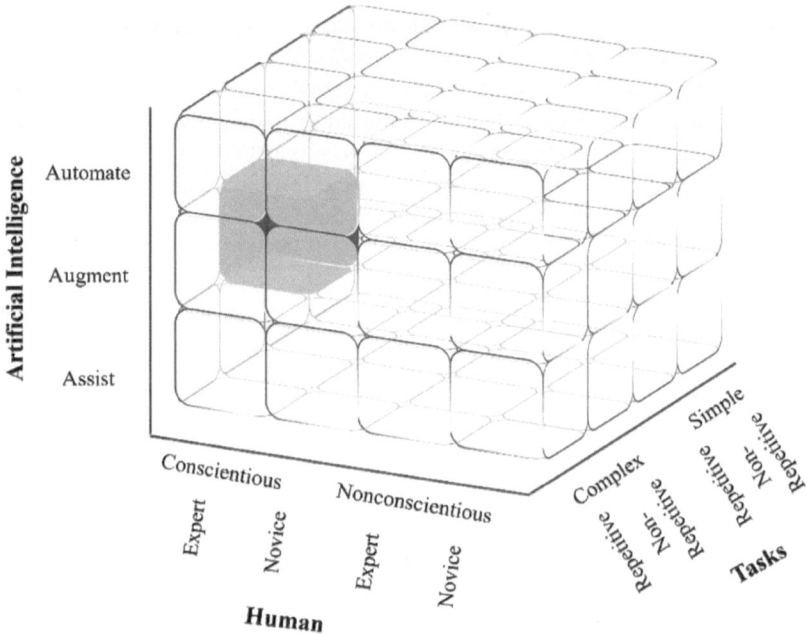

Fig. 4. Location of Chen et al. (2022) within the Cognition Cube

Finally, Jussupow et al. (2021) [25] investigate AI capability to support medical diagnosis decisions in their paper titled "Augmenting Medical Diagnosis Decisions: An Investigation into Physicians' Decision-Making Process." This AI system is designed to assist physicians by providing enhanced analytical insights that aid in clinical decision-making. Physicians are characterized as conscientious due to their meticulous and thoughtful use of the AI system, which aims to ensure accurate and optimal diagnostic outcomes. Further, the paper explores interactions involving both novice and expert physicians with varying medical knowledge and experience, utilizing the AI system to assist in their diagnostic processes. The medical diagnosis tasks explored in this study are non-repeatable due to the uniqueness of each patient case and the varying conditions. Additionally, diagnosing medical conditions is inherently complex, requiring deep analysis, critical thinking, and problem-solving skills. Thus, this paper lies at the intersection of Assist, Conscientious (Novice and Expert), and Non-repetitive and Complex dimensions of AI-Human-Task, respectively. This is illustrated in Fig. 5.

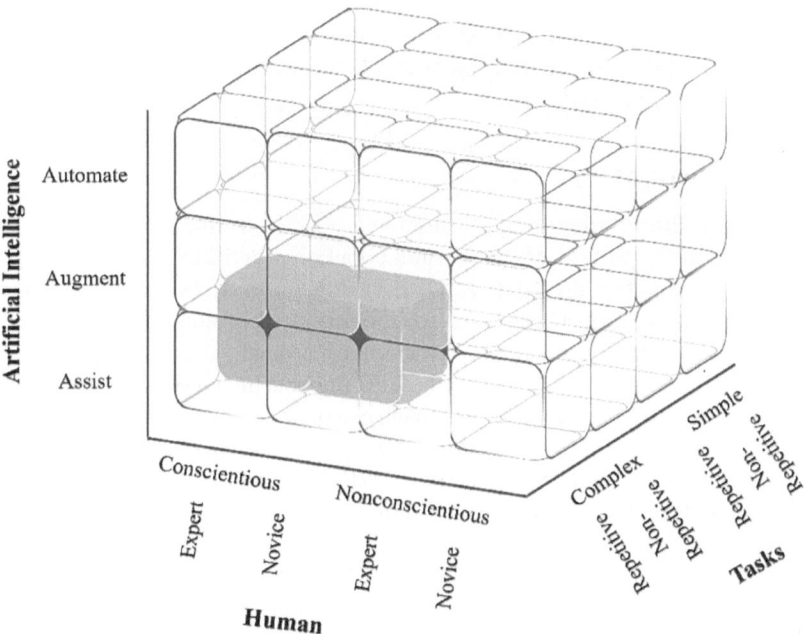

Fig. 5. Location of Jussupow et al. (2021) within the Cognition Cube

6   Avenues for Future Research

6.1   Cognitive Reapportionment

Cognitive Reapportionment refers to "the design of organizational decision-making processes to allocate decision rights and authorities across humans, systems, and combinations of humans and systems in a way that optimizes the use of cognitive resources" [32], a concept extensively studied in prior research [21, 33, 39, 46, 47]. It emphasizes optimizing the synergy between human and machine intelligence to enhance performance and decision-making. Previous studies have called for further exploration, particularly in understanding how cognitive responsibilities can be dynamically allocated in different scenarios [33]. We amplify these calls, urging researchers to delve deeper into Cognitive Reapportionment within the framework of our proposed Cognition Cube. By examining how different configurations of AI roles, human characteristics, and task complexities influence cognitive task distribution, we can gain insights into optimizing human-AI collaboration.

The Cognition Cube, when combined with Cognitive Reapportionment as a design principle, offers a novel perspective on the research and organizational impacts of AI. Each cell within the cube signifies a unique combination of agent, human, and task characteristics, providing fertile ground for the emergence of several research questions. For instance, in a cell characterized by a novice, non-conscientious employee performing a complex task with an augmenting AI system, researchers could investigate optimal patterns of cognitive reapportionment. Questions such as who should take the initial decision, when cognitive reapportionment should occur, and which entity should handle meta-cognition become pertinent.

6.2 GREAT Domains

GREAT (Global, Rural, Emerging, Aspirational, and Transitional) economies encompass a substantial proportion of the world's population and global output [26]. Often characterized by incessant growth [27], GREAT domains have become a growing focus of research [5, 13, 20, 28–31, 44]. As AI continues to revolutionize various sectors, understanding its impact on economic paradigms is crucial.

We encourage researchers to explore how AI impacts interaction in different cells of our Cognition Cube framework. This approach can offer a comprehensive understanding of AI's role in driving organizational outcomes across various contexts. The Cognition Cube aligns seamlessly with the concept of GREAT domains, facilitating comparative analyses across different economic and cultural contexts. This line of inquiry leads to several interesting avenues for future research. For instance, would the outcomes of AI adoption in each cell be consistent across WEIRD (Western, Educated, Industrialized, Rich, and Democratic) societies [24] versus GREAT domains? Investigating the reasons for potential divergences and overlaps can provide valuable insights into how AI's impact varies globally.

6.3 Innovation

Innovation is an enduring topic in IS research, encompassing a vast array of studies focused on understanding the antecedents of innovation within organizations [4, 5, 15, 43]. Despite these efforts, there remain many gaps in our understanding, leading to research questions that become even more prominent in the age of AI. While there is significant ongoing research on the productivity impacts of AI, the transformative potential of cognitive systems lies in their ability to enhance human creativity and innovation. Cognitive systems can assist in generating novel ideas, identifying patterns in large datasets, and providing insights that drive innovative solutions. Despite some research efforts examining the impact of AI on organizational innovation, we are only beginning to scratch the surface.

The Cognition Cube framework offers a robust structure to explore diverse innovation outcomes across its dimensions. By examining each cell of the Cognition Cube, researchers can identify distinct innovation outcomes influenced by the interplay between AI roles, human characteristics, and task nature. This structured approach allows for a comprehensive understanding of how AI drives innovation across different organizational contexts and highlights specific areas where future research can delve deeper.

Exploring these nuanced interactions will enable organizations to harness the full potential of AI, driving both incremental and radical innovations, and ultimately shaping the future of work and technology.

7 Conclusion

In this chapter, we introduced the Cognition Cube, a comprehensive framework designed to classify and organize current research while guiding future inquiries into cognitive systems. Our framework not only categorizes existing research but also outlines three broad areas for future exploration, enriching discussions on the organizational-level antecedents and impacts of AI systems. As we advance towards the cognitive age, the volume of research on these topics is expected to grow significantly. This chapter serves as a guide for researchers, aiming to support and stimulate their contributions to this evolving field.

References

1. Abbasi, A., Parsons, J., Pant, G., Sheng, O.R.L., Sarker, S.: Pathways for design research on artificial intelligence. Inf. Syst. Res. **35**(2), 441–459 (2024)
2. Adamopoulos, P., Ghose, A., Todri, V.: The impact of user personality traits on word of mouth: text-mining social media platforms. Inf. Syst. Res. **29**(3), 612–640 (2018)
3. Allen, R., Choudhury, P.: Algorithm-augmented work and domain experience: the countervailing forces of ability and aversion. Organ. Sci. **33**(1), 149–169 (2022)
4. Andrade-Rojas, M.G., Kathuria, A., Lee, H.-H.: Multilevel synergy of information technology for operational integration: competition networks and operating performance. Prod. Oper. Manag. **33**(5), 1116–1141 (2024)
5. Andrade-Rojas, M.G., Saldanha, T.J.V., Kathuria, A., Khuntia, J., Boh, W.: How information technology overcomes deficiencies for innovation in small and medium-sized enterprises: closed innovation vs. open innovation. Inf. Syst. Res. **0**(0), 1–32 (2024)
6. Bailey, D.E., Barley, S.R.: Beyond design and use: how scholars should study intelligent technologies. Inf. Organ. **30**(2), 100286 (2020)
7. Bailey, D.E., Faraj, S., Hinds, P.J., Leonardi, P.M., von Krogh, G.: We are all theorists of technology now: a relational perspective on emerging technology and organizing. Organ. Sci. **33**(1), 1–18 (2022)
8. Baird, A., Maruping, L.M.: The next generation of research on IS use: a theoretical framework of delegation to and from agentic IS artifacts. MIS Q. **45**(1b), 315–341 (2021)
9. Barrick, M.R., Mount, M.K., Strauss, J.P.: Conscientiousness and performance of sales representatives: test of the mediating effects of goal setting. J. Appl. Psychol. **78**(5), 715 (1993)
10. Bauer, K., von Zahn, M., Hinz, O.: Expl(AI)ned: the impact of explainable artificial intelligence on users' information processing. Inf. Syst. Res. **34**(4), 1582–1602 (2023)
11. Benbya, H., Pachidi, S., Jarvenpaa, S.: Special issue editorial: artificial intelligence in organizations: Implications for information systems research. J. Assoc. Inf. Syst. **22**(2), 10 (2021)
12. Berente, N., Gu, B., Recker, J., Santhanam, R.: Managing artificial intelligence. MIS Q. **45**(3), 1433–1450 (2021)

13. Chaturvedi, D., Karhade, P., Kathuria, A., Rai, A., Naik, N.: IT and the Dual Bottom-Line Objective of Rational Social Enterprises. In: Proceedings of the European Conference on Information Systems (ECIS) (2024)
14. Chen, L., Hsieh, J.J.P.-A., Rai, A.: How does intelligent system knowledge empowerment yield payoffs? uncovering the adaptation mechanisms and contingency role of work experience. Inf. Syst. Res. **33**(3), 1042–1071 (2022)
15. Cho, W., Malik, O., Karhade, P., Kathuria, A.: Need for speed in the sharing economy: how IT capability drives innovation speed? In: Proceedings of the Hawaii International Conference on System Sciences (HICCS). Maui (2022)
16. Choudhury, P., Starr, E., Agarwal, R.: Machine learning and human capital complementarities: Experimental evidence on bias mitigation. Strateg. Manag. J. **41**(8), 1381–1411 (2020)
17. Commerford, B.P., Dennis, S.A., Joe, J.R., Ulla, J.W.: Man versus machine: complex estimates and auditor reliance on artificial intelligence. J. Account. Res. **60**(1), 171–201 (2022)
18. Costello, A.M., Down, A.K., Mehta, M.N.: Machine + man: a field experiment on the role of discretion in augmenting AI-based lending models. J. Acc. Econ. **70**(2), 101360 (2020)
19. Dai, T., Tayur, S.: Designing AI-augmented healthcare delivery systems for physician buy-in and patient acceptance. Prod. Oper. Manag. **31**(12), 4443–4451 (2022)
20. Dasgupta, A., Karhade, P., Kathuria, A., Konsynski, B.: Holding space for voices that do not speak: design reform of rating systems for platforms in GREAT economies. In: Proceedings of the Hawaii International Conference on System Sciences (HICCS). Virtual (2021)
21. Fjeldstad, O.D., Konsynski, B.R.: Reapportionment of cognitive responsibilities in DSS dialogues. Decision Support Systems: A Decade in Perspective, 183–203 (1986)
22. Fügener, A., Grahl, J., Gupta, A., Ketter, W.: Cognitive challenges in human-artificial intelligence collaboration: investigating the path toward productive delegation. Inf. Syst. Res. **33**(2), 678–696 (2022)
23. Gnewuch, U., Morana, S., Hinz, O., Kellner, R., Maedche, A.: More than a bot? the impact of disclosing human involvement on customer interactions with hybrid service agents. Inf. Syst. Res. **35**(3), 936–955 (2024)
24. Henrich, J., Heine, S.J., Norenzayan, A.: The weirdest people in the world? Behavioral and brain sciences **33**(2–3), 61–83 (2010)
25. Jussupow, E., Spohrer, K., Heinzl, A., Gawlitza, J.: Augmenting medical diagnosis decisions? an investigation into physicians' decision-making process with artificial intelligence. Inf. Syst. Res. **32**(3), 713–735 (2021)
26. Karhade, P., Kathuria, A.: Missing impact of ratings on platform participation in India: a call for research in GREAT domains. Commun. Assoc. Inf. Syst. **47**(1), 19 (2020)
27. Karhade, P., Kathuria, A., Dasgupta, A., Malik, O., Konsynski, B.R.: Decolonization of digital platforms: a research agenda for GREAT domains. In: Garimella, A., Karhade, P., Kathuria, A., Liu, X., Xu, J., Zhao, K. (eds.) The Role of e-Business During the Time of Grand Challenges. WEB 2020. Lecture Notes in Business Information Processing, pp. 51–58. Springer, Cham (2021)
28. Kathuria, A., Karhade, P.P., Konsynski, B.R.: In the Realm of Hungry Ghosts: Multi-Level Theory for Supplier Participation on Digital Platforms. J. Manage. Inf. Syst. **37**(2), 396–430 (2020)
29. Kathuria, A., Karhade, P.P., Ning, X., Konsynski, B.R.: Blood and water: information technology investment and control in family-owned businesses. J. Manage. Inf. Syst. **40**(1), 208–238 (2023)
30. Kathuria, A., Mann, A., Khuntia, J., Saldanha, T.J.V., Kauffman, R.J.: A strategic value appropriation path for cloud computing. J. Manage. Inf. Syst. **35**(3), 740–775 (2018)
31. Kathuria, R., Kathuria, N.N., Kathuria, A.: Mutually supportive or trade-offs: An analysis of competitive priorities in the emerging economy of India. J. High Technol. Manage. Res. **29**(2), 227–236 (2018)

32. Konsynski, B., Sviokla, J.: Cognitive reapportionment: Rethinking the location of judgement in managerial decision making. Harvard University, Harvard Business School Discussion Draft (1993)

33. Konsynski, B.R., Kathuria, A., Karhade, P.P.: Cognitive reapportionment and the art of letting go: a theoretical framework for the allocation of decision rights. J. Manag. Inf. Syst. **41**(?), 328–340 (2024)

34. Krakowski, S., Luger, J., Raisch, S.: Artificial intelligence and the changing sources of competitive advantage. Strateg. Manag. J. **44**(6), 1425–1452 (2023)

35. Luo, X., Tong, S., Fang, Z., Qu, Z.: Frontiers: machines vs. humans: the impact of artificial intelligence Chatbot disclosure on customer purchases. Mark. Sci. **38**(6), 937–947 (2019)

36. Man Tang, P., et al.: When conscientious employees meet intelligent machines: An integrative approach inspired by complementarity theory and role theory. Acad. Manage. J. **65**(3), 1019–1054 (2022)

37. Mithas, S., Chen, Z.L., Saldanha, T.J.V., De Oliveira Silveira, A.: How will artificial intelligence and Industry 4.0 emerging technologies transform operations management? Prod. Operat. Manage. **31**(12), 4475–4487 (2022)

38. Nguyen, A., Rai, A., Maruping, L.: Understanding the unintended effects of human-machine moderation in addressing harassment within online communities. J. Manage. Info. Syst. **41**(2), 341–366 (2024)

39. Ning, X., Khuntia, J., Kathuria, A., Konsynski, B.R.: Artificial Intelligence (AI) and cognitive apportionment for service flexibility. In: Xu, J., Zhu, B., Liu, X., Shaw, M.J., Zhang, H., Fan, M. (eds.) The Ecosystem of e-Business: Technologies, Stakeholders, and Connections. WEB 2018. Lecture Notes in Business Information Processing, pp. 182–189. Springer, Cham (2019)

40. Queiroz, M., Anand, A., Baird, A.: Manager appraisal of artificial intelligence investments. J. Manage. Info. Syst. **41**(3), 682–707 (2024)

41. Ray, A., Ghasemkhani, H., Martinelli, C.: Competition and cognition in the market for online news. J. Manage. Info. Syst. **41**(2), 367–393 (2024)

42. Russell, S.: Human compatible: AI and the problem of control. Penguin UK (2019)

43. Saldanha, T.J.V., Sahaym, A., Mithas, S., Andrade-Rojas, M.G., Kathuria, A., Lee, H.-H.: Turning liabilities of global operations into assets: IT-enabled social integration capacity and exploratory innovation. Inf. Syst. Res. **31**(2), 361–382 (2020)

44. Schreieck, M., Huang, Y., Kupfer, A., Krcmar, H.: The effect of digital platform strategies on firm value in the banking industry. J. Manage. Info. Syst. **41**(2), 394–421 (2024)

45. Simon, H.A.: The Sciences of the Artificial, reissue of the third edition with a new introduction by John Laird. MIT Press (2019)

46. Stohr, E.A., Konsynski, B.R.: Information Systems and Decision Processes. IEEE Computer Society Press (1992)

47. Teli, J.S., Rai, A., Lin, Y.-K.: Abnormal returns to artificial intelligence patent infringement litigations. J. Manage. Info. Syst. **41**(2), 422–452 (2024)

48. von Krogh, G.: Artificial intelligence in organizations: new opportunities for phenomenon-based theorizing. Acad. Manage. Discover. **4**(4), 404–409 (2018)

49. Wang, W., Gao, G., Agarwal, R.: Friend or foe? teaming between artificial intelligence and workers with variation in experience. Man. Sci. **70**(9), 5627–6482 (2024)

50. Zhang, S., Mehta, N., Singh, P.V., Srinivasan, K.: Frontiers: can an artificial intelligence algorithm mitigate racial economic inequality? an analysis in the context of Airbnb. Mark. Sci. **40**(5), 813–820 (2021)

How to Strengthen Personal Cyber Security Competencies? Extending the Cyber Security Domain Model (CSDM) to Individuals: A Literature-Based Domain Analysis

Florian Schütz[1]([✉]) [iD], Laura Scholz[1], Simon Hugenberg[1] [iD], Julia Warwas[2] [iD], and Simon Trang[3] [iD]

[1] University of Goettingen, Platz der Göttinger Sieben 5, 37073 Göttingen, Germany
florian.schuetz@uni-goettingen.de
[2] University of Hohenheim, Schloss Hohenheim 1, 70599 Stuttgart, Germany
[3] Paderborn University, Warburger Str. 100, 33098 Paderborn, Germany

Abstract. Companies, public authorities, and private Internet users are increasingly confronted with cyber risks. However, research and practice have focused particularly on cyber security in an organizational context. This ignores the fact that private individuals face cyber risks that differ from those they encounter as part of their job profile in an organizational context. Moreover, it is evident that private individuals behave differently concerning cyber risks, which can be explained by different context-dependent threat awareness as part of multi-dimensional cyber security competencies. Therefore, we extend the Cyber Security Domain Model (CSDM), which was initially established as the prerequisite for building cyber security competencies related to threats within an organizational context, to individuals. We draw on practitioner as well as academic sources to adjust and refine the two dimensions of (1) threat area and (2) threat event in the context of individuals, using a structured literature review.

Keywords: Cyber Security Domain Model · CSDM · Domain Analysis · Cyber Threat · Cyber Security Competencies · SETA

1 Introduction

Along with the widespread use of the Internet [1], consumers are increasingly confronted with security incidents [2]. Although companies are usually the target of cybercriminals, private individuals are also increasingly affected, e.g., in the form of phishing [3]. Consequently, the threat level continues to rise steadily, along with the billions in damage caused by cybercrime [4, 5]. Thereby, human error remains a prime cause of cyber security incidents [6], and humans are considered the "weakest link in the information security chain" [7]. More precisely, many private households do not know enough about cyber security, and their behavior based on this knowledge is inadequate to protect them online [2]. Research and practice, however, have focused primarily on cyber security awareness within organizations [8, 9].

© The Author(s), under exclusive license to Springer Nature Switzerland AG 2025
A. Kathuria et al. (Eds.): WeB 2023, LNBIP 525, pp. 46–62, 2025.
https://doi.org/10.1007/978-3-031-74437-2_5

In the organizational context, Security Education, Training, and Awareness (SETA) programs are conducted with employees to increase cyber security competencies [10, 11]. As part of these SETA programs, employees learn how to deal with security threats and gain knowledge about these threats to increase the level of cyber security of the entire organization [12]. Thereby, individual differences among the employees (e.g., age, gender, mother tongue) may affect their security-related behavior and, thus, the effectiveness of SETA programs [7, 13].

The basis for implementing SETA programs is an organizational security policy (e.g., protection of organizational systems when downloading attachments of unknown e-mails), which employees must adhere to [7]. However, private Internet users such as students or homemakers are not subject to such security policies when using vulnerable assets such as laptops or smartphones [7]. Despite (non-)governmental security awareness campaigns (e.g. sharing videos or displaying posters), there are no structures comparable to organizations to establish cyber hygiene among individuals [8]. Hereby, an individual can be defined as a natural person who uses products, services, or applications privately and for whom cyber risks may arise in the process [14]. However, individuals may not be able to fully transfer the security behaviors taught in corporate SETA programs to their private context since these programs typically cover organizational, non-individual issues [9].

For effective, situationally adequate actions in the face of varying security threats, SETA programs should address conceptual, procedural, and utilizational competencies [11]. Based on evidence from vocational education, the measurement and building of competencies require domain models to give an overview of the requirements and activities within a domain, e.g., job profiles of employees and their daily tasks [15, 16]. While Schütz et al. [15] developed the generalized Cyber Security Domain Model (CSDM) for the cyber security domain as the necessary basis for measuring and promoting competencies for risk-eliminating behaviors in the organizational context, Rampold et al. [17] focus specifically on the organizational context of healthcare providers. However, this does not reflect the reality of life in private households and reveals a gap in research, given the lack of competency-based assessments and SETA programs for individuals. Hence, we aim to extend the CSDM established in practice to the domain of individuals and formulate the following research question: *What security threats should an extended domain model for cyber-secure behavior include regarding individuals?*

We address this research question by conducting a structured literature review based on Moher et al. [18] and using additional best practice recommendations of Vom Brocke et al. [19] and Webster and Watson [20] to analyze the context-specific security threats to individuals. Partially adapting the three-stage process of domain analysis described by Schütz et al. [15], this helps to delineate security threats consisting of threat area (i.e., phone, wearable, IoT device) and threat event (i.e., phishing, malware, DDoS attack). By extending the CSDM to the typical occurrences and devices of individuals' lives, we provide implications for theory and practice. Here, our focus on the security behavior of private individuals not only addresses a blind spot of research but also supports their individual cyber security level with current research findings from the corporate context. In particular, the CSDM for individuals provides the contextual foundation for measuring the cyber security competencies of individuals.

2 Conceptual Background

2.1 Understanding Cybercrime from a Problem-Oriented Angle

Cybercrime is considered a growing concern from the individual's point of view [21]. On the one hand, the BKA [22] defines cybercrime in particular target-focused as a term for crimes (1) committed on the Internet against IT systems or data, such as computer fraud, and (2) those committed with the help of the Internet or use of IT, such as drug trafficking. Al-Khater et al. [23], on the other hand, describe cybercrime as more consequence-focused as a crime that is carried out using a computer or other communication devices to frighten people or harm or destroy their property. In conclusion, cybercrime offenses are directed against computer systems or the like, thus harming the owners and systems.

A glance at crime statistics reveals that private households in Germany are increasingly affected by security incidents [24]. In terms of figures, cybercrime occurs more frequently than any other property crime, with 14.7% of the German resident population aged 16 and over having been victims of such a cybercrime offense in the twelve months prior to the respective survey [25]. From the victim's perspective, eight out of ten Germans affected by cybercrime have suffered a loss (e.g., loss of time, data, or money), with the average financial loss due to cyber fraud amounting to €674 [26]. At the same time, the clearance rate (around 30%) for cybercrime is rather low compared to other offense categories [3]. Another example that the threat of cybercrime has increased in recent years: 144 million new malware variants were noticed in 2021, 22% more than the year before [27], a development that can also be followed in other countries such as the UK [28].

In sum, the reported statistics indicate that the threat level for cybercrime is already high and likely to increase in the following years. However, the competence to handle digital devices is not fully developed among individuals in Germany [2]. Based on self-assessments, it can be concluded that security competencies as a subcategory of digital literacy are also not well-developed among Germans [14]. Moreover, many citizens do not fully implement all the protective cyber security measures they are aware of, e.g. due to the degree of complexity of the security recommendations [29]. This problem-oriented angle informs our research that the CSDM for individuals should cover realistic and common threats encountered by private households in their everyday lives.

2.2 Understanding Cyber Security Competencies from a Process-Oriented Angle

Several studies have identified information security awareness (ISA) as an integral enabler of information security compliance [30]. Similarly, awareness of cyber security threats and security behavior is also the first line of defense for individuals [7, 31]. However, few models holistically assess ISA, and research to date has often only conducted questionnaire-based surveys [6], e.g., the HAIS-Q scale for measuring employee ISA [32]. Moreover, the commonly applied self-report questionnaires used to measure behavioral variables in an organizational context have been criticized regarding common-method variance and, consequently, limited validity [33].

A different approach is learning from the Vocational Education Domain, as Rampold et al. [11] propose, to transfer competence models to the cyber security domain. Following Weinert [34], Köpfer et al. [35] understand cyber security competencies (CSC) as "the (measurable) cognitive abilities and skills that are present (or can be learned) in individuals to act in an IT-secure manner in everyday work, as well as the associated motivational and social dispositions and skills to successfully and responsibly avert or manage a threat in variable situations." Thereby, establishing cyber security competencies requires the development of a domain model and thus goes beyond a mere development of scale [15]. Domain models are used to provide an overview of the requirements and tasks within a domain [16, 36].

More precisely, domain models are often developed as part of the Evidence Centered Assessment Design (ECD) framework to derive design choices for educational assessments and to justify these choices with evidence [37]. Therefore, the ECD framework includes different layers (i.e., domain analysis, domain modeling, conceptual assessment framework, assessment implementation & delivery) that are designed to build on each other [38]. By gathering information about the domain, i.e., common real-world situations, the first layer, "domain analysis," serves to lay the groundwork for further development [42]. Schütz et al. [15] performed such a domain analysis for the cyber security domain already, thus developing the Cyber Security Domain Model (CSDM) as the necessary domain model for establishing employee cyber security competencies [35]. This process-oriented angle informs our research in that the CSDM for individuals can follow the CSDM for SMEs which is already established in practice and thus allows more reliable results.

2.3 Understanding SETA Programs from a Solution-Oriented Angle

According to Li and Siponen [9], IS security research has focused on the organizational rather than the private context, such as security behavior at home. This is also the case for research on SETA since it seems mostly related to the organizational context (e.g., [13, 17]). In general, SETA programs are characterized by their "ongoing efforts to focus employees' attention on information security–related issues, provide employees with crucial knowledge and skills, enable their deep understanding of why security protection is needed, and increase their awareness of security issues" [13]. In the organizational context, the basis for the implementation of a SETA program is often the definition of security policies and the adaptation of a security framework [12]. Often, SETA programs are offered to the entire workforce [13], which means that the programs are not customized to the exact threats or activities of the participants, and consequently participants are not trained on the most relevant risks [15, 17]. Thereby, more effective SETA programs are characterized by being customized to a specific target group [39]. However, private individuals as a target group rarely undergo SETA programs or similar awareness measures. This solution-oriented angle informs our research since the CSDM for individuals must address specific threat vectors and associated real-world action situations that are as realistic as possible. In addition, the current corporate SETA programs are only geared toward organizations and maybe, therefore, not sufficiently tailored to private individuals.

Table 1. Stages of a Domain Analysis for Cyber-Secure Behavior (own illustration, based on Schütz et al. [15]).

	Stage 1: Object Classification	Stage 2: Object Analysis	Stage 3: Object Reduction
Steps	– Determine Objects to be Classified – Investigate Sub-Dimensions of Objects	– Identify new Threat Events and Threat Areas for the Cyber Security Domain	– Determine Threat Vectors – Sort out Unreasonable Threat Vectors
Method	Applied Security Knowledge	Literature Review	Applied Security Knowledge
Source	Literature on Threat Vectors (Schütz et al. [15])	Records on Security Threats	Researchers from the IS Security Domain
Outcome	Security Threat Classification Objects	CSDM for Individuals	Reviewed CSDM for Individuals

3 Research Approach

Unlike the three-stage domain analysis research approach of Schütz et al. [15], we present only the adapted first two stages within the scope of this paper (Table 1). Here, the first stage, "object classification", can be adopted in its entirety (see Chapter 5.1). More precisely, we adopt the two-dimensionality of CSDM consisting of threat area and threat event, which results in threat vectors. The second stage, "object analysis", identifies the threat areas and threat events relevant to individuals through a literature review, including records from practice and academia. In the third stage, "object reduction," all possible threat vectors would be determined based on the identified threat areas and threat events and checked for plausibility, but this is not part of this work.

4 Methodology for a Literature-Based Object Analysis (Stage 2)

As pointed out in the research approach (see Chapter 3) following Schütz et al. [15], we took a literature-based approach for the object analysis. Therefore, we conduct a structured literature review regarding security threats relevant to individuals. In particular, the reporting of the results is based on the PRISMA methodology of Moher et al. [15]. Furthermore, we also draw on best practice recommendations from Vom Brocke et al. [19] and Webster and Watson [20].

The literature review includes both practitioner and academic sources to cover both common and emerging threat events and threat areas. On the one hand, sources from practice (e.g., crime statistics, white papers) were sought that specify currently occurring security threats in the domain of individuals. Since we want to ensure the authenticity of the information obtained, we use primarily publications from organizations (e.g., Deutschland sicher im Netz e.V.) and authorities (e.g., Federal Office for Information Security, Federal Criminal Police Office). The literature review is not limited to German publications but also includes authorities from other European countries, North America, and Australia. Despite local and cultural differences in crime, a global and thus more valid evaluation of current cybercrime can be made. On the other hand, we have searched for academic literature on security threats and assets in three common IS databases (i.e., AISeL, ACM Digital Library, and IEEE Xplore) to identify possible innovative threat areas and threat events that are not yet reflected in common crime statistics in practice. On all three databases, we employed this search string to find matches in abstracts: ("cyber" OR "Information Technology" OR "security") AND ("risk" OR "threat") AND ("individual" OR "consumer" OR "citizen").

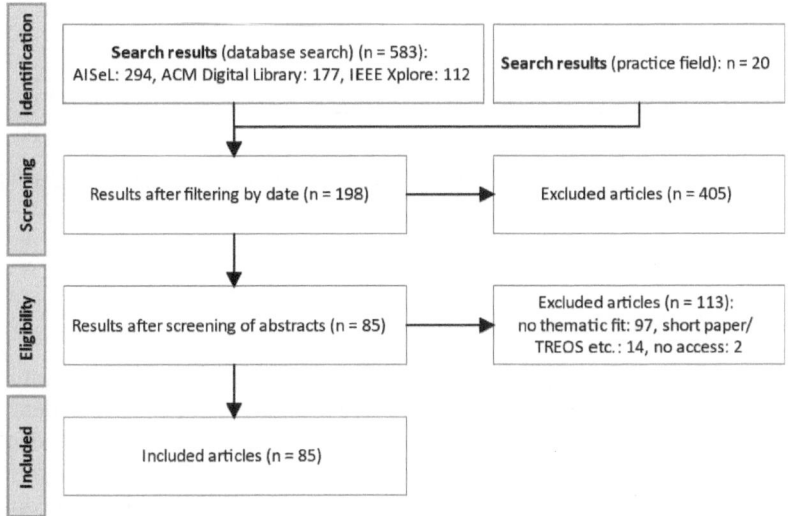

Fig. 1. Overview of the Literature Review (own illustration, based on Moher et al. [18]).

Figure 1 shows the further filtering process of the literature review, focusing on current and relevant literature. Based on the above-mentioned approach, the identified search results (n = 583) are reviewed and all records older than three years and duplicates are sorted out (n = 405). Thus, we focus on literature that has been published since 2020 to best capture today's threats to individuals (n = 198). This also includes the results of the manual search for practitioner literature (n = 20), containing twelve sources from Germany, two sources from the remainder of Europe, five sources from North America, and one source from Australia. The next step is to review the abstracts of the identified literature to decide which paper to analyze in more detail. Articles were excluded (n = 113) due to lack of thematic fit (n = 97), lack of access (n = 2), or unsuitable / too short paper format (n = 14), resulting in n = 85 final relevant sources. Despite the thematic fit of the sources (i.e. dealing with cyber risks and threats), however, they were not always explicitly designed for private individuals.

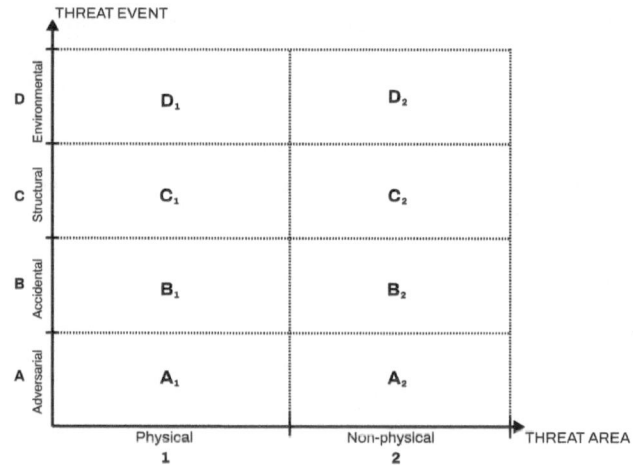

Fig. 2. The CSDM and its two dimensions (own illustration, based on Schütz et al. [15])

5   Results

5.1   Stage 1: Object Classification

Since competent behavior requires the employee to be situationally aware of threatening situations, the initial CSDM consists of two dimensions (Fig. 2) and considers, on the one hand, the assets used in the threat situation, hereafter called threat area, and on the other hand, the threat source, hereafter called threat event [15]. Hereby, a threat area in the cyber security domain can include, among others, Internet-connected computers, applications, telecommunication systems, and any transmitted or stored information in the user's cyber environment [40].

The two dimensions are further subdivided into eight threat clusters (A1 to D2), depending on the threat area and threat event, following the NIST framework 800–30 [41]. Within these eight threat clusters exist several threat vectors, which Schütz et al. [15] define as objects to be classified in the domain model. In terms of threat events, Schütz et al. [15] refer to Blank and Gallagher's [41] resource of threat events, e.g., listing DDoS or phishing attacks. Contrary to Blank and Gallagher [23], the focus here is primarily on adversarial threat events. This decision was made because private households must bear the greater potential damage in the event of adversarial threat events. Moreover, this type of threat event offers the most potential for prevention through SETA programs for individuals.

5.2   Stage 2: Literature-Based Objects Analysis

As outlined above, the CSDM should determine which threat situations the individuals under consideration are exposed to so that SETA programs are best designed for them [15, 17]. Therefore, in this second stage, "object analysis," relevant sources are extracted from the literature review to determine which security threats are described there respectively and which threat events and threat areas may play a role for individuals. We based our approach on the CSDM from Schütz et al. [15], but as stated by Li and Siponen [9], differences exist between organizational context and private context, which also explain the elements in both our two threat dimensions.

Table 2. Threat Areas of the CSDM for Individuals (own illustration)

ID	Threat Area	Exemplary Source
Physical		
TA 1	Computer/Laptop	[24]
TA 2	Smartphone	[24]
TA 3	Tablet	[24]
TA 4	Stationary Connected Devices (e.g., Smart Home)	[24]
TA 5	Mobile Connected Devices (e.g., Smart Watch)	[24]
TA 6	Removable Storage Media (e.g., USB Flash Drive)	[42]
TA 7	Phone	[43]
Non-Physical		
TA 8	E-Mail Service	[24]
TA 9	Messenger Service	[24]
TA 10	Video Conferencing Platform	[44]
TA 11	Social Media Network	[24]
TA 12	Online Dating	[24]
TA 13	Classifieds Platform	[24]
TA 14	Web Browser	[44]
TA 15	Online Banking	[24]
TA 16	Online Shopping	[24]
TA 17	Online Dating	[24]
TA 18	Mobile Payment	[24]
TA 19	Cloud Storage	[45]
TA 20	SMS	[43]
TA 21	Voice Assistant	[24]
TA 22	Application	[44]
TA 23	Streaming Platform (e.g., Video, Music, Podcast)	[24]

Regarding threat areas, we were able to identify twenty-three elements through the literature review (Table 2). In terms of physical threat areas, among others, stationary connected devices (e.g., Smart Home) are added to our CSDM in comparison to the results for organizations of Schütz et al. [15]. In the area of non-physical assets, among others, online shopping and online dating were added. Some key assets in the CSDM for organizations, such as servers or accounting systems [15], could not be adopted in connection with private households. Moreover, a total of thirteen threat events (Table 3) result from the literature review. The results are significantly different from the CSDM for organizations [15], further proving the distinction of the cyber security domain of individuals.

Based on the identified threat areas and threat events, the CSDM finds all possible threat vectors, which then map specific threats, such as a phishing attack on a mailing system[15]. Two more examples of potential threat vectors are shown in Table 4. In sum, a total of thirteen threat events and twenty-three threat areas were identified, allowing for 299 possible threat vectors. In the third and pending stage of the domain analysis (see Chapter 3), these would have to be checked for plausibility, as many combinations may be unlikely or even unfeasible.

6 Discussion

This study aimed to determine which security threats should be addressed when provid-ing SETA programs to private households based on individual cyber risk profiles from an extended domain model of cyber-secure behavior. Following the research approach of Schütz et al. [15], and integrating a literature review following Moher et al. [18], Vom Brocke et al. [19], and Webster and Watson [20], differences between threats to individuals and organizational employees could be identified. This is in line with Li and Siponen's [9] initial proposition that the content of the SETA programs, which has so far been designed primarily for organizations, does not sufficiently address the private domain and thus cannot influence cyber-secure behavior at home. For example, contrary to Schütz et al. [15], individuals do not use systems such as CMS or ERP. Instead, they use platforms for online shopping or dating, which is reflected in their cyber risk profiles. Furthermore, not all threat events from the organizational context, such as elevated data privileges in a collaboration system, are relevant for individuals and, therefore, do not need to be addressed in CSC tests or SETA programs for, e.g., college students.

Based on these findings, we provide the following implications for theory and prac-tice. First, we follow the research call of Li and Siponen [9] by focusing on individuals who, contrary to research about organizational cyber security, have received little atten-tion so far. In contrast to Schütz et al. [15] we are not only contributing to the cyber security literature within IS research but are also addressing the need for digital pro-tection of individuals given advancing digitalization. Therefore, the CSDM identifies security threats to individuals by categorizing 299 possible threat vectors along two dimensions: thirteen threat events and twenty-three threat areas. This extends existing multi-dimensional security threat classifications and reduces complexity by focusing the model on threat events and threat areas as dimensions.

Table 3. Threat Events of the CSDM for Individuals (own illustration)

ID	Threat Event	Definition	Exemplary Source
TE 1	Phishing	"The use of unsolicited email, text messages, and telephone calls purportedly from a legitimate company requesting personal, financial, and/or login credentials."	[46]
TE 2	SIM Swapping	"The use of unsophisticated social engineering techniques against mobile service providers to transfer a victim's phone service to a mobile device in the criminal's possession."	[46]
TE 3	Spam	"unwanted communication intended to be delivered to an indiscriminate target, directly or indirectly, notwithstanding measures to prevent its delivery."	[47]
TE 4	Malware	"Software or code intended to damage, disable, or capable of copying itself onto a computer and/or computer systems to have a detrimental effect or destroy data"	[46]
TE 5	Ransomware	"In a ransomware attack, the attacker reversibly renders the victim's computer or information system inoperable. In practice, most ransomware encrypts computer or system data using cryptographic mechanisms, making it impossible to view or use. The attacker then sends an unencrypted message to the victim offering to provide them with the means to decrypt their data, in exchange for the payment of a ransom."	[42]

(*continued*)

Table 3. (*continued*)

ID	Threat Event	Definition	Exemplary Source
TE 6	Multi-factor Authentication (MFA) Push Exhaustion Attack	"This sees attackers trigger a deluge of MFA acceptance prompts on a user's phone until the user clicks 'Allow' to stop the flood of requests."	[28]
TE 7	Spoofing	"Contact information (phone number, email, and website) is deliberately falsified to mislead and appear to be from a legitimate source. For example, spoofed phone numbers making mass robo-calls; spoofed emails sending mass spam; forged websites used to mislead and gather personal information. Often used in connection with other crime types."	[46]
TE 8	Cyber Harassment	"Repeated words, conduct, or action that serve no legitimate purpose and are directed at a specific person to annoy, alarm, or distress that person. Engaging in a course of conduct directed at a specific person that would cause a reasonable person to fear for his/her safety or the safety of others or suffer substantial emotional distress."	[46]
TE 9	Identity Theft	"Someone steals and uses personal identifying information, like a name or Social Security number, without permission to commit fraud or other crimes and/or (account takeover) a fraudster obtains account information to perpetrate fraud on existing accounts."	[46]

(*continued*)

Table 3. (*continued*)

ID	Threat Event	Definition	Exemplary Source
TE 10	Confidence/Romance Fraud	"An individual believes they are in a relationship (family, friendly, or romantic) and are tricked into sending money, personal and financial information, or items of value to the perpetrator or to launder money or items to assist the perpetrator."	[46]
TE 11	Shopping Fraud	"Payment is sent, and goods or services are never received, or are of lesser quality."	[46]
TE 12	Investment Fraud	"Deceptive practice that induces investors to make purchases based on false information. These scams usually offer the victims large returns with minimal risk."	[46]
TE 13	Credit Card/ Check Fraud	"Credit card fraud is a wide-ranging term for theft and fraud committed using a credit card or any similar payment mechanism (ACH. EFT, recurring charge, etc.) as a fraudulent source of funds in a transaction."	[46]

Table 4. Threat Vector examples (own illustration, based on Schütz et al. [15])

Threat Event (TE)	Threat Area (TA)	Example	Exemplary Source
Malware (TE 4)	Removable Storage Media (e.g., USB Flash Drive) (TA 6)	An adversary places a USB flash drive containing malware where victims will find it	[41]
Phishing (TE 1)	Messenger Service (TA 9)	An adversary sends an instant message to trick the victim into revealing personal information	[41]

Second, the extended CSDM for individuals paves the way to develop valid CSC tests for private individuals within the further layers (i.e., domain modeling, assessment framework, assessment implementation, and delivery) of the ECD Framework, according to Mislevy and Haertel [48]. Thus, the CSDM for Individuals represents the foundation to go beyond the existing self-reported measurement scales and to develop action-oriented, authentic CSC tests. In this way, the criticism of measurement scales based on self-reporting described above [33] could also be addressed.

Third, the domain analysis conducted in this paper presents a suitable starting point for finalizing the third stage of the domain analysis. The possible combinations of the threat areas and events identified here could be analyzed regarding their plausibility to form threat vectors. These threat vectors could be used to better tailor SETA programs to individual cyber risk profiles and the threats at hand. This could increase the effectiveness of SETA programs and the positive impact on CSC of individuals, as they could be prepared specifically for potential threat areas and associated threat events in their everyday lives. For example, a senior citizen who does not use online banking does not need to be trained about phishing as a threat event for effective security behavior in this area. Similarly, time- and thus cost-efficient SETA programs for individuals could be provided on the dangers of using WhatsApp as a social messenger via smartphone if they use it. Overall, this could also prevent cybercrime or at least make it more difficult for attackers to be successful. The higher effectiveness of this competency-based, action-specific design of SETA programs should be investigated in empirical studies and which online experimental studies are suitable for it.

Fourth, the CSDM is compatible with existing KPIs, such as the DsiN security index [2, 24], and can thus further enhance the informative value of those metrics. Thus, the CSDM for Individuals could be precisely adapted by groups with high cyber risk profiles and their most frequent threat vectors. For example, the consumer study DsiN [2] distinguishes five types of individuals exposed to certain risks to varying degrees and thus have different security indexes. This DsiN security index is derived from the threat exposure and the feeling of insecurity as well as the level of protection, the latter calculated from security knowledge and behavior [2], i.e., two dimensions of security competencies [35]. For example, fatalistic users should be addressed in the first step, since they are most frequently affected by security incidents and have too little security knowledge to prevent future incidents [2]. In sum, this makes the CSDM for individuals also suitable for categorizing users with high cyber risk profiles, particularly based on more real-world action situations.

However, our research has some limitations to consider when applying the CSDM to individuals. Since technology and its security threats change rapidly, cyber security research may also use adaptable and flexible frameworks. Analogous to Schütz et al. [15], our extended CSDM for individuals is a snapshot of up-to-date contextualized threat vectors and has to be checked for applicability regularly, which is easily enabled by the two dimensions used. So, despite the intended scalability of the model, there is effort involved in updating the two dimensions.

7   Conclusion

In our study, we contribute to IS security research by providing an extension of CSDM to individuals. Therefore, we adapted the first two stages to the approach presented by Schütz et al. [15] (i.e. object classification and object analysis) to consider the reality of individuals' lives and related threat situations. Through a structured literature review, we deliver insight into the manifestations of the current threat factors at the level of individuals. On the one hand, the CSDM contains twenty-three threat areas for individuals through which they can be exposed to cyber threats. On the other hand, thirteen threat events were identified, which may pose a threat to private individuals and can occur within the above-mentioned threat areas. The combination of both dimensions yields 299 possible threat vectors, which must be further analyzed for their individual plausibility and used in the following steps of the ECD framework.

Acknowledgments. This paper has been developed as part of the project "ITS.kompetent" funded by the German Federal Ministry for Economic Affairs and Climate Action (Grant numbers: 01MS20008A and 01MS20008B). We would like to thank the German Federal Ministry for Economic Affairs and Climate Action for the support.

References

1. Eurostat: Internet use by individuals. Data set. European Commission, Eurostat (2024). https://doi.org/10.2908/TIN00028. Accessed 16 June 2024
2. Deutschland sicher im Netz (DsiN): DsiN Sicherheitsindex 2022. Studie von Deutschland sicher im Netz e.V. zur digitalen Sicherheitslage von Verbraucher:innen in Deutschland. Deutschland sicher im Netz (DsiN), Berlin (2022). https://www.sicher-im-netz.de/dsin-sicherheitsindex-2022. Accessed 7 February 2023
3. Federal Criminal Police Office of Germany (BKA): Bundeslagebild Cybercrime 2021, Wiesbaden (2022). https://www.bka.de/SharedDocs/Downloads/DE/Publikationen/JahresberichteUndLagebilder/Cybercrime/cybercrimeBundeslagebild2021. Accessed 16 September 2022
4. Federal Bureau of Investigation (FBI): Internet Crime Report 2021. Internet Crime Complaint Center (IC3). Federal Bureau of Investigation (FBI) (2021). https://www.ic3.gov/AnnualReport/Reports/2021_IC3Report.pdf. Accessed 24 October 2024
5. Fleck, A.: Cybercrime Expected To Skyrocket in Coming Years. Statista (2022). https://www.statista.com/chart/28878/expected-cost-of-cybercrime-until-2027/. Accessed 7 April 2023
6. Parsons, K., Calic, D., Pattinson, M., Butavicius, M., McCormac, A., Zwaans, T.: The Human Aspects of Information Security Questionnaire (HAIS-Q): Two further validation studies. Comput. Secur. **66**, 40–51 (2017). https://doi.org/10.1016/j.cose.2017.01.004
7. Shah, P., Agarwal, A.: Cybersecurity behaviour of smartphone users in India: an empirical analysis. Info. Comp. Sec. **28**(2), 293–318 (2020). https://doi.org/10.1108/ICS-04-2019-0041
8. Nurse, J.R.C.: Cybersecurity awareness. In: Adams, C., Barg, A., Boneh, D., Bauer, F.L., Benoit, O., Biham, E., Biryukov, A., Black, J., Blakley, R., Bleumer, G., Boeyen, S. (eds.) Encyclopedia of Cryptography and Security. Springer-Verlag, Berlin, Heidelberg (2011). https://doi.org/10.1007/978-3-642-27739-9_1596-1
9. Li, Y., Siponen, M.: A Call For Research On Home Users' Information Security Behaviour. PACIS 2011 Proceedings, 112, pp. 1–11 (2011)

10. Lin, C., Kunnathur, A.: Toward Developing a Theory of End User Information Security Competence. AMCIS 2013 Proceedings, 1, pp. 1–10 (2013)

11. Rampold, F., Schütz, F., Masuch, K., Köpfer, P., Warwas, J.: Are You Aware Of Your Competencies? – The Potentials Of Competence Research To Design Effective SETA Programs. ECIS 2022 Proceedings 134, pp. 1–17 (2022)

12. Whitman, M.E., Mattord, H.J.: Principles of information security, 4th edn. Course Technology Cengage Learning, Stamford, Conn. (2012)

13. Hu, S., Hsu, C., Zhou, Z.: Security education, training, and awareness programs: literature review. J. Comp. Info. Sys. **62**(4), 752–764 (2021). https://doi.org/10.1080/08874417.2021. 1913671

14. Federal Office for Information Security of Germany (BSI): Bericht zum Digitalen Verbraucherschutz 2021, BSI-DVS22/001, Bonn (2022). https://www.bsi.bund.de/SharedDocs/Downloads/DE/BSI/Publikationen/DVS-Berichte/dvs-bericht_2021.pdf?__blob=publicationFile &v=4. Accessed 25 November 2022

15. Schütz, F., et al.: Bridging the Gap between Security Competencies and Security Threats: Toward a Cyber Security Domain Model. Proceedings of the 56th Hawaii International Conference on System Sciences 2023 (HICSS-56), pp. 6118–6127 (2023). https://hdl.handle.net/ 10125/103375. Accessed 24 October 2024

16. Winther, E.: Kompetenzmessung in der beruflichen Bildung. W. Bertelsmann Verlag, Bielefeld (2010). https://doi.org/10.3278/6004148w

17. Rampold, F., Heinsohn, J., Schütz, F., Klein, J., Warwas, J.W.: Custom Solutions for Diverse Needs: Laying the Foundation for Tailored SETA Programs in the Healthcare Domain. Proceedings of the 57th Hawaii International Conference on System Sciences 2024 (HICSS-57), pp. 3719–3728 (2024). https://hdl.handle.net/10125/106832. Accessed 24 October 2024

18. Moher, D., Liberati, A., Tetzlaff, J., Altman, D.G.: Preferred reporting items for systematic reviews and meta-analyses: the PRISMA statement. The BMJ **339**(b2535), 1–8 (2009). https:// doi.org/10.1136/bmj.b2535

19. Vom Brocke, J., et al.: Standing on the shoulders of giants. challenges and recommendations of literature search in information systems research. Comm. Asso. Info. Sys. **37**(9), 205–224 (2015). https://doi.org/10.17705/1CAIS.03709

20. Webster, J., Watson, R.T.: Analyzing the past to prepare for the future. Writ. Lit. Rev. MIS Q. **26**(2), xiii–xxiii (2002)

21. Riek, M., Böhme, R.: The costs of consumer-facing cybercrime: an empirical exploration of measurement issues and estimates†. J. Cybersecurity **4**(1), 1–16 (2018). tyy004, https://doi. org/10.1093/cybsec/tyy004

22. Federal Criminal Police Office of Germany (BKA): Cybercrime. Was ist Cybercrime? (2022) https://www.bka.de/DE/UnsereAufgaben/Deliktsbereiche/Cybercrime/cyberc rime_neu. Accessed 11 November 2022

23. Al-Khater, W.A., Al-Maadeed, S., Ahmed, A.A., Sadiq, A.S., Khan, M.K.: Comprehensive review of cybercrime detection techniques. IEEE Access **8**, 137293–137311 (2020). https:// doi.org/10.1109/ACCESS.2020.3011259

24. Deutschland sicher im Netz (DsiN): DsiN Sicherheitsindex 2023. Studie von Deutschland sicher im Netz e. V. zur digitalen Sicherheitslage von Verbraucher:innen in Deutschland. Deutschland sicher im Netz (DsiN), Berlin (2023). https://www.sicher-im-netz.de/dsin-sic herheitsindex-2023. Accessed 1 November 2023

25. Birkel, C., Church, D., Erdmann, A., Hager, A., Leitgöb-Guzy, N.: Sicherheit und Kriminalität in Deutschland - SKiD 2020. Bundesweite Kernbefunde des Viktimisierungssurvey des Bundeskriminalamts und der Polizei der Länder. Deutschland, Wiesbaden (2023). https://www.bka.de/DE/UnsereAufgaben/Forschung/ForschungsprojekteUndErgebn isse/Dunkelfeldforschung/SKiD/Ergebnisse/Ergebnisse_node.html

26. Onemichl, A., Bolz, C.: Digitalbarometer. Bürgerbefragung zur Cyber-Sicherheit 2022. Kurzbericht zur Studie der Polizeilichen Kriminalprävention der Länder und des Bundes (ProPK) und des Bundesamtes für Sicherheit in der Informationstechnik (BSI), Bonn (2022). https://www.bsi.bund.de/SharedDocs/Downloads/DE/BSI/Digitalbarometer/ Digitalbarometer-ProPK-BSI_2022.pdf. Accessed 31 October 2023

27. Federal Office for Information Security of Germany (BSI): Die Lage der IT-Sicherheit in Deutschland 2021, Bonn (2021). https://www.bsi.bund.de/SharedDocs/Downloads/DE/BSI/ Publikationen/Lageberichte/Lagebericht2021. Accessed 24 October 2024

28. National Cyber Security Centre (NCSC): NCSC Annual Review 2022. Making the UK the safest place to live and work online (2022). https://www.ncsc.gov.uk/collection/annual-rev iew-2022. Accessed 19 November 2023

29. van Nek, L., Bolz, C.: Digitalbarometer 2021. Bürgerbefragung zur Cyber-Sicherheit. Kurzbericht zur Studie der Polizeilichen Kriminalprävention der Länder und des Bundes (ProPK) und des Bundesamtes für Sicherheit in der Informationstechnik (BSI), Bonn (2021). https://www.bsi.bund.de/SharedDocs/Downloads/DE/BSI/Digitalbarometer/ Digitalbarometer-ProPK-BSI_2021.pdf?__blob=publicationFile&v=2. Accessed 9 March 2023

30. Rampold, F., Masuch, K., Warwas, J., Trang, S.: Triad or error? introducing three basic dimensions of competence as a driving force for information security performance. ICIS 2023 Proceedings, 11, pp. 1–17 (2023)

31. Asfoor, A., Rahim, F.A., Yussof, S.: Factors influencing information security awareness of phishing attacks from bank customers' perspective: a preliminary investigation. In: Saeed, F. (ed.) Recent Trends in Data Science and Soft Computing. Proceedings of the 3rd International Conference of Reliable Information and Communication Technology (IRICT 2018), pp. 641– 654 (2019). https://doi.org/10.1007/978-3-319-99007-1_60

32. Parsons, K., McCormac, A., Butavicius, M., Pattinson, M., Jerram, C.: Determining employee awareness using the Human Aspects of Information Security Questionnaire (HAIS-Q). Comput. Secur. **42**, 165–176 (2014). https://doi.org/10.1016/j.cose.2013.12.003

33. Spector, P.E.: Using self-report questionnaires in OB research: a comment on the use of a controversial method. J. Organ. Behav. **15**(5), 385–392 (1994). https://doi.org/10.1002/job. 4030150503

34. Weinert, F.E.: Lehren und Lernen für die Zukunft - Ansprüche an das Lernen in der Schule. Nachrichten der Gesellschaft zur Förderung Pädagogischer Forschung **2**, 4–23 (2000)

35. Köpfer, P., Warwas, J., Schütz, F., Rampold, F., Masuch, K., Trang, S.: A competence-based screening of instructional designs in trainings for IT-security at the workplace. AERA **2023**, 1–11 (2023). https://doi.org/10.5281/zenodo.8300825

36. Warwas, J., et al.: Developing and validating an online situational judgment test on the stress coping competence of nursing apprentices. Empirical Res. Vocat. Edu. Train. **15**(5), 1–24 (2023). https://doi.org/10.1186/s40461-023-00145-x

37. Mislevy, R.J., Almond, R.G., Lukas, J.F.: A brief introduction to evidence-centered design. ETS Research Report Series **2003**(1), 1–29 (2003). RR-03-16, https://doi.org/10.1002/j.2333-8504.2003.tb01908.x

38. Mislevy, R.J.: Evidence-centered design for simulation-based assessment. Mil. Med. **178**(10), 107–114 (2013). https://doi.org/10.7205/MILMED-D-13-00213

39. Tsohou, A., Karyda, M., Kokolakis, S.: Analyzing the role of cognitive and cultural biases in the internalization of information security policies: Recommendations for information security awareness programs. Comput. Secur. **52**, 128–141 (2015). https://doi.org/10.1016/j. cose.2015.04.006

40. von Solms, R., van Niekerk, J.: From information security to cyber security. Comput. Secur. **38**, 97–102 (2013). https://doi.org/10.1016/j.cose.2013.04.004

41. Blank, R.M., Gallagher, P.D.: NIST Special Publication 800-30. Revision 1. Guide for Conducting Risk Assessments. National Institute of Standards and Technology (NIST), Gaithersburg (2012). https://doi.org/10.6028/NIST.SP.800-30r1

42. Agence nationale de la sécurité des systèmes d'information (ANSSI): Ransomware attacks, all concerned. How to prevent them and respond to an incident, ANSSI-GP-077-EN (2021). https://cyber.gouv.fr/sites/default/files/2021/08/anssi-guide-ransomware_a ttacks_all_concerned-v1.0.pdf. Accessed 21 October 2024

43. Federal Office for Information Security of Germany (BSI): Bericht zum Digitalen Verbraucherschutz 2022, BSI-DVS23/001, Bonn (2023). https://www.bsi.bund.de/SharedDocs/Downlo ads/DE/BSI/Publikationen/DVS-Berichte/dvs-bericht_2022.pdf. Accessed 31 October 2023

44. Deutschland sicher im Netz (DsiN): Basisschutz digital. https://www.sicher-im-netz.de/bas isschutz-digital (2023). Accessed 1 November 2023

45. Federal Office for Information Security of Germany (BSI): Die Lage der IT-Sicherheit in Deutschland 2022, Bonn (2022). https://www.bsi.bund.de/SharedDocs/Downloads/DE/BSI/ Publikationen/Lageberichte/Lagebericht2022. Accessed 16 February 2023

46. Federal Bureau of Investigation (FBI): Internet Crime Report 2022. Internet Crime Complaint Center (IC3) (2022). https://www.ic3.gov/AnnualReport/Reports/2022_IC3Report. pdf. Accessed 21 October 2024

47. Cormack, G.V.: Email Spam Filtering: A Systematic Review. Foundations and Trends® in Information Retrieval **1**(4), 335–455 (2006). https://doi.org/10.1561/1500000006

48. Mislevy, R.J., Haertel, G.D.: Implications of evidence-centered design for educational testing. Educ. Meas. Issues Pract. **25**(4), 6–20 (2006). https://doi.org/10.1111/j.1745-3992.2006.000 75.x

An Exploratory Analyses of Consumers' Digital Focus on Bitcoin Price and Activity

B. Muralikrishnan, Abhinav Mathur$^{(\boxtimes)}$, N. Govindrajan, and Anita Manda

Indian School of Business, Hyderabad 500032, India
{muralikrishnan_b,abhinav_mathur,govind_n,anita_manda}@isb.edu

Abstract. Existing literature attempting to model the determinants of Bitcoin pricing has used a combination of economic, transactional, and technical factors as the independent variables. We seek to build on this body of knowledge by narrowing our investigation to the impact of Consumers' Digital Focus, which we conceptualize as a multidimensional construct that constitutes the volume, sentiment, and engagement of social media mentions and web search trends on Bitcoin prices, volatility, and growth. Specifically, we hypothesize that Tweet volumes (mentions), impressions, positive tweet sentiment, and engagement (immediate and lagged effect) for regular and verified users and internet search volume positively impact Bitcoin prices. We also hypothesize that Tweets with negative sentiment have a counter effect. Our study uses primary data from Blockchain, Twitter, and Google Search to test these hypotheses. Regression analysis finds broad support for our research model. Overall, we uncover novel insights that challenge conventional thinking regarding engagement and sentiment and present fresh insights into the influence of web searches and Twitter impressions on Bitcoin pricing.

Keywords: Digital Consumer Persona · Bitcoin Volatility · Cross-Sectional Analysis

1 Introduction

Cryptocurrencies, especially Bitcoins, are heralded as a decentralized alternative to fiat currencies, a store of value that can serve as an effective inflation hedge, a medium exchange, and an alternative asset class. The popularity of Bitcoins peaked in November 2021 with a total market capitalization of $ 1.28 Trillion (compared to the NYSE Market cap of $ 28 Trillion) and 85 million wallets created on bitcoin.com (growth of 30.30% in 5 years). Given the digital-by-design nature of Bitcoins, the interest in Cryptocurrency amongst the Technology-savvy connected populace is natural. Understanding the role of internet searches and social media interest in influencing the price of Bitcoins and trade activity can help traders and investors adjust their trading strategy based on predicted price movements. An internal Twitter analysis finds that there have been over a billion tweets about Bitcoin since 2020, and Bitcoin still maintains a high index search ranking across Google search volume.

© The Author(s), under exclusive license to Springer Nature Switzerland AG 2025
A. Kathuria et al. (Eds.): WeB 2023, LNBIP 525, pp. 63–82, 2025.
https://doi.org/10.1007/978-3-031-74437-2_6

Existing literature has modeled Bitcoin pricing determinants using economic, transactional, social media mentions, and technical factors. Transactional factors include Bitcoin addresses, exchange-to-trade ratio, hash rate, and difficulty [1, 2]. Technical factors incorporate hash rate and bitcoin mining difficulty [3]. The rise in the popularity of Bitcoin and other cryptocurrencies has led to increased internet activity on platforms like Google Search, Twitter, Reddit, and Wikipedia [4, 5]. Researchers have worked to identify the impact of this surge in user interest on Bitcoin's price.

Our work aims to enhance this body of knowledge by focusing on the influence of social media mentions, especially on Twitter, and web search trends. We use primary data from Blockchain, Twitter, and Google Search. Past research has delved into the impact of social media on trading volume, volatility, returns, sentiments, and more [6, 7]. While several studies have looked at tweet volume, few have explored the lag effect of searches and tweets on Bitcoin pricing or the influence of Twitter impressions and engagement on Bitcoin's price [5, 8].

Our work seeks to build on this body of knowledge by narrowing our focus to the impact of social media mentions on Bitcoin prices and trade volumes. For this purpose, we use Twitter (now known as X) as a source, considering its popularity amongst celebrities and average users, the high volume of posts on the platform. Further, we examine the impact of the tweet's sentiment and overall engagement received on the tweet and understand the impact this has on Bitcoin prices and transaction volumes. We look at the impact that user interest has had on the growing number of Bitcoin users and the impact this has had on Bitcoin pricing. We also use web search trends (specifically, google search trends) as another source.

Our study uses primary data from the Blockchain as well as Twitter and Google Search data to test the hypotheses that Tweet volumes (mentions), impressions, positive tweet sentiment, and engagement (immediate as well as lagged effect) for regular as well as verified users as well as Google search volume have a positive impact on Bitcoin prices, with negative sentiment having the counter effect. We have used OLS regression, Stepwise regression using Akaike Information Criteria (AIC), and ensemble ML algorithms such as GBM XgBoost models to asses our hypotheses. Further, our hypothesis tests whether the abovementioned variables influence total Bitcoin trade volume and the number of Bitcoin wallets created. The scope of the paper encompasses not just Bitcoin pricing but also trade volumes, wallets and search trends on Ethereum (a competitor to Bitcoin), both of which are relevant to a Bitcoin investor.

Our approach resulted in a significant OLS model and a GBM backtested on 2022 daily predictions until 21 October 2023. The OLS model has a p-value < 0.05 and has a MAPE of 38% for the total back-tested data; the GBM model performs better with a MAPE of 22%. Both models predict the Bitcoin price with a lesser error for a 4-month prediction with a MAPE of 22% and 14%, respectively, as expected due to data drift from long-term predictions.

Our approach has also improved existing literature by capturing lag effects. The data preparation for Model training included standard NLP pre-processing and sentiment analysis with Vader, along with metrics such as tweet impressions and engagements and various derived metrics such as reduction of tweet impact chronologically. The approach also considers daily search volumes. Our model found that tweet volume and search trends impact bitcoin prices; surprisingly, the model does not show a relationship between sentiment and bitcoin prices. Another curious finding was that one-day search lags affect bitcoin prices negatively, while two-day lags positively affect prices. We have consciously not considered the lag effects of the previous day's price in the model training.

The paper is structured as follows. We start with a synthesis of the existing literature studying the determinants of Bitcoin pricing and identify the research gaps of (i) Lack of consolidated data sources, (ii) Limited work on lag effects of tweets and searches, (iii) Possibility of tweets and search damping using depreciation effects. We then lay out the hypothesis of the factors determining Bitcoin pricing being studied by us, describe the data preparation, modelling, and analysis results, and discuss the findings, limitations, and future research direction.

2   Historical and Theoretical Background on Bitcoin

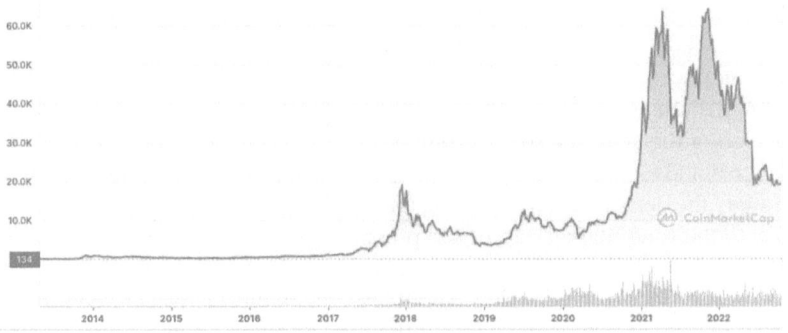

Fig. 1. Daily closing price of Bitcoin in USD

After an uneventful start, where Technology enthusiasts were primarily exploring Bitcoin, Bitcoin started seeing regulatory scrutiny with increasing transaction volumes and suspicions of Bitcoins being used in illegal activities (example - Silk Road). Over time, up until 2016, Bitcoin continued to gain user and merchant interest, with an increasing number of online merchants accepting Bitcoin payments for online transactions. A discussion paper titled 'A History of Bitcoin' [9] traces the history of Bitcoin and other Cryptocurrencies, highlighting the Regulatory intervention across the world leading up to the big Bitcoin bubble, which started in late 2017 when the price of Bitcoin topped the USD 19,000 mark[1], which fueled investor and trading interest and set the stage for the mainstream acceptance of Bitcoin. The promise of a new world currency that is decentralized and not controlled by a central authority (like central banks which control fiat currency) and hence not subject to the whims of macro-economic and monetary policy uncertainty attracted a set of investors and anarchists who had lost faith in traditional currencies due to the successive devaluation due to inflation. At the same time, the

---

[1] Source for figure and historical prices: https://coinmarketcap.com/currencies/bitcoin/.

volatility in Bitcoin prices and the lure of becoming overnight millionaires in this new 'Crypto Gold Rush' attracted traders looking for quick short-term gains. The emerging view of Bitcoin as an asset class also attracted Institutional interest, and significantly higher transaction value and volumes came with it. However, following this bull run, there was also a big crash in Bitcoin prices. By the end of 2018, Bitcoin prices had crashed to USD 3,866, reducing the market capitalization of Bitcoin from over USD 300 Billion to less than USD 70 billion (Fig. 1).

The onset of the COVID-19 pandemic unleashed an unprecedented bull run in the prices of Bitcoin and other Cryptocurrencies, with millions of individuals constrained by lockdowns finding an outlet. This new 'Gold rush' was also aided by Governments and Central banks providing unprecedented stimulus to support economic demand, which was being impacted by COVID spread and the resultant lockdowns [10, 11]. This bull run, which started in October 2020, eventually increased the price of Bitcoin to over USD 63,500 and a market cap of over USD 1.18 Trillion. Subsequently, Bitcoin has been part of the mainstream conversation even as it continued a boom-and-bust cycle being impacted at various points of time by Inflationary concerns, the rapid spread of the COVID-19 Delta wave, concerns of Global recession in 2022, and, more recently, the collapse of a Stablecoin TerraUSD. Bitcoin prices hit a peak of USD 67,566.82 and a peak market capitalization of USD 1.28 Trillion in Nov 2021. Subsequently, from this peak, Bitcoin prices fell to less than USD 20,000 in October 2022 and a Market cap of ~ USD 370 Billion.

Considering the attention that Cryptocurrencies have received not just as a medium of exchange but also as a store of value and an alternate asset class, attempts have been made to study the determinants of pricing and, more specifically, with Bitcoin contributing ~40% to the total market cap of Cryptocurrencies. Such attempts at modeling the determinants of Bitcoin price have used a combination of economic, transactional, and technical factors as the independent variables. Economic factors include the demand and supply of bitcoins, money supply, inflation, price of oil and gold, stock market returns, exchange rates, and economic policy uncertainty [12, 13]. The transactional factors include the number of Bitcoin addresses, exchange-to-trade ratio, hash rate, and difficulty [2, 4]. Technical factors include hash rate and bitcoin mining difficulty [3].

With the popularity of Bitcoin and other Cryptocurrencies, the interest of general users has increased significantly, as evidenced by the number of wallet addresses transacting Bitcoins (Bitcoin: Active Addresses - Glassnode Studio [14]. This interest in Bitcoin and Cryptocurrencies from individual investors has also resulted in a substantial increase in Internet search and referencing activity on Google Search, Twitter, Reddit, and Wikipedia, amongst others [4, 5, 12] and researchers have tried to establish the impact of such manifestation of user interest and attractiveness on the price of Bitcoin. However, existing research utilizes these user interest and attractiveness variables as one of the many variables. More specifically, extant literature needs to address the question of the impact of social media and web search trends on Bitcoin price immediately and with a lag.

Our work seeks to build on this body of knowledge by narrowing our focus to the impacts of social media mentions (using Twitter as a source considering its popularity amongst celebrities as well as average users and the high volume of posts on the platform) and web search trends (using google search trends as the source). Our objective is to focus on the effect of social media interest and search trends on short-term price and transaction volatility, apart from user activity of bitcoin. Various researchers have analyzed the impact of social media, including Twitter, on trading volume volatility and returns [6, 7]. Specific research comparing the volume of a tweet over the sentiment has been carried out, resulting in volume having a more significant impact than the sentiment on the price [8]. Past research has also proved that price and the size of the price change are predictable based on the sentiment, with a day's lag as the indicator [5]. An analysis concluded that while the change in the price of crypto depends on the sentiment in social media and Google trends, a hybrid model like Google trends combined with negative sentiments is the best predictor [15]. A paper analyzed the emotion on Twitter impacting the bitcoin market and summarized that emotion reflects on bitcoin's market movements [16]. Another study has also concluded that the silent majority (to the extent of 95%) are primary drivers apart from internet forums and are more impactful than Twitter from the perspective of the future value of bitcoin [17]. A specific "Musk Effect" study concluded that dogecoin-related tweets have significance in price and not much in Bitcoin [18].

Research has also shown that the technology and economic determinants are better predictors of the exchange rate of Bitcoin than the previous rate [19]. A study on the short-term price prediction of Bitcoin against buys and sell orders results in future fluctuations [20]. An article evaluated how economic policy uncertainty impacts on Bitcoin volatility and returns and summarized having a positive impact on returns and a negative impact on long-term fluctuations [21]. A paper evaluating the impact of news coverage on the Bitcoin return has certain interesting observations, like the positive news on unemployment and durables having a negative impact on Bitcoin price compared to equity returns, wherein it had a positive impact. The negative news on the same criterion positively impacted Bitcoin price [22].

A study conducted to explore Bitcoin as a safe haven during extreme markets compared to commodities like Gold after analysis resulted in a weak safe haven and varies with time as well with different indices [23]. A study evaluated Bitcoin as part of a diversified portfolio instead of Gold, particularly during volatility in oil prices. The study concluded that instead of oil, both Gold and Bitcoin are safer as a hedge [24]. A study comparing the G7 stock market with bitcoin and Gold resulted in bitcoin and Gold as a safer hedge. This study also resulted in Gold as compared to Bitcoin being safer as a hedge compared to Bitcoin, which has relevance in certain countries like Canada [25].

In sum, past studies have analyzed the price of bitcoin against tweet volumes, volatility, returns, search trends, sentiments, influencer impact, as a haven, against the news, and economic policy uncertainty, amongst other factors. However, a few vital aspects need to be further studied. While several researchers studied tweet volume, research has not explored the lag effect of searches and tweets on Bitcoin pricing nor the impact of Twitter impressions and engagement on Bitcoin price. The verified status of the Twitter user making the post still needs to be studied as an independent variable.

3 Hypothesis Development

Our key thesis is that *Consumers' Digital Focus* is associated with the popularity of bitcoin. Specifically, *Consumers' Digital Focus* is associated with the price, the volume of trade, and wallet creation of bitcoin. We conceptualize *Consumers' Digital Focus* as a multidimensional construct comprising the volume, sentiment, and engagement of social media mentions and web search trends. Based on our literature survey, we identify three aspects of bitcoin trading to be explored in the study.

3.1 The Price of Bitcoin

Our first hypothesis relates to the price of Bitcoin. We propose that the price of bitcoin is a direct function of the search volume of the term "Bitcoin" on the internet, tweet impressions (calculated by the depreciated number of followers of the tweet), tweet engagement (likes, retweets, replies), impressions of tweets by verified users, engagement on tweets by verified users and positive sentiment of the tweet. Further, Bitcoin price is hypothesized to be an inverse function of negative sentiment on the tweet and engagement on negative sentiment tweets.

H1o: Consumers' Digital Focus on Bitcoin is associated with Bitcoin price.

H1a: Search volume focused on Bitcoin is positively associated with Bitcoin price.

H1b: Impressions of tweets focused on Bitcoin are positively associated with Bitcoin price.

H1c: Verified users' impressions of tweets focused on Bitcoin are positively associated with Bitcoin price.

H1d: Engagement of tweets focused on Bitcoin is positively associated with Bitcoin price.

H1e: Verified users' engagement of tweets focused on Bitcoin is positively associated with Bitcoin price.

H1f: Positive sentiment of tweets focused on Bitcoin is positively associated with Bitcoin price.

H1g: Negative sentiment of tweets focused on Bitcoin is negatively associated with Bitcoin price.

H1h: Verified users' engagement of negative sentiment tweets focused on Bitcoin is negatively associated with Bitcoin price.

3.2 The Volume of Bitcoin Trades

Our second hypothesis relates to the total volume of Bitcoin trades. We propose that the volume of Bitcoin is a direct function of the search volume of Bitcoin terms on the internet, tweet impressions (calculated by the depreciated number of followers of the tweet), tweet engagement (likes, retweets, replies), impressions of tweets by verified users, engagement on tweets by verified users and positive sentiment of the tweet. Bitcoin volume is hypothesized to be an inverse function of negative sentiment of tweets and engagement on tweets with negative sentiment.

H2o: Consumers' Digital Focus on Bitcoin is associated with Bitcoin trade volume.

H2a: Search volume focused on Bitcoin is positively associated with Bitcoin trade volume.

H2b: Impressions of tweets focused on Bitcoin are positively associated with Bitcoin trade volume.

H2c: Verified users' impressions of tweets focused on Bitcoin are positively associated with Bitcoin trade volume.

H2d: Engagement of tweets focused on Bitcoin is positively associated with Bitcoin trade volume.

H2e: Verified users' engagement of tweets focused on Bitcoin is positively associated with Bitcoin trade volume.

H2f: Positive sentiment of tweets focused on Bitcoin is positively associated with Bitcoin trade volume.

H2g: Negative sentiment of tweets focused on Bitcoin is negatively associated with Bitcoin trade volume.

H2h: Verified users' engagement of negative sentiment tweets focused on Bitcoin is negatively associated with Bitcoin trade volume.

3.3   The Creation of Bitcoin Wallets

Our final hypothesis relates to the daily creation of new Bitcoin wallets. We propose that the number of new wallets is a direct function of the search volume of Bitcoin on the internet, tweet impressions (calculated by the depreciated number of followers of the tweet), tweet engagement (likes, retweets, replies), impressions of tweets by verified users, engagement on tweets by verified users and positive sentiment of the tweet. Bitcoin price is hypothesized to be an inverse function of negative sentiment on tweets and engagement on tweets with negative sentiment.

H3o: Consumers' Digital Focus on Bitcoin is associated with Bitcoin wallet creation.

H3a: Search volume focused on Bitcoin is positively associated with Bitcoin wallet creation.

H3b: Impressions of tweets focused on Bitcoin are positively associated with Bitcoin wallet creation.

H3c: Verified users' impressions of tweets focused on Bitcoin are positively associated with Bitcoin wallet creation.

H3d: Engagement of tweets focused on Bitcoin is positively associated with Bitcoin wallet creation.

H3e: Verified users' engagement of tweets focused on Bitcoin is positively associated with Bitcoin wallet creation.

H3f: Positive sentiment of tweets focused on Bitcoin is positively associated with Bitcoin wallet creation.

H3g: Negative sentiment of tweets focused on Bitcoin is negatively associated with Bitcoin wallet creation.

H3h: Verified users' engagement of negative sentiment tweets focused on Bitcoin is negatively associated with Bitcoin wallet creation.

4   Methods

4.1   Data Sources

We collected data from three different primary sources. First, we scraped 1,500 daily tweets from Jan 01, 2018, to Oct 22, 2022, using the SNS scrape library and Python. This resulted in a total dataset of 2,635,756 tweets. Second, we manually downloaded data from Google Search Trends[2] in batches of 6 months, each with date ranges from Jan 01, 2018, to Oct 22, 2022, with overlaps in subsequent months. This was done to normalize the data by incorporating a common multiplication factor between periods. Google Trends data is scaled for relative periods, and discontinuous data across periods would have different scales. Third, Blockchain data was downloaded manually from NASDAQ (Wallets data) and Yahoo Finance (Adjusted Closing Price, Volume) for all days between Jan 01, 2018, to Oct 22, 2018.

4.2   Data Preparation

Our study employs Python's Pandas framework to consolidate daily Twitter datasets into a singular data frame for rigorous preprocessing. Utilizing Vader, a rule-based model optimized for social media sentiment analysis, we derive four sentiment scores—Positive, Negative, Neutral, and Compound—for each tweet, subsequently classifying them along with their engagements (likes and replies) into positive, negative, or neutral categories. This is in line with prior work that utilizes Natural Language Processing for analyzing text data in the information systems research [26, 27]. We assign double weightage to verified tweets and their engagements, hypothesizing their heightened influence on Bitcoin prices. A temporal damping factor is applied to metrics from previous years, such as 2018, depreciating their values by 80%. Interaction variables like replies per follower and likes per follower are generated to gauge tweet engagement, which indicates content relevance. Finally, all metrics are amalgamated into a daily-level dataset for comprehensive analysis.

For our analysis, Google Trends data was incorporated as-is, while daily Bitcoin metrics such as adjusted closing prices and trading volume from Yahoo Finance were merged with total wallet counts from NASDAQ. New user counts were calculated through a day-over-day differential from cumulative wallet data. The final dataset, which included both independent and dependent variables, amalgamated Twitter, Google Trends, and Bitcoin data on a daily basis. To rigorously assess the model's predictive efficacy and generalizability, we demarcated the training period from January 1, 2018, to December 31, 2021, and the validation period from January 1, 2022, to October 21, 2022.

---

[2] https://trends.google.com/trends/.

4.3   Estimation Approach and Econometric Model

We developed initial baseline models using Ordinary Least Square (OLS) regression models to predict the adjusted closing price of Bitcoin. The baseline model was significant, with the model p-value < 0.05. The baseline model was put through a stepwise regression as a next step. The stepwise regression resulted in only the most significant variables used.

5   Results

Our study aimed to examine the effects of consumers' digital focus on Bitcoin. The reduced model results are as follows: model Significance: 2.2e−16 and Model Adjusted R Square: 0.7647. We present our results in Table 1.

Table 1. Results of the Bitcoin Price Model

Variable	Description	Estimate	p-value
(Intercept)	Constant value from linear regression	17,180.00	0.0962
BTC [H1a]	SVI (scaled from 01/01/2018) for Bitcoin currency on google trends	155.60	0.0000
people_impressions	Sum of weighted (linear depreciation) followers for the username of the tweet on a daily granularity	0.00	0.0007
replies [H1d]	Sum of reply counts to the tweet on a daily granularity	4.08	0.0000
likes [H1d]	Sum of likes counts to the tweet on a daily granularity	1.20	0.0000
retweets	Sum of retweet counts to the tweet on a daily granularity	−2.39	0.0000
verified_likes	Sum of likes counts to verified user tweets on a daily granularity	−1.12	0.0000
verified_retweets [H1e]	Sum of retweet counts of verified user tweets on a daily granularity	1.98	0.0449

(*continued*)

Table 1. (*continued*)

Variable	Description	Estimate	p-value
verified_replies	Sum of reply to verified user tweets on a daily granularity	0.55	0.6841
verified_impressions	Sum of followers for the verfied username of the tweet on a daily granularity	−0.000169	0.0837
positive_tweet	sum of all positive weighted tweets considered with maximum positivite scores at a daily granularity	−64.06	0.0789
neutral_tweet	sum of all negative weighted tweets considered with maximum positive scores at a daily granularity	−17.04	0.0196
positive_likes_lag1	Sum of weighted likes (linear depreciation) likes counts to a tweet identified as a positive on a daily granularity for the previous day	−175.80	0.2665
negative_likes_lag1	Sum of weighted likes (linear depreciation) likes counts to a tweet identified as a negative on a daily granularity for the previous day	65.46	0.0999
negative_likes_lag2	Sum of weighted likes (linear depreciation) likes counts to a tweet identified as a negative on a daily granularity for 2 days earlier	6.50	0.0051

(*continued*)

Table 1. (*continued*)

Variable	Description	Estimate	p-value
positive_replies_lag2	Sum of weighted replies (linear depreciation) likes counts to a tweet identified as a positive on a daily granularity for the previous day	227,50	0.0222
people_impressions_lag1	Sum of weighted (linear depreciation) followers for the username of the tweet on a daily granularity for the previous day	0.00	0.0000
people_impressions_lag2	Sum of weighted (linear depreciation) followers for the username of the tweet on a daily granularity for 2 days earlier	0.00	0.0000
BTC_lag2	SVI (scaled from 01/01/2018) for Bitcoin currency on google trends for 2 days earlier	101.60	0.0010
positive_engagement_lag1	sum of all interactions with the tweet (likes, replies, retweets) for all tweets at a daily granularity for the previous day	173.50	0.1867
negative_engagement_lag1	sum of all interactions with the tweet (likes, replies, retweets) for all tweets at a daily granularity for 2 days before	−50.52	0.1308

The Q-Q plot (Fig. 2) analysis suggests a presence of slight heteroscedasticity and the presence of autocorrelation in the dependent variable, as confirmed by using an ACF test.

An ensemble approach using a gradient boosting machine was also tried for the data, and the backtest results are shown in Fig. 3 below.

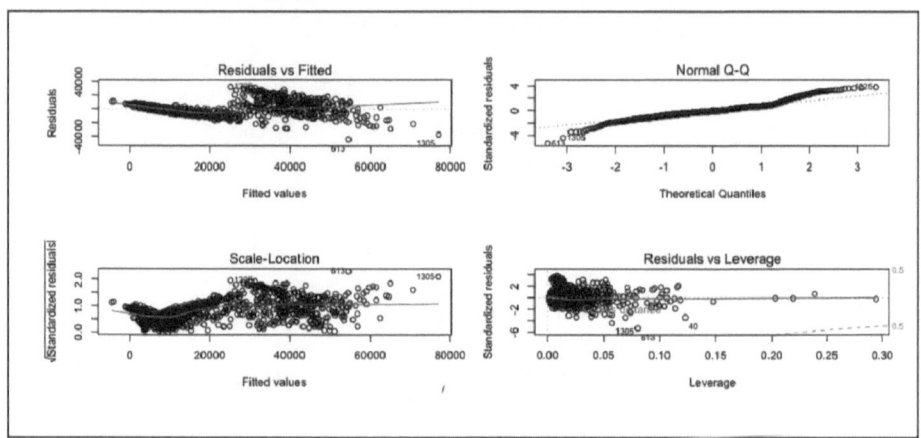

Fig. 2. QQ Plot for Bitcoin Price Model

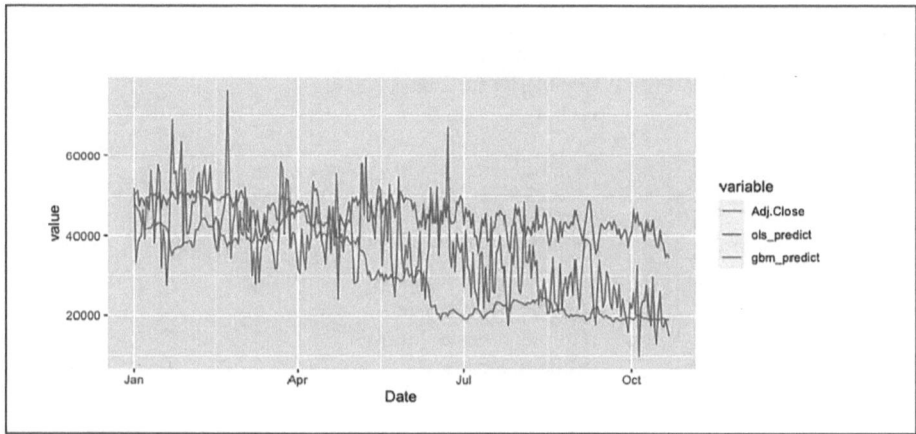

Fig. 3. Backtest Results of GBM for Bitcoin Price

The OLS regression for predicting the volume of trade had the model significance of <2.2e−16 and the model adjusted R square of 0.571 with the estimates as presented in the Table 2 below.

Table 2. Results of Bitcoin Volume Model

Variable	Estimate	p value
(Intercept)	1.62E + 11	0
btc [H2a]	8.21E + 08	0
people_impressions [H2b]	1157.939	0
verified_impressions	−990.3733	0
positive_tweet	−2.66E + 08	0
neutral_tweet	−1.14E + 08	0
neutral_replies	−2,026,494	0
negative_likes_lag1	−1.52E + 08	0.006
people_impressions_lag1 [H2b]	277.07	0
engagement_lag1	−41,797.9	0.007
btc_lag1	−3.77E + 08	0
negative_engagement_lag1	1.28E + 08	0.006

The linear regression model has no heteroscedasticity and could be considered except for the autocorrelation of the volume of Bitcoin trade volume (Fig. 4).

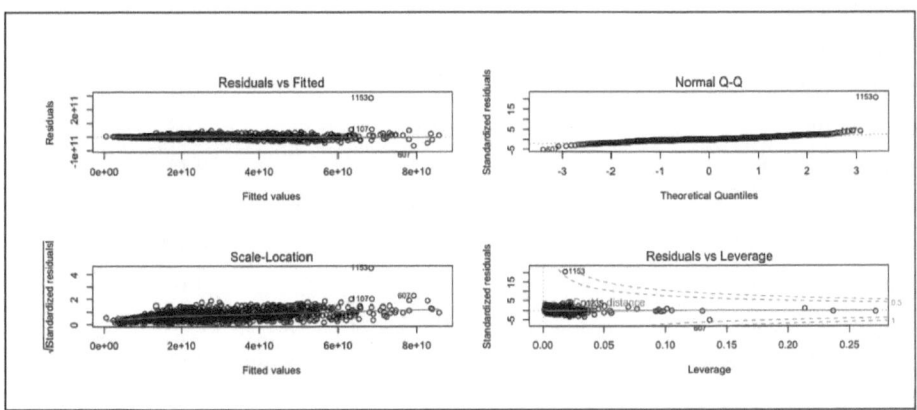

Fig. 4. QQ Plot for Bitcoin Volume Model

The results of backtesting with the similar GBM model are as presented in Fig. 5.

A similar approach was followed to predict new wallets created with the results in Table 3 with the modelling significance of $<2.2e-16$ and model adjusted R square of 0.1085.

The Q-Q plot analysis presented in Fig. 6 suggests a presence of heteroscedasticity and autocorrelation in the dependent variable (new wallets), as confirmed by using an ACF test.

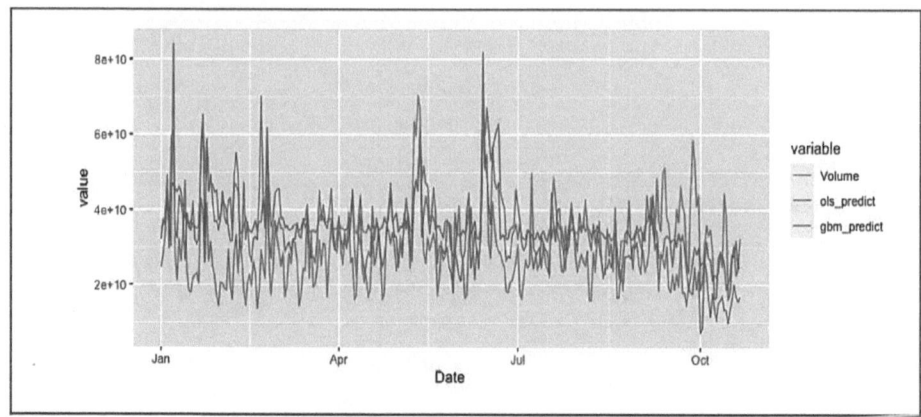

Fig. 5. Backtest Results of GBM for Bitcoin Volume

Table 3 Results of Bitcoin Wallets Model

Variable	Estimate	p value
(Intercept)	250,300.00	0.00
people_impressions [H3b]	0.00026	0.02
engagement [H3d]	0.59	0.01
negative_tweet	647.00	0.08
neutral_tweet	−156.00	0.00
positive_replies	−1521.00	0.01
positive_likes	231.20	0.03
positive_retweet	−1405.00	0.13
neutral_retweet	−3.68	0.01
positive_likes_lag1	1192.00	0.04
negative_likes_lag1	−12.01	0.16
negative_likes_lag2	−14.84	0.08
people_impressions_lag1	0.00	0.13
verified_impressions_lag1	0.00	0.09
verified_impressions_lag2	0.00	0.14
engagement_lag1	−0.52	0.02
engagement_lag2	−0.34	0.12
verified_engagement_lag1	0.67	0.05
verified_engagement_lag2	0.60	0.08

(*continued*)

Table 3 (*continued*)

Variable	Estimate	p value
BTC_lag1	481.60	0.00
BTC_lag2	−213.20	0.15
positive_engagement_lag1	−982.60	0.04

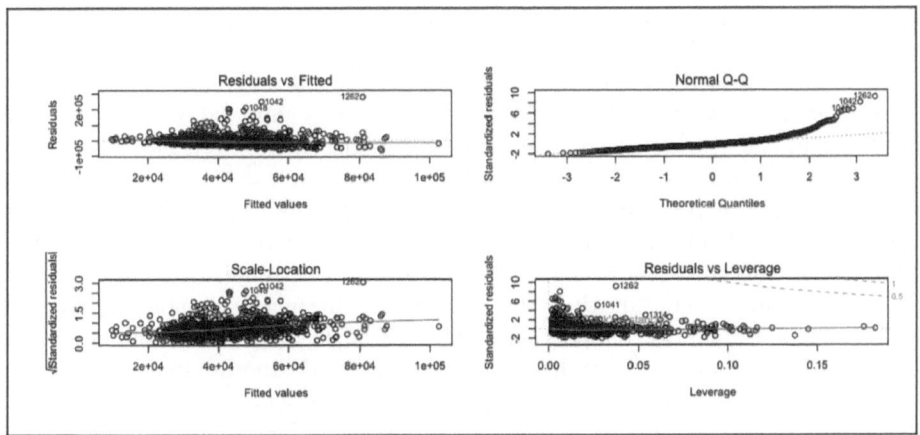

Fig. 6. QQ Plot for Bitcoin Wallets Model

A similar approach using GBM experimented with the predictions on the backtest as presented in Fig. 7.

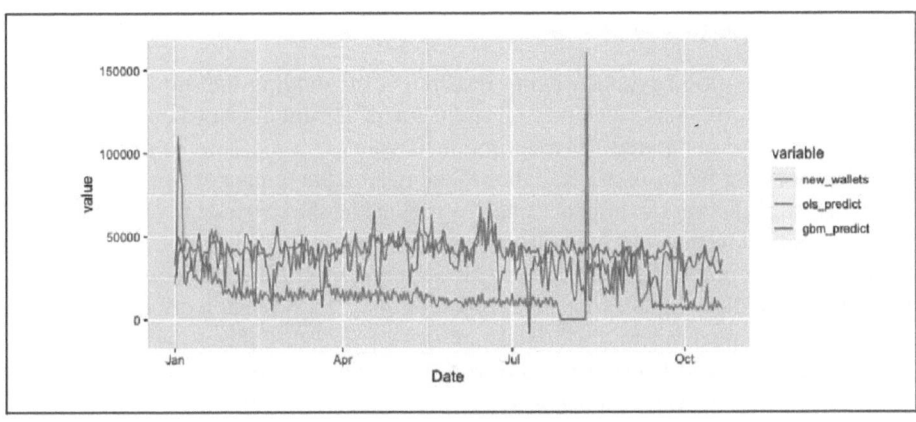

Fig. 7. Backtest Results of GBM for Bitcoin Wallets

6 Discussion

6.1 Summary of Findings

In the present study, we meticulously curated a multi-source dataset comprising Twitter data— sampled at a rate of 1,500 tweets per day containing mentions of Bitcoin— as well as daily Google Trends data and a comprehensive array of Bitcoin metrics, including price, trading volume, and wallet counts. The temporal scope of the dataset spans from January 1, 2018, to October 20, 2022. Rigorous data preprocessing measures were enacted to eradicate outliers and conduct temporal rescaling to ensure the cross-period comparability of Google Trends data.

First, we confirmed our hypotheses H1a and H1d. Specifically, we discovered a positive correlation between Bitcoin's price and both search volume and tweet engagement related to Bitcoin. This suggests that heightened online interest, reflected in searches and active engagement with Bitcoin-related content, can drive up its price. Second, our analysis validated hypotheses H2a and H2b, revealing a positive association between search volume and Bitcoin's trade volume, as well as between tweet impressions and trade volume. This underscores the role of online visibility in stimulating trading activity. Finally, our findings for the third hypothesis highlighted the impact of online engagement on user adoption. Both tweet impressions (H3b) and engagement (H3d) were positively linked to Bitcoin wallet creation, indicating that increased exposure to and interaction with Bitcoin-related content can encourage new users to join the ecosystem.

Our empirical findings substantiate the correlational relationship between Twitter impressions concerning Bitcoin and key market indicators such as price, trading volume, and user adoption rates. Moreover, we have ascertained the lagged influence of Google search trends on both Bitcoin pricing and new user adoption. Intriguingly, the study also unearths counterintuitive insights concerning the nuanced interplay between tweet sentiment and its ramifications on Bitcoin market dynamics.

6.2 Contributions to Theory

Our novel contribution beyond existing research is in studying the impact of Bitcoin-related Tweet impressions (which is an indicator of the number of people who have viewed a tweet) as compared to tweet volume (which is a measure of the number of tweets and does not factor in the visibility of the tweet), the impact of tweets by verified users and also assessing the impact of such variables on the dependent variables with a lag effect (same day, one and 2-day lag).

More broadly, our work contributes to the large streams of literature on social media, social platforms, digital platforms, and cryptocurrency. Significant work has been done to assess various phenomena on digital platforms [27–39]. Other work studies cryptocurrency platforms [40–44]. Yet more work has examined social media, both from a consumer [45–48], as well as a business perspective [39, 45, 49].

6.3   Implications for Practice and Policy

Our work will be significant to Crypto investors, traders, regulators, and the media fraternity as they seek to understand the drivers of Bitcoin pricing and transaction volume and prepare strategies to leverage Bitcoin as an alternative asset class.

6.4   Limitations and Future Research

Tweet sentiment (positive, negative, or neutral) surprisingly has not shown to have any relationship with Bitcoin price, volume, or new users. This is counter-intuitive and needs to be analyzed further in subsequent research. Further, Google search trends with a one-day lag impact Bitcoin volume negatively but significantly positively impact price and new users. This counter-intuitive impact of the lagged Google search trends on Bitcoin transaction volume must be understood further.

Subsequent research in this field can include more popular social media platforms like Facebook and Reddit to capture more comprehensive user perspectives. The Twitter data used in our analysis is limited to 1,500 sampled tweets daily; subsequent research can extend the understanding using a larger Twitter dataset using APIs.

OLS regressions are usually the most used models for regressions due to their intuitive nature, high degree of interpretation, and ability to produce highly generalized outcomes. However, OLS regressions cannot take advantage of the longitudinal nature of our data. We will incorporate rigorous dynamic panel regression models to address endogeneity and reverse causality concerns.

7   Conclusion

In this paper, we have attempted to establish the relationship between Web Search trends, social media (Twitter) trends, and Bitcoin Price, Volume, and number of new users. Besides, we also attempted to validate hypotheses on the impact of tweet sentiment on the dependent variables. Our findings through OLS regression models and the GBM approach show that Google searches positively impact Bitcoin price and new users (wallets). Twitter impressions have a positive relationship with Bitcoin price, volume, and new users, and retweets of tweets by verified users also positively impact price.

Exploratory work to include lagged price variables drastically improve the fit and predictability of the model suggesting the development of a panel linear model. Further research could also be done to explore which effects in a PLM model are ideal for this research.

References

1. Béjaoui, A., Mgadmi, N., Moussa, W., Sadraoui, T.: A short-and long-term analysis of the nexus between Bitcoin, social media and Covid-19 outbreak. Heliyon **7**(7), e07539 (2021)
2. Kristoufek, L.: What are the main drivers of the Bitcoin price? Evidence from wavelet coherence analysis. PLoS ONE **10**(4), e0123923 (2015)
3. Guizani, S., Nafti, I.K.: The determinants of bitcoin price volatility: an investigation with ardl model. Procedia Comput. Sci. **164**, 233–238 (2019)

4. Bouoiyour, J., Selmi, R.: The Bitcoin price formation: Beyond the fundamental sources (2017)
5. Critien, J.V., Gatt, A., Ellul, J.: Bitcoin price change and trend prediction through twitter sentiment and data volume. Financ. Innov. **8**(1), 1–20 (2022)
6. Matta, M., Lunesu, I., Marchesi, M.: Bitcoin spread prediction using social and web search media. In: UMAP Workshops (2015)
7. Shen, D., Urquhart, A., Wang, P.: Does twitter predict Bitcoin? Econ. Lett. **174**, 118–122 (2019)
8. Abraham, J., Higdon, D., Nelson, J., Ibarra, J.: Cryptocurrency price prediction using tweet volumes and sentiment analysis. SMU Data Sci. Rev. **1**(3), 1 (2018)
9. Chohan, U.W.: Cryptocurrencies and inequality. In: Cryptofinance: A New Currency for a New Economy, pp. 49–62. World Scientific (2022)
10. Divakaruni, A., Zimmerman, P.: Uncovering retail trading in bitcoin: the impact of COVID-19 stimulus checks. Manage. Sci. **70**(4), 2066–2085 (2024)
11. Náñez Alonso, S.L., Jorge-Vázquez, J., Echarte Fernández, M.Á., Forradellas, R.R.: Cryptocurrency mining from an economic and environmental perspective. Analysis of the most and least sustainable countries. Energies **14**(14), 4254 (2021). https://doi.org/10.3390/en1414 4254
12. Ciaian, P., Ivanov, A., Kancs, A.: Long-run economic, budgetary and fiscal effects of Roma integration policies. In: JRC Working Papers in Economics and Finance (2018)
13. Panagiotidis, T., Stengos, T., Vravosinos, O.: The effects of markets, uncertainty and search intensity on bitcoin returns. Int. Rev. Financ. Anal. **63**, 220–242 (2019)
14. Studio, G.: Glassnode Studio (2022). https://studio.glassnode.com/home
15. Wołk, K.: Advanced social media sentiment analysis for short-term cryptocurrency price prediction. Expert. Syst. **37**(2), e12493 (2020)
16. Kaminski, J.: Nowcasting the bitcoin market with twitter signals. arXiv preprint arXiv:1406.7577 (2014)
17. Mai, F., Shan, Z., Bai, Q., Wang, X., Chiang, R.H.: How does social media impact Bitcoin value? A test of the silent majority hypothesis. J. Manag. Inf. Syst. **35**(1), 19–52 (2018)
18. Ante, L., Fiedler, I., Strehle, E.: The impact of transparent money flows: effects of stablecoin transfers on the returns and trading volume of Bitcoin. Technol. Forecast. Soc. Chang. **170**, 120851 (2021)
19. Chen, T., Lau, C.K.M., Cheema, S., Koo, C.K.: Economic policy uncertainty in China and bitcoin returns: evidence from the COVID-19 period. Front. Public Health **9**, 651051 (2021)
20. Guo, T., Antulov-Fantulin, N.: Predicting short-term Bitcoin price fluctuations from buy and sell orders. arXiv preprint arXiv:1802.04065 (2018)
21. Wan, Y., Song, Y., Zhang, X., Yin, Z.: Asymmetric volatility connectedness between cryptocurrencies and energy: dynamics and determinants. Front. Environ. Sci. **11**, 1115200 (2023)
22. Corbet, S., Larkin, C., Lucey, B.M., Meegan, A., Yarovaya, L.: The impact of macroeconomic news on Bitcoin returns. Eur. J. Finance **26**(14), 1396–1416 (2020)
23. Shahzad, S.J.H., Bouri, E., Roubaud, D., Kristoufek, L., Lucey, B.: Is Bitcoin a better safe-haven investment than gold and commodities? Int. Rev. Financ. Anal. **63**, 322–330 (2019)
24. Selmi, R., Mensi, W., Hammoudeh, S., Bouoiyour, J.: Is Bitcoin a hedge, a safe haven or a diversifier for oil price movements? A comparison with gold. Energ. Econ. **74**, 787–801 (2018)
25. Shahzad, S.J.H., Bouri, E., Roubaud, D., Kristoufek, L.: Safe haven, hedge and diversification for G7 stock markets: gold versus bitcoin. Econ. Model. **87**, 212–224 (2020)
26. Sonpatki, R., Kathuria, A., Sethi, S.: Earnings call transcripts as a source and resource for information systems research. In: Kathuria, A., Karhade, P.P., Zhao, K., Chaturvedi, D. (eds.)

Digital Transformation in the Viral Age: 21st Workshop on e-Business, WeB 2022, Copen-hagen, Denmark, December 10, 2022, Revised Selected Papers, pp. 38–63. Springer Nature Switzerland, Cham (2024). https://doi.org/10.1007/978-3-031-60003-6_4

27. Karhade, P., Kathuria, A., Dasgupta, A., Malik, O., Konsynski, B.R.: Decolonization of digital platforms: a research agenda for GREAT domains. In: Garimella, A., Karhade, P., Kathuria, A., Liu, X., Xu, J., Zhao, K. (eds.) The Role of e-Business during the Time of Grand Challenges: 19th Workshop on e-Business, WeB 2020, Virtual Event, December 12, 2020, Revised Selected Papers, pp. 51–58. Springer International Publishing, Cham (2021). https://doi.org/10.1007/978-3-030-79454-5_5

28. Bonina, C., Koskinen, K., Eaton, B., Gawer, A.: Digital platforms for development: foundations and research agenda. Inf. Syst. J. 31(6), 869–902 (2021)

29. Sutherland, W., Jarrahi, M.H.: The sharing economy and digital platforms: a review and research agenda. Int. J. Inf. Manage. 43, 328–341 (2018)

30. De Reuver, M., Sørensen, C., Basole, R.C.: The digital platform: a research agenda. J. Inf. Technol. 33(2), 124–135 (2018)

31. Fu, X., Avenyo, E., Ghauri, P.: Digital platforms and development: a survey of the literature. Innov. Dev. 11(2–3), 303–321 (2021)

32. Karhade, P., Kathuria, A., Malik, O., Konsynski, B.: Digital platforms and infobesity: a research agenda, In: Garimella, A., Karhade, P., Kathuria, A., Liu, X., Xu, J., Zhao, K. (eds.) The Role of e-Business During the Time of Grand Challenges. WEB 2020. Lecture Notes in Business Information Processing, pp. 67–74. Springer: Cham (2020)

33. Karhade, P., Kathuria, A., Konsynski, B.L When choice matters: assortment and participation for performance on digital platforms. In: Proceedings of the Hawaii International Conference on System Sciences (HICCS). Virtual (2021)

34. Kathuria, A., Karhade, P.P., Konsynski, B.R.: In the realm of hungry ghosts: multi-level theory for supplier participation on digital platforms. J. Manag. Inf. Syst. 37(2), 396–430 (2020)

35. Dasgupta, A., Karhade, P., Kathuria, A., Konsynski, B.: Holding space for voices that do not speak: design reform of rating systems for platforms in GREAT economies. In: Proceedings of the Hawaii International Conference on System Sciences (HICCS). Virtual (2021)

36. Karhade, P., Kathuria, A.: Missing impact of ratings on platform participation in India: a call for research in GREAT domains. Commun. Assoc. Inf. Syst. 47(1), 19 (2020)

37. Kathuria, A., Saldanha, T., Khuntia, J., Andrade Rojas, M., Mithas, S., Hah, H.: Inferring supplier quality in the gig economy: the effectiveness of signals in freelance job markets. In: Proceedings of the Hawaii International Conference on System Sciences (HICCS). Virtual (2021)

38. Kathuria, A., Saldanha, T., Khuntia, J., Andrade Rojas, M.G., Hah, H.: Strategic intent, contract duration, and performance: evidence from micro-outsourcing. In: Proceedings of the International Conference on Information Systems (ICIS). Fort Worth (2015)

39. Vitzthum, S., Kathuria, A., Konsynski, B.: Real commerce in virtual worlds. In: Proceedings of the International Conference on Information Systems (ICIS). Phoenix (2009)

40. Caliskan, K.: Data money: The socio-technical infrastructure of cryptocurrency blockchains. Econ. Soc. 49(4), 540–561 (2020)

41. Zutshi, A., Grilo, A., Nodehi, T.: The value proposition of blockchain technologies and its impact on Digital Platforms. Comput. Ind. Eng. 155, 107187 (2021)

42. Ilk, N., Shang, G., Fan, S., Leon Zhao, J.: Stability of transaction fees in bitcoin: a supply and demand perspective. MIS Q. 45(2), 563–692 (2021). https://doi.org/10.25300/MISQ/2021/15718

43. Benjamin, V., Valacich, J.S., Chen, H.: DICE-E: a framework for conducting darknet identification, collection, evaluation with ethics. MIS Q. 43(1), 1–22 (2019). https://doi.org/10.25300/MISQ/2019/13808

44. Kathuria, A., Fontaine, A., Prietula, M.: Acquiring IT competencies through focused technology acquisitions. In: Proceedings of the International Conference on Information Systems (ICIS). Shanghai (2011)
45. Saldanha, T.J., Sahaym, A., Mithas, S., Andrade-Rojas, M.G., Kathuria, A., Lee, H.-H.: Turning liabilities of global operations into assets: IT-enabled social integration capacity and exploratory innovation. Inf. Syst. Res. 31(2), 361–382 (2020)
46. Chaturvedi, D., Karhade, P., Kathuria, A., Rai, A., N. Naik, A.: IT and the dual bottom-line objective of rational social enterprises. In: 2024 in Proceedings of the European Conference on Information Systems (ECIS)
47. Hutton, G., Fosdick, M.: The globalization of social media: consumer relationships with brands evolve in the digital space. J. Advert. Res. 51(4), 564–570 (2011)
48. Santos, Z.R., Cheung, C.M., Coelho, P.S., Rita, P.: Consumer engagement in social media brand communities: a literature review. Int. J. Inf. Manage. 63, 102457 (2022)
49. Andrade-Rojas, M.G., Kathuria, A., Lee, Hs.-H.: Multilevel synergy of information technology for operational integration: competition networks and operating performance. Product. Operat. Manage. 33(5), 1116–1141 (2024). https://doi.org/10.1177/10591478241239005

Drivers of Perceived Value of Cryptocurrency: Comparing Stablecoins and Non-Stable Cryptocurrency

Gerrard Li[1], Cheuk Hang Au[2]([envelope]) [ID], Kevin K. W. Ho[3] [ID], and Kris M. Y. Law[4] [ID]

[1] Department of Information Management, National Chung Cheng University, Chiayi, Taiwan
[2] School of Business and Law, Edith Cowan University, Perth, Australia
c.au@ecu.edu.au
[3] Institute of Business Sciences, University of Tsukuba, Tokyo, Japan
[4] Institute of Intelligent Systems Research and Innovation, Deakin University, Geelong, Australia

Abstract. While cryptocurrencies gain popularity, many lose value over time. To harness the benefits of launching a new cryptocurrency, identifying factors influencing its perceived value is crucial. Our in-progress study, based on the Technology-Organisation-Environment (TOE) framework and trust-related literature, revealed that (1) security, transaction speed, supply, gifting, trust, user critical mass, and issuer interaction impact cryptocurrency value directly or indirectly, (2) Technical aspects matter less compared to organizational and environmental factors, (3) Drivers of value differ slightly between stablecoins and non-stablecoins, (4) Some factors influence value indirectly through trust, with no significant direct impact.

Keywords: Cryptocurrency · Stablecoin · Bitcoin · Initial Coin Offering (ICO)

1 Introduction

Cryptocurrency (crypto), secured by cryptography [1], gained prominence post-Bitcoin's 2008 debut [2]. Its 2023 market cap exceeds $1.18 trillion [3], significantly impacting finance. It promotes financial inclusion, aiding the un/underbanked [1], aligning with the United Nations' Social Development Goals. Governments and entities, e.g., Central African Republic and El Salvador, introduce their cryptos for unbanked support [4]. Also, cryptocurrency issuance lures capital via initial coin offerings (ICOs), attracting high-return-seeking investors [5].

However, not all cryptocurrency ventures succeed. For example, LUNA's May 2022 collapse due to value peg issues costed investors significantly [6] and weakened public confidence on cryptocurrencies. In addition, past cryptocurrency research misses the difference between stablecoin and non-stablecoin, which nevertheless affect value, usage, and risks for all parties. Thus, it is vital to examine cryptocurrency success factors.

A higher perceived value boosts cryptocurrency adoption and ownership, fostering success [7, 8]. This paper aims to study those drivers behind the perceived value of

© The Author(s), under exclusive license to Springer Nature Switzerland AG 2025
A. Kathuria et al. (Eds.): WeB 2023, LNBIP 525, pp. 83–91, 2025.
https://doi.org/10.1007/978-3-031-74437-2_7

cryptocurrency, with the difference between stablecoins and non-stablecoins considered. In turn, it helps investors identify lasting cryptocurrencies, aiding issuers in seizing opportunities. Thus, our research question is, "What drives cryptocurrencies' perceived value?".

2 Literature Review

Cryptocurrencies, secured by cryptography [9], initially offered secure online transactions without intermediaries, often free from central authorities [10]. Blockchain technology ensures transaction data integrity [1, 11]. Self-regulating cryptocurrencies offer speed, convenience, and cross-border capabilities [12]. Their value hinges on market belief in long-term viability [4]. Table 1 lists key cryptocurrency advantages, features, and success factors. These elements interact with cryptocurrency's perceived value, shaping investor trust and overall worth [13].

Cryptocurrency businesses are on the rise [23], with ICOs being popular for raising capital [24]. Yet, crypto prices fluctuate due to decentralization. To address this, stablecoins, linked to assets like USD, enhance adoption and price stability [25, 26]. Common stablecoins include USDT, USDC, and BUSD, while non-stable cryptocurrencies include BTC, EOS, and Litecoin. However, prior research has limitations. For example, Narayanan, Bonneau [13] suggested cryptocurrency value factors, but was unbacked by data. The difference between stablecoins and non-stablecoins receive insufficient scrutiny, while opinion-based or single-case studies [1, 23] lack statistical breadth. More empirical research is needed to fathom cryptocurrency value drivers, their merits, and potential.

3 Theoretical Framework

Tornatzky and Fleischer's TOE framework, assessing tech innovation adoption in organizations, considers technical, organizational, and environmental factors [27]. It pinpoints determinants and hurdles in adoption, shaping strategies and policies. TOE is well-recognized and used in diverse studies like banking web services [28] and online gaming [29]. Table 2 outlines the three TOE dimensions.

We classified factors in Table 1 into one of the categories listed in Table 2, and argue that these factors positively influence cryptocurrency perceived value. Trust is a vital moderator [8] which directly impact owners' decisions and is critical for stakeholders who aim to promote cryptocurrency acceptance and use [30]. Figure 1 shows our theoretical model.

4 Research Methods

We used survey to test our model. We used established items from previous research to survey cryptocurrency users, assuring the model's construct measurement's reliability and validity. For example, trust and gamification measurement items were borrowed from Maier, Laumer [31] and Feng, Ye [32]. Each construct contained a minimum of three items (See **Table 3** for a list of sample measurement items adopted).

Table 1. A Selected List of Dimensions of Cryptocurrencies

Dimensions	Description
Advantages	
Transaction Speed	Cryptocurrency transactions are speedy, usually taking minutes compared to days for wire transfers, ensuring convenience and minimizing vulnerability to attacks and financial risks Dierksmeier and Seele [14]
Low Cost	Cryptocurrency transactions incur low costs Lee, Guo and Wang [15], and creating cryptocurrency wallets is simpler than opening traditional bank accounts, which require extensive documentation Jagtiani and Lemieux [16]
Critical Success Factors	
Security	Security measures implemented by cryptocurrency issuers ensure the security and protection of user assets and data, instilling confidence in the system's integrity Reyna, Martín [17]
Gifting	Gifting refers to distributing coins to users in the early stages. This increases the number of users who own cryptocurrencies Li and Au [18]
Trust	Trust is vital in cryptocurrencies on decentralized networks with secure cryptographic transactions, but it encounters hurdles from security, regulatory, and market volatility concerns Nakamoto [2] and Swan [19]
Convertibility	A high convertibility of cryptocurrencies enables users to acquire or sell them in exchange for other cryptocurrencies or fiat currencies, which may be influenced by market demand and regulation Brenig and Müller [20]
Critical Mass of User	Reaching a critical user mass spurs network effects and cryptocurrency adoption, enhancing credibility, liquidity, and value. However, this necessitates marketing and education efforts Moin, Sekniqi and Sirer [21]
Interaction with Issuers	Thriving cryptocurrencies offer open communication, stimulating user collaboration for innovation and improvement, boosting transparency, accountability, and community involvement Ali, Vecchio [22] and Swan [19])

We employed Amazon MTurk for data collection, a method endorsed by esteemed information systems journals [33], known for its efficiency compared to traditional approaches [31]. MTurk is suitable for generalizing diverse cognition studies, as per Jia, Steelman and Reich [34], and facilitates access to hard-to-reach subjects [35]. Nonetheless, we recognize potential issues like self-selection bias, attentiveness, ability, and social desirability [34, 36]. We included attention and ability tests to filter out ineligible responses. Specifically, for the ability test, respondents named a top-ten and a failed cryptocurrency; only correct answers were accepted.

Table 2. Description of the Three Dimensions of the TOE Framework

Dimensions	Description
Technology	This refers to characteristics and attributes of the technology itself, such as complexity, compatibility, the relative advantage of the innovation, as well as the level of technological knowledge and expertise required for adoption
Organisation	This refers to internal characteristics of the organisation, such as structure, resources, communication channels, capabilities, and readiness and willingness to adopt and integrate the innovation
Environment	These are external influences on innovation adoption, including industry norms, regulations, competition, customer needs, and socio-economic contexts

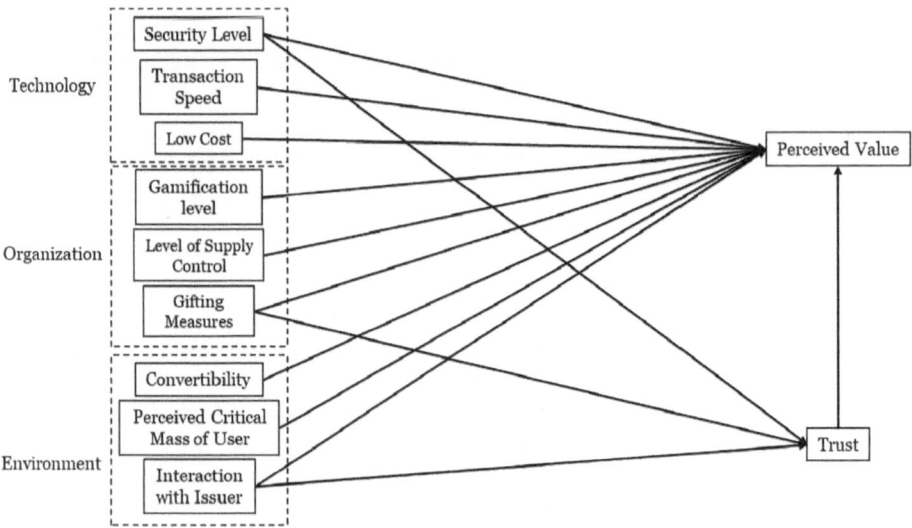

Fig. 1. Theoretical Model of Perceived Value of Cryptocurrency

Table 3. List of sample measurement items adopted

Constructs	Sample Measurement Items
Security	I feel confident in the security measures implemented by the issuer and blockchain of this cryptocurrency
Transaction Speed	I believe that using this cryptocurrency will improve the speed of transactions

(continued)

We tested our model using SmartPLS. In addition, we split users into stablecoins vs. non-stablecoins. By considering these subgroup distinctions, we sought to ascertain potential boundary conditions influencing the effects of the identified factors.

Table 3. (*continued*)

Constructs	Sample Measurement Items
Low Cost	I expect this cryptocurrency to provide cost-effective alternatives to traditional financial transactions
Gamification	Participating in tasks of earning this cryptocurrency brings me a lot of fun
Control Supply	I perceive a controlled limit on the quantity of this cryptocurrency
Gifting	My friends and/or I have effortlessly received a large quantity of this cryptocurrency in the past
Trust	I trust this cryptocurrency
Convertibility	There are convenient and hassle-free conversion options for this cryptocurrency
Perceived Critical Mass of User	Many people will continue to use this cryptocurrency
Interaction with Issuers	The issuer of this cryptocurrency offers open and accessible communication channels
Perceived Value	Taking everything together, I consider this cryptocurrency useful

5   Preliminary Findings

We gathered 1,100 responses, with 636 deemed valid after eliminating incomplete or contradictory entries. Most participants (94%) were from the United States, with the remaining from Australia, Albania, India, Brazil, or other countries. On average, participants had been investing in cryptocurrencies for 17.7 months, with a median of 10 months. Using a 9-point scale, they reported an average activity frequency of 7.5 and a median of 8. Top choices for non-stable cryptocurrencies were Bitcoin and ETH, and for stablecoins, they preferred USDT and USDC, consistent with market popularity as indicated by coinmarketcap.com. Of the valid responses, 310 chose stablecoins, and 326 selected non-stable cryptocurrencies, enabling our comparative analysis between two of them (see Table 4 for the results, including t-statistics and p-values). Moreover, composite reliability exceeded 0.8, affirming construct reliability.

Our result illustrates that security and supply control levels influence trust, but their effect on perceived value is not significant. Transaction speed significantly affects the perceived value of non-stablecoins only, while low cost and convertibility have insignificant effects on the perceived value of both stablecoins and non-stablecoins. Gamification, trust, and perceived user critical mass influence perceived value for both types. Gifting measures marginally impact the perceived value of cryptocurrency, but impacts are insignificant when considering only one data subset. Finally, interactions play a direct and significant role in cryptocurrency value for the entire dataset and non-stablecoins subset but aren't significant for the stablecoin dataset alone. However, the impact of interactions is significant for both cryptocurrency types when trust acts as a mediator.

Table 4. Testing Results of Our Theoretical Model, Including Overall Sample and Comparison between Stablecoins and Non-stable Cryptocurrencies

Hypotheses	Overall		Stablecoins		Non-stablecoins	
	t-statistics	p-value	t-statistics	p-value	t-statistics	p-value
Security Level → Perceived Value	0.760	0.448	0.568	0.570	0.613	0.540
Security Level → Trust	4.483	0.000***	3.665	0.000***	3.908	0.000***
Transaction Speed → Perceived Value	1.574	0.116	0.769	0.442	2.011	0.044*
Low Cost → Perceived Value	0.997	0.319	0.089	0.929	0.821	0.412
Gamification → Perceived Value	2.883	0.004**	2.208	0.027*	2.071	0.038*
Level of Supply Control → Perceived Value	0.308	0.758	0.977	0.329	0.079	0.937
Level of Supply Control → Trust	3.384	0.001**	2.548	0.011*	2.417	0.016*
Gifting → Perceived Value	1.781	0.075#	1.173	0.241	1.516	0.130
Trust → Perceived Value	2.485	0.013*	2.480	0.013*	1.488	0.137
Convertibility → Perceived Value	0.496	0.620	0.506	0.613	0.362	0.718
Perceived Critical Mass of User → Perceived Value	3.882	0.000***	3.258	0.001**	3.128	0.002**
Interaction with Issuer → Perceived Value	2.478	0.013*	0.584	0.559	2.213	0.027*
Interaction with Issuer → Trust	7.018	0.000***	5.351	0.000***	5.262	0.000***

Note: ***$p < 0.001$, **$p < 0.01$, *$p < 0.05$, #$p < 0.1$

6 Discussion and Conclusion

In our ongoing research, we identified several factors linked to cryptocurrency's perceived value, including security level, transaction speed, level of supply, gifting, trust, perceived critical mass of user, and interaction with the issuer. Of these factors, technical aspects exert less influence on perceived value compared to organizational and environmental factors. For instance, security's impact on perceived value is indirect through trust, with an insignificant direct effect. This suggests that user perceptions are predominantly shaped by factors tied to issuers, market conditions, and the broader economic and regulatory environment in which cryptocurrencies operate. Technical strengths are necessary but not sufficient for cryptocurrency success.

Second, we found variations in the determinants of perceived value for stablecoins and non-stablecoins. Notably, speed influences the perceived value of non-stablecoins but not stablecoins. This dissimilarity can be attributed to the volatile nature of non-stablecoins. If transaction speed isn't adequately swift, price shifts can swiftly impact traders' earnings. In contrast, stablecoins offer stability, reducing the risk of transaction outcomes being influenced by speed-related concerns. Third, we also found that certain factors, typically seen as direct drivers of perceived value, actually influence it indirectly through trust as a mediator, but had no significant direct impact on perceived value. This underscores trust's pivotal role as a mediator in shaping the perception on cryptocurrencies.

Our results aid issuers in promoting cryptocurrency adoption, enabling governments and investors to identify less promising cryptocurrencies. However there may be differences in factors that influence cryptocurrency perceived value across different socioeconomic environment [37, 38]. Such differences have been witnessed across several digital context [38–46] resulting in multiple call for research papers [39, 47, 48]. Future efforts may involve broader data collection and encompass various cryptocurrency types, so that we can enhance cryptocurrency success, making its benefits more accessible to a wider range of users, particularly in terms of financial inclusion.

Acknowledgements. The authors have no competing interests to declare that are relevant to the content of this article.

References

1. Li, X., Whinston, A.B.: Analyzing cryptocurrencies. Inf. Syst. Front. **22**, 17–22 (2020)
2. Nakamoto, S.: Bitcoin: A peer-to-peer electronic cash system. Satoshi Nakamoto (2008)
3. CoinMarketCap. Global Live Cryptocurrency Charts & Market Data (2023). https://coinmarketcap.com/charts/
4. Zhang, Y., Li, B., Qian, S.: Ridesharing and digital resilience for urban anomalies: evidence from the new york city taxi market. Inform. Syst. Res. **34**(4), 1775–1790 (2023). https://doi.org/10.1287/isre.2023.1212
5. Haleem, A., Javaid, M., Singh, R.P., Suman, R., Rab, S.: Blockchain technology applications in healthcare: an overview. Int. J. Intell. Netw. **2**, 130–139 (2021)
6. Briola, A., Vidal-Tomás, D., Wang, Y., Aste, T.: Anatomy of a Stablecoin's failure: the terra-Luna case. Financ. Res. Lett. **51**, 103358 (2023)

7. Abooleet, S., Fang, X.: Investigating Users' Continuous Adoption of Cryptocurrency (2023)
8. Alsmadi, A.A., Shuhaiber, A., Al-Omoush, K.S.: Risky? So, why people are getting back to invest in cryptocurrencies? The United Arab Emirates as a case. Kybernetes (2023)
9. Lansky, J.: Possible state approaches to cryptocurrencies. J. Syst. Integr. **9**(1), 19 (2018)
10. Huang, H.H., Kerstein, J., Wang, C.: The impact of climate risk on firm performance and financing choices: an international comparison. J. Int. Bus. Stud. **49**, 633–656 (2018)
11. Di Pierro, M.: What is the blockchain? Comput. Sci.Eng. **19**(5), 92–95 (2017)
12. Mendoza-Tello, J.C., Mora, H., Pujol-López, F.A., Lytras, M.D.: Disruptive innovation of cryptocurrencies in consumer acceptance and trust. IseB **17**, 195–222 (2019)
13. Narayanan, A., Bonneau, J., Felten, E., Miller, A., Goldfeder, S.: Bitcoin and cryptocurrency technologies: a comprehensive introduction. (2017)
14. Dierksmeier, C., Seele, P.: Cryptocurrencies and business ethics. J. Bus. Ethics **152**, 1–14 (2018)
15. Lee, D.K.C., Guo, L., Wang, Y.: Cryptocurrency: a new investment opportunity? J. Altern. Investments **20**(3), 16 (2018)
16. Jagtiani, J., Lemieux, C.: Do fintech lenders penetrate areas that are underserved by traditional banks? J. Econ. Bus. **100**, 43–54 (2018)
17. Reyna, A., Martín, C., Chen, J., Soler, E., Díaz, M.: On blockchain and its integration with IoT. Challenges and opportunities. Future Gener. Comput. Syst. **88**, 173–190 (2018)
18. Li, G., Au, C.H.A.: What drive the successes and adoption of cryptocurrencies (2022)
19. Swan, M.: Blockchain thinking: the brain as a decentralized autonomous corporation [commentary]. IEEE Technol. Soc. Mag. **34**(4), 41–52 (2015)
20. Brenig, C., Müller, G.: Economic analysis of cryptocurrency backed money laundering (2015)
21. Moin, A., Sekniqi, K., Sirer, E.G.: SoK: A classification framework for stablecoin designs. In: Financial Cryptography and Data Security: 24th International Conference, FC 2020, Kota Kinabalu, Malaysia, 10–14 Feb 2020 Revised Selected Papers 24. Springer (2020)
22. Ali, M.S., Vecchio, M., Pincheira, M., Dolui, K., Antonelli, F., Rehmani, M.H.: Applications of blockchains in the Internet of Things: a comprehensive survey. IEEE Commun. Surv. Tutorials **21**(2), 1676–1717 (2018)
23. Au, C.H., Law, K.M., Chiu, D.K., Ho, K.K.: Investigating mainstreaming strategies of hot cryptocurrencies-wallet (2022)
24. Preston, J.: Initial coin offerings: innovation, democratization and the SEC. Duke L. & Tech. Rev. **16**, 318 (2017)
25. Hsu, W.S., Au, C.H., Shieh, P.-H.: Can Stablecoins Foster Cryptocurrencies adoption? A Preliminary Study from the Push-Pull-Mooring Model Perspective (2022)
26. Mita, M., Ito, K., Ohsawa, S., Tanaka, H.: What is stablecoin?: A survey on price stabilization mechanisms for decentralized payment systems. In: 2019 8th International Congress on Advanced Applied Informatics (IIAI-AAI). IEEE (2019)
27. Wang, J., Gao, F., Ip, W.: Measurement of resilience and its application to enterprise information systems. Enterp. Inform. Syst. **4**(2), 215–223 (2010)
28. Subramanian, N., Chaudhuri, A., Kayıkcı, Y., Subramanian, N., Chaudhuri, A., Kayıkcı, Y.: Blockchain applications in retail supply chain. Blockchain and Supply Chain Logistics: Evolutionary Case Studies, pp. 49–56 (2020)
29. Au, C.H., Ho, K.K.: The anti-ageing secret of massively multiplayer online game: Managing its lifecycle. Aust. J. Manag. **46**(4), 652–671 (2021)
30. Hamm, P.: Cryptocurrencies, stablecoins and central bank digital currencies: The impact of trust and perceived risk (2023)
31. Maier, C., Laumer, S., Wirth, J., Weitzel, T.: Technostress and the hierarchical levels of personality: a two-wave study with multiple data samples. Eur. J. Inf. Syst. **28**(5), 496–522 (2019)

32. Feng, Y., Ye, H.J., Yu, Y., Yang, C., Cui, T.: Gamification artifacts and crowdsourcing participation: examining the mediating role of intrinsic motivations. Comput. Hum. Behav. **81**, 124–136 (2018)
33. Mattke, J., Maier, C., Reis, L., Weitzel, T.: Bitcoin investment: a mixed methods study of investment motivations. Eur. J. Inf. Syst. **30**(3), 261–285 (2021)
34. Jia, R., Steelman, Z.R., Reich, B.H.: Using mechanical turk data in IS research: risks, rewards, and recommendations. Commun. Assoc. Inf. Syst. **41**(1), 14 (2017)
35. Smith, N.A., Sabat, I.E., Martinez, L.R., Weaver, K., Xu, S.: A convenient solution: using MTurk to sample from hard-to-reach populations. Ind. Organ. Psychol. **8**(2), 220–228 (2015)
36. Cheung, J.H., Burns, D.K., Sinclair, R.R., Sliter, M.: Amazon Mechanical Turk in organizational psychology: an evaluation and practical recommendations. J. Bus. Psychol. **32**, 347–361 (2017)
37. Karhade, P., Kathuria, A., Dasgupta, A., Malik, O., Konsynski, B.R.: Decolonization of digital platforms: a research agenda for GREAT domains. In: Garimella, A., Karhade, P., Kathuria, A., Liu, X., Xu, J., Zhao, K. (eds.) The Role of e-Business during the Time of Grand Challenges: 19th Workshop on e-Business, WeB 2020, Virtual Event, December 12, 2020, Revised Selected Papers, pp. 51–58. Springer International Publishing, Cham (2021). https://doi.org/10.1007/978-3-030-79454-5_5
38. Dasgupta, A., Karhade, P., Kathuria, A., Konsynski, B.: Holding space for voices that do not speak: design reform of rating systems for platforms in GREAT economies. In: Proceedings of the Hawaii International Conference on System Sciences (HICCS). Virtual (2021)
39. Karhade, P., Kathuria, A.: Missing impact of ratings on platform participation in India: a call for research in GREAT domains. Commun. Assoc. Inf. Syst. **47**(1), 19 (2020)
40. Yadav, N., Meenakshi, N., Banerjee, P.: Exploring governance issues between online food delivery platforms and restaurant partners in India. Digit. Policy, Regul. Gov. **24**(3), 292–308 (2022)
41. Celly, N., Kathuria, A., Subramanian, V.: Overview of Indian multinationals. In: Thite, M., Wilkinson, A., Budhwar, P. (eds.) Emerging Indian multinationals: Strategic players in a multipolar world, pp. 54–101. Oxford University Press (2016). https://doi.org/10.1093/acprof:oso/9780199466467.003.0003
42. Kathuria, R., Kathuria, N.N., Kathuria, A.: Mutually supportive or trade-offs: an analysis of competitive priorities in the emerging economy of India. J. High Technol. Managem. Res. **29**(2), 227–236 (2018)
43. Ali, J.R., Aitchison, J.C.: Greater India. Earth Sci. Rev. **72**(3–4), 169–188 (2005)
44. Srivastava, S.C., Shainesh, G.: Bridging the service divide through digitally enabled service innovations. MIS Q. **39**(1), 245–268 (2015)
45. Venkatesh, V., Sykes, T., Zhang, X.: Development in rural india: a longitudinal study of women's health outcomes. MIS Q. **44**, 605–629 (2020)
46. Venkatesh, V., Bala, H., Sykes, T.A.: Impacts of information and communication technology implementations on employees' jobs in service organizations in India: a multi-method longitudinal field study. Prod. Oper. Manag. **19**(5), 591–613 (2010)
47. Sonpatki, R., Kathuria, A., Sethi, S.: Earnings call transcripts as a source and resource for information systems research. In: Kathuria, A., Karhade, P.P., Zhao, K., Chaturvedi, D. (eds.) Digital Transformation in the Viral Age: 21st Workshop on e-Business, WeB 2022, Copenhagen, Denmark, December 10, 2022, Revised Selected Papers, pp. 38–63. Springer Nature Switzerland, Cham (2024). https://doi.org/10.1007/978-3-031-60003-6_4
48. Chaturvedi, D., Karhade, P., Kathuria, A., Rai, A., Naik, N.: IT and the dual bottom-line objective of rational social enterprises. In: Proceedings of the European Conference on Information Systems (ECIS) (2024)

Digital Product Design and Customer Experience: Setting the Stage for Interdisciplinary Research Based on Value Co-Creation and Organizational Routines

Himanshu Warudkar[✉]

DBA, Indian School of Business and Senior Industry Professional, Pune, India
himanshu_warudkar2024@efpm.isb.edu

Abstract. We are in a digital economy, and the ever-increasing use of digital products in our daily lives has left us wanting a superlative customer experience [1, 2]. An engaging customer experience results from a conscious embodiment of several factors across multiple disciplines. In this paper, I set the stage for an interdisciplinary research program to study the interactional effects of two seminal constructs in management value co-creation and organisational routines. This research is critical for furthering our understanding of digital product design.

1 Introduction

Customer experience is a complex phenomenon with several antecedents ranging from prior expectations of customers, having a zone of tolerance, awareness of organisational service offerings, and actor engagement [3]. Popular products from a variety of industry domains, such as food delivery, travel, e-commerce and digital governance, are competing to provide a customer experience that is frictionless, intuitive and provides all-round value to the users. However, much of the experience delivery in digital products relies on two fundamental constructs, i.e., value co-creation and organisational routines [4–9].

Organisational routines have been called "grammar of action" and are a core topic in organisational behaviour research [10]. Since the 1950s, routines have been a source of organisational stability and change. Initially conceptualised by R. R. Nelson and Sidney Winter in 1982, organisational routines have been described as *"a pattern of behaviour that is followed repeatedly but is subject to change if conditions change"*.

Value co-creation, a fundamental construct within service-dominant logic, gives us an axiom stating that *"value co-creation is coordinated through actor-generated institutions and institutional arrangements"* [9, 11–13]. I equate these institutional arrangements to organisational routines.

Following are some of the questions to which interdisciplinary answers need to be found in the context of digital product design, and I have answered a few through my research. *How can an organisational understanding of customer value co-creation behaviours influence changes in organisational routines when transitioning from physical to digital products? How can organisations utilise flexibility in organisational routines for optimal customer satisfaction? When designing digital products, how should an*

© The Author(s), under exclusive license to Springer Nature Switzerland AG 2025
A. Kathuria et al. (Eds.): WeB 2023, LNBIP 525, pp. 92–105, 2025.
https://doi.org/10.1007/978-3-031-74437-2_8

organisation decide which organisational routines to keep within administrative bound-
aries and which ones to outsource to the customer (or other stakeholders)? How does
change in practices (practice theoretical lens) affect organisational routines?

This paper provides a strong foundation for an interdisciplinary research program
and links Marketing and Information Systems to customer value co-creation behaviours
and organisational routines. Customer value co-creation behaviours is a key construct
in Marketing the delivery mechanism of value co-creation is in organizational routines
[4, 5, 7, 14, 15]. Considering digitalization of many services the context in which these
organizational routines need to be looked at falls under the Information Systems domain
[2, 16–18]. Understanding customer behaviours from the lens of organisational routines
provides a strong lever for leaders and managers to continuously evolve the mechanisms
through which digital product experience is delivered.

2 Digital Products – A Confluence of Three Key Elements

We are in a digital economy, and the ever-increasing use of digital products in our
daily lives has left us wanting a superlative customer experience. An engaging customer
experience results from embodying several factors across multiple disciplines. However,
three critical elements are fundamental to delivering a great customer experience for any
digital product – design, digital and data.

Research on technology adoption within digital products relies on four concepts –
digital product innovation, product meaning, product component, and digital-physical
interactions [19]. Further, artificial intelligence, data analytics, robotics, digital platforms, social media, blockchain, and 3-D printing are reshaping human action and interaction. These have cascading effects on how digital products are designed. Many of
these technological advances carry new opportunities and organising constraints [20].
Concepts such as digital twin, which is defined as "an integrated multiphysics, multi-
scale, probabilistic simulation of a complex product, which functions to mirror the life
of its corresponding twin", have allowed product designers to bridge the physical world
and digital world [21]. The increasing use of artificial intelligence (chatbots) is bringing
new paradigms into how humans and machines interact [22], and an agency theoretical
view provides us with direction on how the entire decision-making process is changing
[23].

The importance of design (in particular user experience and service design) is critical for building great digital products [24]. Designing experiences for digital products
is complicated. This is because of the challenges associated with a wide range of user
demographics, reduced attention spans, the need for instant gratification, and challenges
in getting users to interact with and engage with the product for value creation. Therefore,
design thinking as a way of designing products must be integrated with strategy-making.
One reason to do this is to help with the product-market fit problem. This problem relates
to how organisations construct products relevant to their customers. Product-market fit
is particularly acute in innovation contexts, where organisations either re-imagine existing products and services or create new offerings [25]. Simply translating a physical
experience to a digital experience is not the answer, and the digital twin way of concep-
tualising digital products is helpful. Experiences are personal, emotional, and ephemeral

— the subjective perception of a particular moment. Knowingly or unknowingly, product designers are in the user experience business. Every product creates an experience for its users [26].

The creation of digital platforms has enabled organisations to provide an increasing range of services and content through value-creating interactions between external producers and consumers [27–29]. The digital platform does not necessarily hold physical assets as infrastructure resources nor generate value through product sales [30]. I equate these infrastructure resources to organisational routines [31–34]. As such, much of the experience delivery in digital products relies on two fundamental constructs, i.e., value co-creation and organisational routines. The proposition that the "customer is the primary creator of the value" is critical to designing any digital product experience [35, 36]. For example, the Uber app doesn't have any value unless the user can book a cab from point A to B at a desired price range, driver safety rating, wait time and journey time. Fig. 1 below provides a conceptual model of the interaction of the three dimensions of digital products.

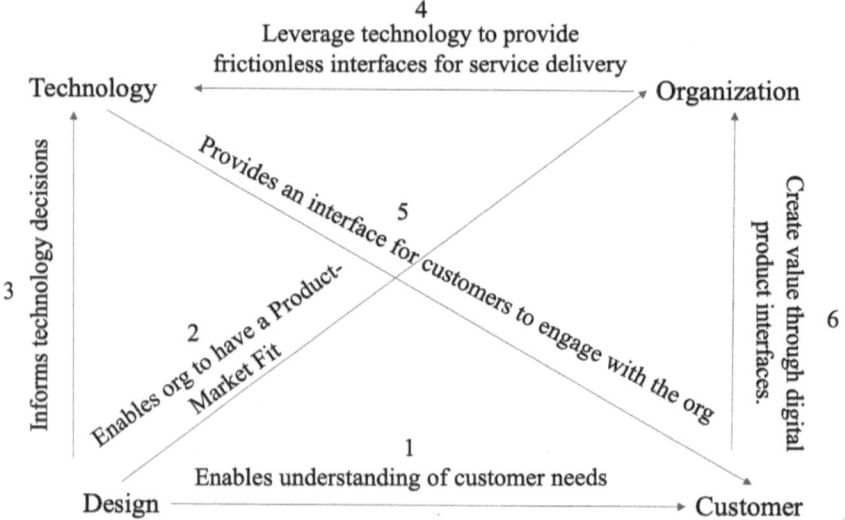

Fig. 1. Conceptual Model of Interaction of the Three Dimensions of Digital Products

Prior research also informs us that customer experience has several antecedents [37–39]. Popular products from a variety of industry domains, such as food delivery[1], music[2], travel, e-commerce and digital governance, are competing to provide a customer experience that is frictionless, intuitive and provides all-round value to the users. These experiences are enabled through effective use design and technology (engineering).

The confluence of these critical issues leads us to the interdisciplinary nature of research that is required to identify factors that affect the success of a digital product (one

---

[1] https://blog.zomato.com/category/technology.

[2] https://engineering.atspotify.com/.

outcome measure being customer satisfaction). These disciplines are value co-creation (Marketing), organizational routines (Organizational Behavior), service dominant logic (Marketing). As such, this paper provides a strong foundation for undertaking a research program linking two critical factors, i.e., customer value co-creation behaviours and organisational routines. Understanding customer behaviours from the lens of organisational routines provides a strong lever for leaders and managers to continuously evolve the mechanisms through which digital product experience is delivered.

3 Key Construct Definitions

Organizational routines have been called grammar of action [10] and has been a core topic in organizational behaviour research. Tracing its roots back to 1950s [10], routines have been seen as a source of both organizational stability and change [40]. Initially conceptualised by R. R. Nelson and Sidney Winter in 1982, organizational routines are *"a pattern of behaviour that is followed repeatedly but is subject to change if conditions change"* [41]. Over the past two decades, organizational routines community of practice [42] has produced a rich body of research which has taken the journey from early conceptualisation of routines as stable, reliable and quasi-automatically performed patterns of actions to a practice theoretical view of dynamic capabilities view offered by research on routine dynamics [43]. However, for the most part, routines research has focused on an organizational view of how routines change, their interdependence, relationship with learning and innovation.

Value co-creation [44] has played a central role in service-dominant logic [9] whereby *customer is seen as the primary value co-creator*. Further, *value is co-created and coordinated through actor-generated institutions and institutional arrangements* [45] which I equate to organizational routines.

Customer satisfaction, which is a key measure of success of a digital product (or service) can be broadly characterised as a *"post-purchase evaluation of product quality given prepurchase expectations"* [46, 47]. With a rich history that dates back to 1960s it has been seen as a means of evaluating quality. A rich literature review of customer satisfaction and the main antecedents identified by consumer research: expectations, perceived quality, and disconfirmation [48].

High customer satisfaction ratings are widely believed to be the best indicator of a company's future profits [46, 47]. Firms increasingly use customer satisfaction as a criterion for diagnosing product or service performance and often tie customer satisfaction ratings to both executive and employee compensation. However, providing incentives to maximise customer satisfaction is detrimental to the firm. Understanding the link between the antecedents of satisfaction and satisfaction's behavioural and economic consequences is necessary to encourage actions that will lead to an optimal level of satisfaction.

Taking these distinct streams of work, I conducted an interdisciplinary search [42] of over 150 research articles on organisational routines and value co-creation research to bring new insights into the organisational understanding of customers' value co-creation behaviours. In doing so, I posed questions about how organisations could benefit from changes in organisational routines, for example, by knowing their customer's value co-creation behaviours [49]. I also aimed to provide a new perspective on how organisations can effectively use customer satisfaction data [50, 51] to bring changes in institutional practices and make customers allies in bringing about institutional change. All of these are key when aiming to design a great digital product [52, 53].

4 Digital Product or Digital Service

In researching digital products, it is essential to understand the distinction (if any) between a digital product and a digital service. As such, a few essential concepts need to be understood.

The first concept is that *"customers do not buy goods or services: they buy offerings which render services which create value.* The traditional division between goods (products) and services is long outdated. It is not a matter of redefining services and seeing them from a customer perspective; activities render services, and things render services. The shift in focus to services is from the means and the producer perspective to the utilization and the customer perspective."* [54]. This is an important concept as it allows us to start thinking about customer behaviours as one of the critical drivers of value creation. For example, electric vehicles are increasingly seen as a platform and services business [55].

The second concept is, *"actors do business by performing boundary-crossing activities that generate business exchange."* [56]. This concept has also been elaborated further (perhaps independently) in identifying mandatory, voluntary, and replaceable activities for value creation. [57]. For example, when travelling via airline one has the option of getting oneself registered for biometric check-in/security which is a voluntary participation with a digital product[3].

The third concept is *"value (utility) which came to be understood in terms of value-in-exchange."* This is in comparison to *value-in-exchange,* which has been dealt with separately and used as another means to create value for customers, more so as "value-added". In many situations, *"value-in-use, which was a higher order concept than exchange value,"* service is defined in terms of customer-defined benefit. As such, assistance is accorded a superordinate position in marketing (in comparison to goods), and value-in-use also takes a superordinate position about value-in-exchange and the service/goods relationship is clarified. A good summary of the above description is that *"value shift is inherently customer-oriented"* and consumer is endogenous to the value-creation process [58].

The fourth concept is that *"service in S-D logic is defined in terms of applied resources."* Service-dominant logic (SDL) was introduced by Stephen Vargo and Robert Lusch (2004a) in a Journal of Marketing (JM) article titled "Evolving to a New Dominant Logic for Marketing" [59]. Its beginning, though, can be traced to much earlier and deeply rooted in marketing and marketing-associated literature. S-D logic is intended to capture and extend a convergence of apparently diverse thought that has shifted the dominant logic of marketing and economic thought away from a primary concern with tangible resources, output in the form of firm-created value (goods), and transactions. The central tenet of S-D logic (S-D Logic) is that reciprocal service, defined as the

---

[3] https://digiyatrafoundation.com/.

application of competencies for the benefit of another party, is the fundamental basis of economic exchange. Service is exchanged for service [45].

In S-D logic, service is defined as *"the application of specialized competencies (operant resources—knowledge and skills), through deeds, processes, and performances for the benefit of another entity or the entity itself"*. It is important to note that S-D logic uses the singular term, "service," which reflects the process of doing something beneficial for and in conjunction with some entity, rather than units of output—immaterial goods—as implied by the plural "services." Therefore, according to S-D logic, goods and service are not alternative forms of products. Goods (or digital products) are tools and distribution mechanisms that serve as alternatives to direct service provision. Service represents the common denominator of the exchange process; service is what is constantly exchanged. Goods, when employed, are aids to the service-provision process. Marketing occurs as parties (individuals, organizations, etc.) exchange in markets. This exchange involves each party using its resources for the (current or eventual) benefit of the other party. This use of resources for another party's help is *"service."* [58].

Therefore, when researching digital product design, we must consider digital service delivery enabled through customer value co-creation behaviors and organizational routines. These aligns with prior research that tenents from IS [60–63].

5   Integrating Value Co-creation and Organizational Routines Research

Having laid down the core construct definitions, I put forward the need to bring together research in organisational routines, value co-creation and customer satisfaction. This redirection is required because although the individual streams of research take perspectives on familiar themes, their interactional effects still need to be studied. For example, a research gap exists in studying the interaction between value co-creation (behaviours) and organisational routines. Firms' usage of customer satisfaction data has been researched [51]. It does provide some commentary on how customer satisfaction information usage (CSIU) may provide an essential mechanism for directing the firm's resource deployments and the behaviour of its personnel. However, a gap exists in conducting an empirical study on the relationship between organisational routines and customer satisfaction information usage. A relatively recent study of the evolution and prospects of service-dominant (S-D) logic provides us with a view that there are islands of research within the S-D logic [64].

Figure 2 below shows the thematic synthesis and associations between four constructs and takes me closer to formulating a hypothesis.

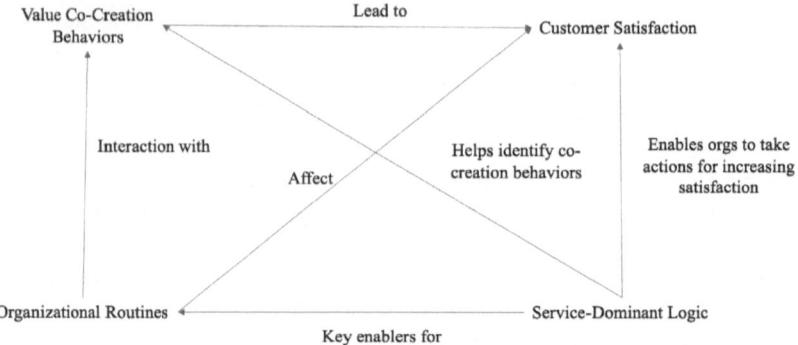

Fig. 2. Thematic Synthesis of Key Construct Definitions

6   Value Co-Creation Behaviours for Digital Product Design

To unite S-D logic, value co-creation researchers have defined the behaviour of customer co-creation as a construct comprising two differentiated types of consumer behaviour: participation behaviour and citizenship behaviour [49]. The first of these dimensions (participation behaviour) refers to the customer's behaviour during the service encounter. This is considered necessary to attain an appropriate performance in value co-creation.

The second relates to citizenship behaviour as a type of behaviour that can create a higher value for the organisation but is not necessary for value co-creation [65, 66]. Each of these dimensions comprises four factors on the original scale: information seeking, information sharing, responsible behaviour, and personal interaction in the framework of participation behaviour and feedback, advocacy, helping, and tolerance of citizenship behaviour.

These eight behaviour dimensions are [49]:

1. *Information Seeking*: The customers need to have access to the information related to the service's basic characteristics that they are going to receive. This knowledge is going to facilitate their integration in the value co-creation process.
2. *Information Sharing*: The customers must participate actively, supplying information to the employees about the needs they wish to satisfy and the specifications of the service they expect to receive.
3. *Responsible Behaviour*: In value co-creation, customers must cooperate with the employees, following their guidelines and orientations.
4. *Personal Interaction*: Interpersonal relations between customers and employees based on courtesy, friendliness, and respect are fundamental for the success of the value co-creation process.
5. *Feedback*: The information that customers supply to the employees (suggestions and orientations) and which facilitates the long-term improvement of the service provision.
6. *Advocacy*: The recommendation of the firm or its employees to family and friends.
7. *Helping*: The willingness to advise or give information to the rest of the users contributes to improving the service without the employees needing to intervene.

8. *Tolerance*: Refers to the customers being patient when the service provision does not meet their expectations.

The role of higher value creation for customers in the firm's competitiveness is evident [13]. Customers that engage with digital products are more informed and educated, selective and demanding and have a greater capacity for choice. This new consumer demand warrants a different lens through which one should study the design of digital products. Therefore, developing our understanding of customer value creation is necessary to design digital products effectively.

Taking examples of products in domains such as travel and tourism[4] each of these value co-creation behaviours is critical for effective customer engagement and participation in the value creation activities from a digital product perspective.

7 Organisational Routines and Digital Product Design

Effective delivery of services through digital products relies on a well-coordinated orchestra of organisational routines. Routines are repetitive patterns of interdependent actions [67, 68]. Since the foundational work of the Carnegie School i.e., James March, Richard Cyert and Herbert Simon [69, 70], scholars have acknowledged routines as core components of organisational life and have explored the characteristics of routines, their effects on firm performances, and their downsides [10, 40, 71, 72]. There are two main perspectives to the analysis of routines and two related communities of practice [73] or "camps" as the authors dubbed them [74]. One is a so-called "capability perspective" led by organisational economists that studies routine effects on firms, and a "practice perspective" led by organisational theorists focused on how routines work in practice. The capability aspect of organizational routines as relates to digital products is in building the capabilities to engage with and create value using digital products. For example, the capability to scan a QR code is essential for users to make a digital payment.[5]

Another lens through which one can study this phenomenon is practice theory which gives us an understanding of how "materials, meaning and competencies" change over time and how digital products can drive societal change (Fig. 3). Researchers engaging with the first perspective view routines as "black boxes" and explore their impact on firm performance, while scholars adopting the second perspective focus on action enactment and how routines operate in practice. These perspectives have also been called "ostensive aspect", which represents a routine as it is. The actual enactment of a routine is called its "performative aspect" [68].

Organisational routines research has covered various perspectives over the past two decades. These perspectives have evolved from an early definition of routines as multi-actor, interlocking, reciprocally-triggered sequences of actions [75] to research that utilizes routines as a mechanism underlying organizational practices that lead to IS outcomes [43, 76]. Organisational routines researchers have applied various theoretical and methodological lenses such as a practice theoretical view [43], studying the intentional nature of routines [77], studying how an understanding-based redesigning of routines

---

[4] www.makemytrip.com.

[5] https://www.npci.org.in/what-we-do/upi/product-overview.

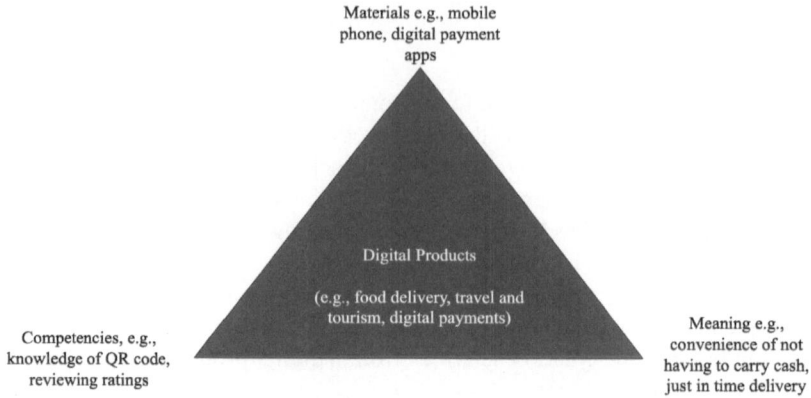

Fig. 3. Practice Theoretical Lens of Digital Products

improves the effectiveness of a routine by facilitating the actions and interactions of routine participants [78].

Other studies have focussed on various organizational aspects of routines example, routine regulation as a source of balancing conflicting organizational goals [79], inertia in routines as a source of variation [80], role of artifacts in changes to routines [81]. A few studies have attempted to study the relationships between consumers and organizational routines. One such example covers consumers response and adjustment to the unease that arises when their normal routines are disrupted [82]. Relationship between organizational routines and experience has been explored from a learning perspective [83]. Work on organizational boundaries identifies conditions under which organizations may want to outsource certain part of routine execution to customers [57]. These diverse perspectives provide me with a strong theoretical ground to extract first order themes in organizational routines research and subsequently link them to other areas of research.

Understanding how organizational routines operate, designing digital products in isolation without taking into consideration the need for process re-engineering of existing routines could result in degradation in experience, challenges in scalability. Understanding customer value co-creation behaviours in conjunction with organizational routines would give organizations a strong lever for increasing customer satisfaction.

8   Setting the Stage for Inter-Disciplinary Research on Digital Product Design

Bringing all of the above topics together, there is a strong case to conduct inter-disciplinary research on digital product design. In today's age of "everything" digital – creation of value through actor engagement (often consumers and their associated social networks) interacting with organizing actors (often firms and their associated organizational ecosystem) has shifted from a physical space to a joint space of interactive system-environments. Prevalence of digital platforms (Amazon, Uber) over the past several years has led to development of a novel conceptualization of an offering as an evolving digitalized networked arrangement of artifacts, persons, processes, and interfaces. This is referred to as a digitalized interactive platform (DIP).

To that extent, there has not been a more important time for practically using our knowledge of customer value co-creation behaviors and organizational routines. As far as customers are concerned, organizations must move from keeping routines as a black box for customers to a more transparent view which allows customers to actively feedback on the routines, understand the complexities involved and even help organizations in resolving problems faced during the execution of routines. As such, this interdisciplinary research is critical for furthering our understanding of digital product design. In summary, this paper provides a strong foundation for an interdisciplinary research program linking customer value co-creation behaviours and organisational routines. Understanding customer behaviours from the lens of organisational routines provides a strong lever for leaders and managers to continuously evolve the mechanisms through which digital product experience is delivered.

References

1. Bolton, R.N., et al.: Customer experience challenges: bringing together digital, physical and social realms. J. Serv. Manag. **29**(5), 776–808 (2018)
2. Brynjolfsson, E., Collis, A.: How should we measure the digital economy. Harvard Bus. Rev. **97**(6), 140–148 (2019)
3. Anderson, E.W., Sullivan, M.W.: The antecedents and consequences of customer satisfaction for firms. Market. Sci. **12**(2), 125–143 (1993)
4. Ramaswamy, V., Ozcan, K.: What is co-creation? An interactional creation framework and its implications for value creation. J. Bus. Res. **84**, 196–205 (2018)
5. Storbacka, K., Brodie, R.J., Böhmann, T., Maglio, P.P., Nenonen, S.: Actor engagement as a microfoundation for value co-creation. J. Bus. Res. **69**(8), 3008–3017 (2016)
6. Alves, H., Fernandes, C., Raposo, M.: Value co-creation: concept and contexts of application and study. J. Bus. Res. **69**(5), 1626–1633 (2016)
7. Jaakkola, E., Alexander, M.: The role of customer engagement behavior in value co-creation. J. Serv. Res. **17**(3), 247–261 (2014)
8. Pinho, N., Beirão, G., Patrício, Lia, Fisk, Raymond P.: Understanding value co-creation in complex services with many actors. J. Serv. Manag. **25**(4), 470–493 (2014). https://doi.org/10.1108/JOSM-02-2014-0055
9. Vargo, S.L., Maglio, P.P., Akaka, M.A.: On value and value co-creation: a service systems and service logic perspective. Eur. Manag. J. **26**(3), 145–152 (2008)
10. Pentland, B.T., Rueter, H.H.: Organizational routines as grammars of action. Adm. Sci. Q. **39**(3), 484 (1994). https://doi.org/10.2307/2393300
11. Vargo, S.L., Lusch, R.F.: Institutions and axioms: an extension and update of service-dominant logic. J. Acad. Mark. Sci. **44**(1), 5–23 (2015)
12. Edvardsson, B., Tronvoll, B., Gruber, T.: Expanding understanding of service exchange and value co-creation: a social construction approach. J. Acad. Mark. Sci. **39**, 327–339 (2011)
13. Payne, A.F., Storbacka, K., Frow, P.: Managing the co-creation of value. J. Acad. Market. Sci. **36**(1), 83–96 (2007)
14. Ranjan, K.R., Read, S.: Value co-creation: concept and measurement. J. Acad. Market. Sci. **44**(3), 290–315 (2014)
15. Galvagno, M., Gummesson, E., Mele, C., Polese, F., Dalli, D.: Theory of value co-creation: a systematic literature review. Managing Serv. Qual. **24**(6), 643–683 (2014)

16. Lanzolla, G., Lorenz, A., Miron-Spektor, E., Schilling, M, Solinas, G., Tucci, C.L.: Digital Transformation: What is New if Anything? Emerging Patterns and Management Research, pp. 341–350. Academy of Management Briarcliff Manor, NY (2020)

17. Wulf, J., Blohm, I.: Fostering value creation with digital platforms: a unified theory of the application programming interface design. J. Manag. Inform. Syst. **37**(1), 251–281 (2020)

18. Tabrizi, B., Lam, E., Girard, K., Irvin, V.: Digital transformation is not about technology. Harvard Bus. Rev. **13**(March), 1–6 (2019)

19. Wang, G., Henfridsson, O., Nandhakumar, J., Yoo, Y.: Product meaning in digital product innovation. MIS Q. **46**(2), 947–976 (2022)

20. Bailey, D.E., Faraj, S., Hinds, P.J., Leonardi, P.M., von Krogh, G.: We are all theorists of technology now: a relational perspective on emerging technology and organizing. Organ. Sci. **33**(1), 1–18 (2022)

21. Glaessgen, E., Stargel, D.: The digital twin paradigm for future NASA and US Air Force vehicles. In: 53rd AIAA/ASME/ASCE/AHS/ASC structures, structural dynamics and materials conference 20th AIAA/ASME/AHS adaptive structures conference 14th AIAA (2012).

22. Konsynski, B.R., Kathuria, A., Karhade, P.P.: Cognitive reapportionment and the art of letting go: a theoretical framework for the allocation of decision rights. J. Manag. Inform. Syst. **41**(2), 328–340 (2024)

23. Murray, A., Rhymer, J., Sirmon, D.G.: Humans and technology: forms of conjoined agency in organizations. Acad. Manag. Rev. **46**(3), 552–571 (2021)

24. Wetter-Edman, K., Sangiorgi, D., Edvardsson, B., Holmlid, S., Grönroos, C., Mattelmäki, T.: Design for value co-creation: Exploring synergies between design for service and service logic. Serv. Sci. **6**(2), 106–121 (2014)

25. Knight, E., Daymond, J., Paroutis, S.: Design-led strategy: how to bring design thinking into the art of strategic management. Calif. Manage. Rev. **62**(2), 30–52 (2020)

26. Garrett, J.J.: Customer loyalty and the elements of user experience. Des. Manag. Rev. **17**(1), 35–39 (2006)

27. Kathuria, A., Karhade, P.P., Konsynski, B.R.: In the realm of hungry ghosts: multi-level theory for supplier participation on digital platforms. J. Manage. Inform. Syst. **37**(2), 396–430 (2020)

28. Karhade, P., Kathuria, A., Malik, O., Konsynski, B.: Digital platforms and infobesity: a research agenda. In: Garimella, A., Karhade, P., Kathuria, A., Liu, X., Xu, J., Zhao, K. (eds.) The Role of e-Business during the Time of Grand Challenges: 19th Workshop on e-Business, WeB 2020, Virtual Event, December 12, 2020, Revised Selected Papers, pp. 67–74. Springer International Publishing, Cham (2021). https://doi.org/10.1007/978-3-030-79454-5_7

29. Dasgupta, A., Karhade, P., Kathuria, A., Konsynski, B.: Holding space for voices that do not speak: design reform of rating systems for platforms in GREAT economies. In: Proceedings of the Hawaii International Conference on System Sciences (HICCS).Virtual (2021)

30. Constantinides, P., Henfridsson, O., Parker, G.G.: Introduction—platforms and infrastructures in the digital age. Inform. Syst. Res. **29**(2), 381–400 (2018). https://doi.org/10.1287/isre.2018.0794

31. Howard-Grenville, J., Rerup, C.: A Process Perspective On Organizational Routines*. In: Langley, A., Tsoukas, H. (eds.) The SAGE Handbook of Process Organization Studies, pp. 323–337. SAGE Publications Ltd, 1 Oliver's Yard, 55 City Road London EC1Y 1SP (2016). https://doi.org/10.4135/9781473957954.n20

32. Feldman, M.S., Pentland, B.T., D'Adderio, L., Lazaric, N.: Beyond routines as things: introduction to the special issue on routine dynamics. Organ. Sci. **27**(3), 505–513 (2016)

33. Pentland, B.T., Hærem, T.: Organizational routines as patterns of action: implications for organizational behavior. Annu. Rev. Organ. Psychol. Organ. Behav. **2**(1), 465–487 (2015)

34. Pentland, B.T.: Organizational routines as a unit of analysis. Ind. Corp. Change **14**(5), 793–815 (2005)

35. Wibowo, A.J.I., Sumarwan, U., Suharjo, B., Simanjuntak, M.: 17 years of service-dominant logic: Vargo and Lusch's contributions. Bus.: Theory Pract. **22**(2), 482–492 (2021)
36. Vargo, S.L., Lusch, R.F., Akaka, M.A., He, Y.: Service-dominant logic: a review and assessment. Rev. Market. Res. **6**, 125–167 (2017)
37. Zha, D., Marvi, R., Foroudi, P.: Synthesizing the customer experience concept: a multimodularity approach. J. Bus. Res. **167**, 114185 (2023). https://doi.org/10.1016/j.jbusres.2023.114185
38. Verleye, K.: The co-creation experience from the customer perspective: its measurement and determinants. J. Serv. Manag. **26**(2), 321–342 (2015). https://doi.org/10.1108/JOSM-09-2014-0254
39. Verhoef, P.C., Lemon, K.N., Parasuraman, A., Roggeveen, A., Tsiros, M., Schlesinger, L.A.: Customer experience creation: determinants, dynamics and management strategies. J. Retail. **85**(1), 31–41 (2009)
40. Feldman, M.S.: Organizational routines as a source of continuous change. Organ. Sci. **11**(6), 611–629 (2000)
41. Becker, M.C.: Organizational routines: a review of the literature. Ind. Corp. Change **13**(4), 643–678 (2004)
42. Cronin, M.A., George, E.: The why and how of the integrative review. Organ. Res. Methods **26**(1), 168–192 (2020)
43. Wenzel, M., Danner-Schröder, A., Spee, A.P.: Dynamic capabilities? Unleashing their dynamics through a practice perspective on organizational routines. J. Manag. Inq. **30**(4), 395–406 (2021)
44. Prahalad, C.K., Ramaswamy, V.: Co-creation experiences: the next practice in value creation. J. Interact. Market. **18**(3), 5–14 (2004)
45. Vargo, S.L., Lusch, R.F.: Service-dominant logic 2025. Int. J. Res. Market. **34**(1), 46–67 (2017)
46. Kotler, P., Saliba, S., Wrenn, B.: Marketing Management: Analysis, Planning, and Control: Instructor's Manual. Prentice-hall (1991)
47. Barich, H., Kotler, P.: A framework for marketing image management. MIT Sloan Manag. Rev. **32**(2), 94 (1991)
48. Yi, Y.: A critical review of consumer satisfaction. Rev. Market. **4**(1), 68–123 (1990)
49. Yi, Y., Gong, T.: Customer value co-creation behavior: scale development and validation. J. Bus. Res. **66**(9), 1279–1284 (2013)
50. Otto, A.S., Szymanski, D.M., Varadarajan, R.: Customer satisfaction and firm performance: insights from over a quarter century of empirical research. J. Acad. Market. Sci. **48**(3), 543–564 (2019)
51. Morgan, N.A., Anderson, E.W., Mittal, V.: Understanding firms' customer satisfaction information usage. J. Market. **69**(3), 131–151 (2005)
52. Tuunanen, T., Lumivalo, J., Vartiainen, T., Zhang, Y., Myers, M.D.: Micro-level mechanisms to support value co-creation for design of digital services. J. Serv. Res. **27**(3), 381–396 (2023). https://doi.org/10.1177/10946705231173116
53. Liu, Q., Yang, M.: Sustainable value co-creation in the circular economy through digitalization. In: Academy of Management Proceedings. Academy of Management Briarcliff Manor, NY 10510 (2023).
54. Gummesson, E.: Truth and myths in service quality. J. Qual. Participation **18**(6), 18 (1995)
55. Anderson, E.G., Bhargava, H.K., Boehm, J., Parker, G.: Electric vehicles are a platform business: what firms need to know. Calif. Manag. Rev. **64**(4), 135–154 (2022)
56. Håkansson, H., Prenkert, F.: Exploring the Exchange Concept in Marketing (2004)
57. Santos, F.M., Eisenhardt, K.M.: Organizational boundaries and theories of organization. Organ. Sci. **16**(5), 491–508 (2005)

58. Vargo, S.L., Lusch, R.F.: Why "service"? J. Acad. Market. Sci. **36**(1), 25–38 (2007)
59. Vargo, S.L., Lusch, R.F.: Evolving to a new dominant logic for marketing. J. Market. **68**(1), 1–17 (2004)
60. Chaturvedi, D., Kathuria, A., Andrade, M., Saldanha, T.: Navigating the paradox of IT novelty and strategic conformity: the moderating role of industry dynamism. In: Proceedings of the International Conference on Information Systems (ICIS), Hyderabad (2023)
61. Ramakrishnan, T., Kathuria, A., Khuntia, J., Konsynski, B.: IoT value creation through supply chain analytics capability. In: Proceedings of the International Conference on Information Systems (ICIS). Copenhagen (2022)
62. Saldanha, T.J., Kathuria, A., Khuntia, J., Konsynski, B.R.: Ghosts in the machine: how marketing and human capital investments enhance customer growth when innovative services leverage self-service technologies. Inform. Syst. Res. **33**(1), 76–109 (2022)
63. Saldanha, T.J., Kathuria, A., Khuntia, J.: Digital service flexibility and performance of credit unions. In: Proceedings of the Americas Conference on Information Systems (AMCIS). Chicago (2013)
64. Wilden, R., Akaka, M.A., Karpen, I.O., Hohberger, J.: The evolution and prospects of service-dominant logic. J. Serv. Res. **20**(4), 345–361 (2017)
65. Bove, L.L., Pervan, S.J., Beatty, S.E., Shiu, E.: Service worker role in encouraging customer organizational citizenship behaviors. J. Busi. Res. **62**(7), 698–705 (2009)
66. Groth, M.: Customers as good soldiers: examining citizenship behaviors in internet service deliveries. J. Manage. **31**(1), 7–27 (2005)
67. Feldman, M.S., Pentland, B.T.: Reconceptualizing organizational routines as a source of flexibility and change. Adm. Sci. Q. **48**(1), 94–118 (2003)
68. Feldman, M.S.: A performative perspective on stability and change in organizational routines. Ind. Corp. Change **12**(4), 727–752 (2003)
69. Cyert, R.M., March, J.G.: A behavioral theory of the firm. Englewood Cliffs, NJ **2**(4), 169–187 (1963)
70. March, J.G., Simon, H.A.: Organizations. John Wiley & Sons (1993)
71. Windrum, P., Reinstaller, A., Bull, C.: The outsourcing productivity paradox: total outsourcing, organisational innovation, and long run productivity growth. J. Evol. Econ. **19**, 197–229 (2009)
72. Zollo, M., Reuer, J.J., Singh, H.: Interorganizational routines and performance in strategic alliances. Organ. Sci. **13**(6), 701–713 (2002)
73. Elsbach, K.D., van Knippenberg, D.: Creating high-impact literature reviews: an argument for 'integrative reviews.' J. Manage. Stud. **57**(6), 1277–1289 (2020)
74. Parmigiani, A., Howard-Grenville, J.: Routines revisited: exploring the capabilities and practice perspectives. Acad. Manage. Ann. **5**(1), 413–453 (2011)
75. Cohen, M.D., Bacdayan, P.: Organizational routines are stored as procedural memory: evidence from a laboratory study. Organ. Sci. **5**(4), 554–568 (1994)
76. Andrade-Rojas, M.G., Saldanha, T.J., Kathuria, A., Khuntia, J., Boh, W.: How information technology overcomes deficiencies for innovation in small and medium-sized enterprises: closed innovation vs. open innovation. Inform. Syst. Res. (2024)
77. Makowski, P.T.: Routines: towards the Complexity of Organizational Intentionality. Rev. Philos. Psychol. **13**(4), 1059–1080 (2021)
78. Bapuji, H., Hora, M., Saeed, A.M.: Intentions, intermediaries, and interaction: examining the emergence of routines. J. Manage. Stud. **49**(8), 1586–1607 (2012)
79. Salvato, C., Rerup, C.: Routine regulation: balancing conflicting goals in organizational routines. Adm. Sci. Q. **63**(1), 170–209 (2017)
80. Yi, S., Knudsen, T., Becker, M.C.: Inertia in routines: a hidden source of organizational variation. Organ. Sci. **27**(3), 782–800 (2016)

81. Glaser, V.L.: Design performances: how organizations inscribe artifacts to change Routines. Acad. Manage. J. **60**(6), 2126–2154 (2017)
82. Phipps, M., Ozanne, J.L., Fischer, E., Thompson, C.: Routines disrupted: reestablishing security through practice alignment. J. Consum. Res. **44**(2), 361–380 (2017)
83. Espedal, B.: Do organizational routines change as experience changes? J. Appl. Behav. Sci. **42**(4), 468–490 (2016)

An Instructive Guide for Extracting Digital and IT Competence of Firms Using Natural Language Processing on Earnings Call Transcripts

Sai Rithwik Mahateja Ambatipudi(iD), Harish Ramadurgam(✉)(iD),
and Abhishek Kathuria(iD)

Indian School of Business, Hyderabad, India
{sairithwik_ambatipudi,harish_ramadurgam,
abhishek_kathuria}@isb.edu

Abstract. Earnings Call Transcripts are a valued data source across the fields of accounting, finance, strategic management, corporate governance, and corporate social responsibility. Researchers in the field of information systems have asserted the importance of ECT as a source and resource to understand firms' digital endowments and strategies. The objective of this chapter is to provide a description and instructive guide for extracting digital and IT-related constructs of firms using natural language processing on ECTs. We explore the implementation of the text-mining and natural language processing techniques of bag-of-words, word2vec, lexical, semantic, and combined analyses to interpret a firm's proclivity towards the utilization of digital and information technology. We discuss the strengths and limitations of employing ECT. Finally, we provide an extensive explication of alternative approaches and avenues for future research related to the use of earnings call transcripts in the field of information systems.

Keywords: Text-mining · NLP Techniques · Natural Language Processing · Earning Call Transcripts · Business Value of IT · Digital Competence

1 Introduction

The Internet and mass media have enabled firms to divulge and manipulate information about their firm through various sources. Given the proliferation of outlets for information about firms, financial investors, business analysts, and enthusiasts must deliberate several channels to identify reliable, trusted sources of information. The primary channel through which the majority of firms report their management sentiments and financial stability are *Earnings Call Transcripts*, henceforth termed ECT. ECTs are published year-on-year or quarter-on-quarter and discuss, emphasize, and display the expectations and performances of publicly traded firms. Firms also file annual (10-K), quarter (10-Q), or current (8-K) reports at the U.S. Securities and Exchange Commission (SEC). Any firm with assets over $10 million and 500 or more shareholders is required to file Form 10 with the SEC.

© The Author(s), under exclusive license to Springer Nature Switzerland AG 2025
A. Kathuria et al. (Eds.): WeB 2023, LNBIP 525, pp. 106–125, 2025.
https://doi.org/10.1007/978-3-031-74437-2_9

ECTs capture the sentiment and strategic orientation of the C-suite leadership, firms' growth strategy, go-to-market strategy for product/service launches, market expansion plans, and analyst inquiries on firm performance [1]. These transcripts allow readers to:

1. Glean the company's revenue, strategic direction, etc., directly from comments from company leadership.
2. Understand the company's proactive and reactive positioning ("optics" and "spin").
3. Discover issues analysts are probing via their questions to determine what industry insiders deem crucial for understanding the company's performance (Companies can manipulate what questions analysts can ask in these scenarios as well) [2].

Extensive study of ECTs helps gauge the factors that firms consider critical, such as potential pitfalls, industry trend effects on the firm, revenue breakdown across product lines/geographies, and concerns of analysts regarding the outlook of specific strategy implementations within the firm. The reports capture investment information, market trends & conditions, competitive dynamics, strategic evaluations and initiatives, forecasting expectations like market & growth expansion, and governance practices. Studying ECTs provides a holistic view of the financial health, investment decisions, and strategic trajectory of the firm [3, 4].

Earnings calls are scheduled several days or even weeks in advance, allowing interested parties to plan their attendance. This scheduling moderates investors' decisions to adjust trades frequently and prompts equity analysts to update their earnings estimates. Earnings calls are typically held in the form of teleconference calls or webcasts following an official press release summarizing the key point of the company's financial performance. ECTs contain a safe harbor statement by the firm's management regarding foresight for the upcoming quarter or year. This is a disclaimer statement that is intended to alert participants that estimates based on these forward-looking statements might significantly deviate from actual results, aiming to limit the company's liability in case of such discrepancies. After the safe harbor statement, the next section of the quarterly earnings conference call is termed the prepared remarks section. Here, managers of the company, typically represented by C-level executives, with the CEO and CFO being consistent fixtures, discuss the financial results for the specified reporting period. They also provide insights into upcoming company goals and anticipated impact on future performance [5]. The latter part of an earnings call is a Q&A session where participants, including investors and analysts, ask questions about the financial results. Each participant typically asks 2–3 questions, and the call concludes with closing remarks from the management.

Quarterly earnings conference calls typically span 45 to 60 min, and no statutory guidelines dictate its duration. The length of the call largely hinges on the duration of the Q&A session, the extent of information shared by the management, and the company's performance during the specified period.

Having understood the nuances of information within ECTs, we now explore the importance of ECTs as a valuable source across domains and how to create a streamlined flow of analysis for the benefactors interested and invested in the firms.

ECTs have been used in prior research work across different fields like Accounting, Finance, Information Systems, Strategic Management, Corporate Governance, and Corporate Social Responsibility, among others. ECTs provide a wealth of information for research across domains like financial health, accounting disclosures, auditor interaction, strategic outlook, investor sentiment, management biases, stock prices, trading volumes, market reactions, and efficiency. Emerging issues on management transparency, accountability, behavior, and sustainability initiatives, environment, social, and governance are also captured that help scholars study the governance and social responsibility in the firms [6, 7]. Especially, calls for further use of ECTs in information systems research using the NLP techniques for exploration [5] have been a recurring theme. The versatility of ECTs presents a credible and reliable data source that provides an avenue for future IS researchers.

Table 1. Text-Mining & NLP Techniques Used for ECT Analysis in this Chapter

Bag of Words (BoWs)	Simplified representation of text data where each unique word is counted without considering grammar or word order, often used in text classification
Word2Vec Models	Dense vector representations of words are termed as embeddings in continuous vector space. The model helps capture semantic and syntactic nuances of the words/sentences in lower dimensions for computational efficiency
Lexical Analysis	Degree of resemblance or overlap between two linguistic units, such as words or phrases, in terms of their form, meaning, or both, often used in spell checking and phonetic matching
Semantic Analysis	Degree of likeness or relatedness between two pieces of text based on the meaning of their content rather than just surface similarity, often used in sense disambiguation, question answering
Combined Analysis (Semantic + Lexical)	Utilizing both techniques will help understand nuances of words and sentence-level sentiment and enable to comprehend domain-specific and domain-agnostic information

The purpose of this chapter is to provide a description and instructive guide for extracting digital and IT-related constructs of firms using natural language processing (NLP) on ECTs. Among various NLP techniques to analyze ECT, we explore Bag of Words (BoWs), Word2Vec, Lexical Analysis, Semantic Analysis, and Combined Analysis. These are described in brief above in Table 1.

The rest of this chapter is organized as follows. We start by giving an overview of the automation analysis process, following up with the importance of data preprocessing. As the saying goes, "Garbage in, garbage out." Preprocessing text-heavy documents like ECT is crucial for limiting the noise/irrelevant data present within the documents. We examine the preprocessing techniques commonly used in text-mining, stemming, and lemmatization and compare the two, demonstrating the working of the techniques with a firm's ECT as an example. It is essential to analyze the data after data preprocessing with appropriate techniques. Thus, in the further parts of the chapter, we explore the Bag of Words and explain the necessity and working of the technique, followed by a TF-IDF analysis of a variation of the same technique. We then list the limitations of the technique to capture the context-level information and suggest NLP techniques of Word2Vec that use word embeddings for tackling the same.

The subsequent section gives a picture of the implementation of techniques like lexical, semantic, and combined. All these techniques result in vector-based representations, which are hard to interpret; hence, simplifications/reductions like cosine similarity are illustrated following them. ECTs are structured, and utilizing an analytical process for large volumes is similar; in the final parts of the chapter, we will discuss automating the process for ECT at a huge scale and discuss efficiencies around them.

The intention of the chapter is to describe the use of ECT to measure the digital and IT competence of the firms using text-mining and NLP techniques that aid the scholars, researchers, analysts, and managers to leverage the current technological trends and apply them to identify the digital transformations happening across firms. For this purpose, we will be using ECTs of S&P 500 firms across the years 2006 to 2021.

2   Process Flow Overview of the Automation Analysis

This section presents an overview of the automation process being followed for sourcing and retrieving ECTs from listing websites such as Capital IQ for US-based firms and BSE for India-based firms. This involves downloading and storing ECTs in PDF format within firm-year-specific folders, accessing and converting the files into text-analyzable data, ultimately to be used during text-mining or NLP techniques. This process will eventually enable the extraction of information pertaining to the digital and IT implementations of the firms.

In the specific context of studying S&P 500 companies, we source data from the Capital IQ website from 2006 to 2021 and store each respective firm's year-level reports in the data processing and extraction machine. This data, sourced across all the firms and years, acts as a central repository for analysis. The available data will be converted to text-readable information using inbuilt text extraction and manipulation tools in Python, such as PDFMiner and PyPDF2. The text preprocessed data will then be analyzed using text-mining and NLP algorithms to gauge the digital and information technology keywords captured within the specific ECT. In this process, we explore the associated algorithms and techniques of BoWs, Word2Vec, lexical, semantic, and combined similarities. A visualization of the process flow is represented in the flowchart depicted in Fig. 1.

3   Preprocessing (Stemming & Lemmatization)

No matter which technique has been chosen for the analysis of text in the ECT, the most important and crucial step is to preprocess and clean the data for modeling. ECT is content and text heavy, containing sections such as Headers, Footers, Table of Contents, Call Participants, Presentation and Question & Answer, Source related Copyright information. [See Figs. 2, 3, 4 and 5] Considering the abundance of rich data available, streamlining the processing is essential to sift through and discern respective sections, thereby deriving valuable insights. The analysts/programmers codify the text accessing, extracting, preprocessing, modeling, and archiving software for each of the techniques.

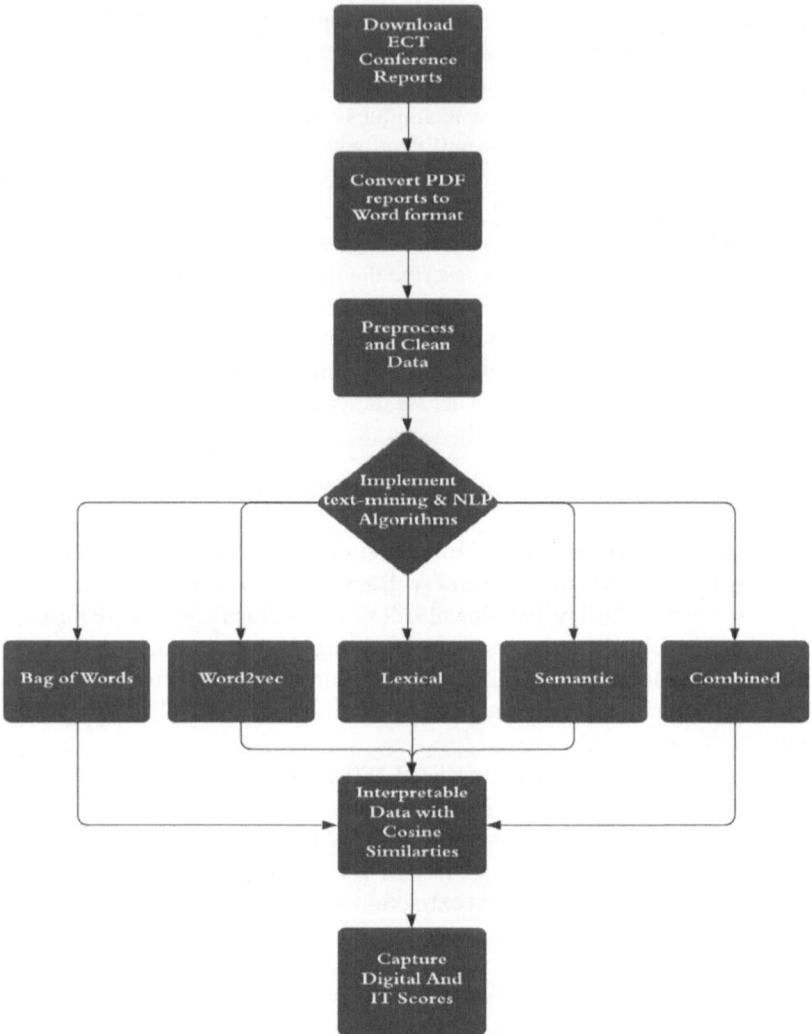

Fig. 1. Process for Automation of ECT Analysis

Among these, removing HTML tags, special characters, non-ASCII characters, end-of-sentence characters, tokenization, stop word removal, and normalizing (Stemming and Lemmatization) is standard across all the techniques.

Within ECT, the valuable source of information for business enthusiasts, financial investors, and analysts is generally listed under the Presentation and Q&A sections. Hence additional information in the ECT is discarded in further analysis. Particularly for our study, the sections containing financial information, Table of Contents, and Call Participants will not be regarded in the analysis, though they may contain insightful sources of information for future avenues of research. In addition, the presentation and Q&A

The Continental High Table India BSE:007
FQ1 2023 Earnings Call Transcripts
Thursday, March 24, 2023, 6:45 AM GMT
S&P Global Market Intelligence Estimates

	-FQ1 2023-			-FQ2 2023-	-FY 2023-	-FY 2024-
	CONSENSUS	ACTUAL	SURPRISE	CONSENSUS	CONSENSUS	CONSENSUS
EPS Normalized	2.40	2.28	▼ (5.00 %)	-	9.08	9.78
Revenue (mm)	13118.20	13337.60	▲ 1.67	11164.00	49706.25	52532.00

Currency: INR
Consensus as of Mar-15-2023 7:57 AM GMT

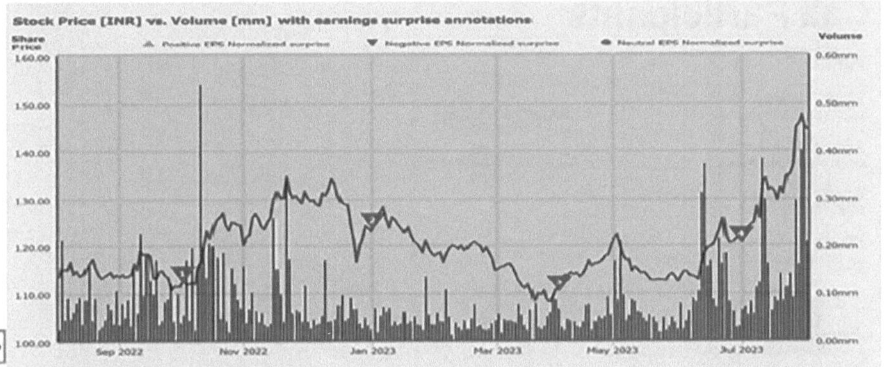

Stock Price [INR] vs. Volume [mm] with earnings surprise annotations

	CONSENSUS	ACTUAL	SURPRISE
FQ3 2022	2.20	1.89	▼ (14.09 %)
FQ4 2022	2.20	1.95	▼ (11.36 %)
FQ1 2023	2.50	2.05	▼ (18.00 %)
FQ2 2023	2.40	2.28	▼ (5.00 %)

Fig. 2. Additional Financial Information Captured Within An ECT

sections contain the management sentiments, financial stability, and strategic decision-making statements that will be analyzed within the main analysis. The snapshots below represent typical information contained under each of the sections.

Text-mining algorithms are efficient in handling smaller texts, but ECT is text-heavy. Further, essential information like management sentiments, strategic orientation, firms' growth, go-to-market strategy, market expansion plans, and responses to analyst inquiries on firm performance is generally obscured within presentations and discussions and willingly obfuscated to conceal the firm's advantage to maintain a strategic moat.

Essentially, to capture the digital constructs, such as digital competency or digital orientation of a firm, a naïve approach is to find out the relevant words that commonly occur within each ECT and assign a score. To achieve the objective of finding the occurrence of specific words in the text, we need to reduce the heavy text into smaller units called tokens using the process of tokenization. The process can be done with words, sub-words, characters, or phrases which results in text segmentations at the respective

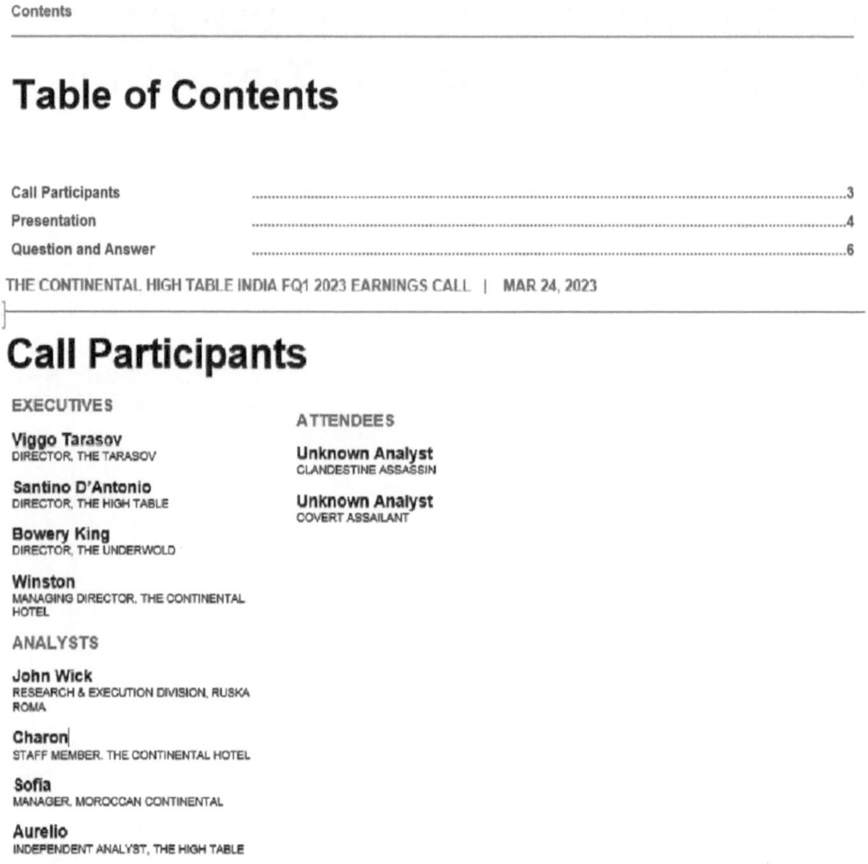

Table of Contents

THE CONTINENTAL HIGH TABLE INDIA FQ1 2023 EARNINGS CALL | MAR 24, 2023

Call Participants

EXECUTIVES

Viggo Tarasov
DIRECTOR, THE TARASOV

Santino D'Antonio
DIRECTOR, THE HIGH TABLE

Bowery King
DIRECTOR, THE UNDERWOLD

Winston
MANAGING DIRECTOR, THE CONTINENTAL
HOTEL

ANALYSTS

John Wick
RESEARCH & EXECUTION DIVISION, RUSKA
ROMA

Charon|
STAFF MEMBER, THE CONTINENTAL HOTEL

Sofia
MANAGER, MOROCCAN CONTINENTAL

Aurelio
INDEPENDENT ANALYST, THE HIGH TABLE

ATTENDEES

Unknown Analyst
CLANDESTINE ASSASSIN

Unknown Analyst
COVERT ASSAILANT

Fig. 3. Additional Content within ECTs

task necessary level. Let us consider the snapshots of the sections present within the ECT that capture the information within the presentation and QA sections where further processing can be explored on the mentioned distinction.

Meaningful information can be captured by scanning against the information that also contains noise that is random/unwanted. Having excessive content of uncorrelated data/noise might skew and bias the results of the study. Hence discretion must be made regarding which content has to be considered as information relevant to the context. Based on those criteria, we use a standard approach to defining the "Stopwords" dictionary in English, which contains the most occurring words in the language and captures essential information from the ECT. This allows us to create the bag containing the information necessary for our study. Further processing of reducing the bag to a standard representation of text needs to be done to capture the occurrences of words, which is done by stemming and lemmatization techniques.

Stemming & Lemmatization are text-mining & NLP preprocessing steps involved in reducing words to their root or base form that help capture the abstracted take or intention of the strategy, finance, market, or technology. Though similar in purpose,

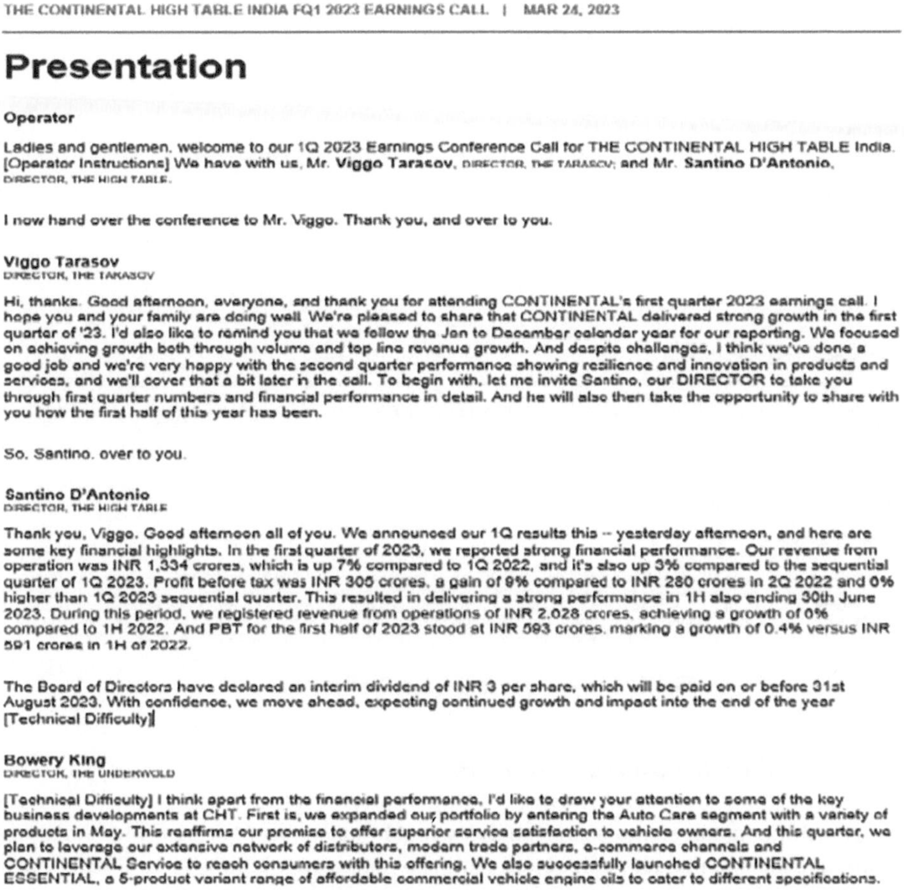

THE CONTINENTAL HIGH TABLE INDIA FQ1 2023 EARNINGS CALL | MAR 24, 2023

Presentation

Operator

Ladies and gentlemen, welcome to our 1Q 2023 Earnings Conference Call for THE CONTINENTAL HIGH TABLE India. [Operator Instructions] We have with us, Mr. **Viggo Tarasov**, DIRECTOR, THE TARASOV; and Mr. **Santino D'Antonio**, DIRECTOR, THE HIGH TABLE.

I now hand over the conference to Mr. Viggo. Thank you, and over to you.

Viggo Tarasov
DIRECTOR, THE TARASOV

Hi, thanks. Good afternoon, everyone, and thank you for attending CONTINENTAL's first quarter 2023 earnings call. I hope you and your family are doing well. We're pleased to share that CONTINENTAL delivered strong growth in the first quarter of '23. I'd also like to remind you that we follow the Jan to December calendar year for our reporting. We focused on achieving growth both through volume and top line revenue growth. And despite challenges, I think we've done a good job and we're very happy with the second quarter performance showing resilience and innovation in products and services, and we'll cover that a bit later in the call. To begin with, let me invite Santino, our DIRECTOR to take you through first quarter numbers and financial performance in detail. And he will also then take the opportunity to share with you how the first half of this year has been.

So, Santino, over to you.

Santino D'Antonio
DIRECTOR, THE HIGH TABLE

Thank you, Viggo. Good afternoon all of you. We announced our 1Q results this – yesterday afternoon, and here are some key financial highlights. In the first quarter of 2023, we reported strong financial performance. Our revenue from operation was INR 1,334 crores, which is up 7% compared to 1Q 2022, and it's also up 3% compared to the sequential quarter of 1Q 2023. Profit before tax was INR 305 crores, a gain of 9% compared to INR 280 crores in 2Q 2022 and 0% higher than 1Q 2023 sequential quarter. This resulted in delivering a strong performance in 1H also ending 30th June 2023. During this period, we registered revenue from operations of INR 2,028 crores, achieving a growth of 0% compared to 1H 2022. And PBT for the first half of 2023 stood at INR 593 crores, marking a growth of 0.4% versus INR 591 crores in 1H of 2022.

The Board of Directors have declared an interim dividend of INR 3 per share, which will be paid on or before 31st August 2023. With confidence, we move ahead, expecting continued growth and impact into the end of the year [Technical Difficulty]

Bowery King
DIRECTOR, THE UNDERWORLD

[Technical Difficulty] I think apart from the financial performance, I'd like to draw your attention to some of the key business developments at CHT. First is, we expanded our portfolio by entering the Auto Care segment with a variety of products in May. This reaffirms our promise to offer superior service satisfaction to vehicle owners. And this quarter, we plan to leverage our extensive network of distributors, modern trade partners, e-commerce channels and CONTINENTAL Service to reach consumers with this offering. We also successfully launched CONTINENTAL ESSENTIAL, a 5-product variant range of affordable commercial vehicle engine oils to cater to different specifications.

Fig. 4. The Presentation Section of an ECT

both serve different functions. Stemming is used to reduce the word form by removing suffixes. Lemmatization is used to reduce the word form to standard dictionary format. Consideration must be given to both techniques regarding the accuracy and speed of processing. While stemming is faster and easier on computation, the interpretability is lost, and lemmatization is slower and has higher computational costs with context-specific interpretations. We use both techniques in processing the data to achieve the standard representation of the words [8–10]. Once the standard representation has been achieved, we use the BoWs and Word2Vec techniques to extract and interpret the digital orientation of the firms. We explore how BoWs work in the next section.

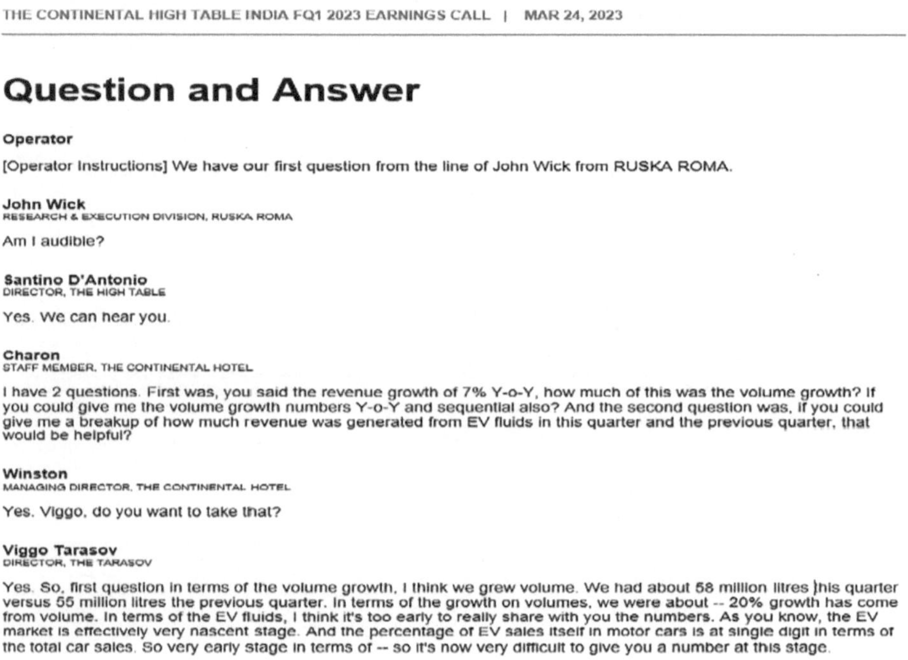

Question and Answer

Operator

[Operator Instructions] We have our first question from the line of John Wick from RUSKA ROMA.

John Wick
RESEARCH & EXECUTION DIVISION, RUSKA ROMA

Am I audible?

Santino D'Antonio
DIRECTOR, THE HIGH TABLE

Yes. We can hear you.

Charon
STAFF MEMBER, THE CONTINENTAL HOTEL

I have 2 questions. First was, you said the revenue growth of 7% Y-o-Y, how much of this was the volume growth? If you could give me the volume growth numbers Y-o-Y and sequential also? And the second question was, if you could give me a breakup of how much revenue was generated from EV fluids in this quarter and the previous quarter, that would be helpful?

Winston
MANAGING DIRECTOR, THE CONTINENTAL HOTEL

Yes. Viggo, do you want to take that?

Viggo Tarasov
DIRECTOR, THE TARASOV

Yes. So, first question in terms of the volume growth, I think we grew volume. We had about 58 million litres this quarter versus 55 million litres the previous quarter. In terms of the growth on volumes, we were about -- 20% growth has come from volume. In terms of the EV fluids, I think it's too early to really share with you the numbers. As you know, the EV market is effectively very nascent stage. And the percentage of EV sales itself in motor cars is at single digit in terms of the total car sales. So very early stage in terms of -- so it's now very difficult to give you a number at this stage.

Fig. 5. Presentation and Q&A Section of an ECT

4 Bag of Words (BoWs) Analysis

Asset/Portfolio managers, Research analysts, and Finance/Accounting professionals are becoming experimental and competent with new-age technologies for analyzing documents. Machine learning and artificial intelligence techniques are being seen as a go-to solution to analyze financial documents as systematic text processing using the techniques will help mitigate subjective human interpretations and biases [11]. A stream of research has been conducted to interpret and utilize rich textual data within ECTs, among which text-mining and NLP techniques are observed to perform better. A popular technique for analysis is bag-of-words (BoWs). Bag-of-words (BoWs) model is a technique used in natural language processing (NLP) to represent text or images in a way that can be used by machine learning algorithms. Conceptually, the text or an image is treated as a "bag" of unordered words or features, ignoring their order and focusing on their presence and frequency [12, 13]. In NLP, it represents documents as a vector of word counts. Each element in the vector corresponds to a word in the vocabulary, and the value represents how many times that word appears in the document. This allows machine learning algorithms to analyze and compare documents based on their word content.

Another method for extracting significant words or phrases from documents by counting the frequency of words or phrases and weighing their impact with inverse relative frequencies across all the documents within a corpus is TF-IDF (Term Frequency-Inverse Document Frequency) [14]. A document term matrix representation against a standard seed wordlist is used to calculate the score of occurrences for each document against a corpus for the implementation. The seed wordlist is essential in this methodology as it captures the respective words within the document being searched across, which captures the relevant information for the study.

In the context of digital transformation, the aptitude and inclination of the firm to transform into a digitally savvy organization can be captured using text-mining approaches. In both approaches, a comprehensive seed wordlist is created by reviewing ECTs across industries, domains, and geographies. The essence of the seed wordlist is to identify words that capture the digital transformation and digital competency of firms. Hence it comprises assorted keywords from technology, digital, platforms, and systems; the idea for creating the same is to capture the word-level association in the context of discussion between executives and analysts [15–17]. Though the approach is plain and simple, it has the caveats of not capturing contextual information by tokenizing the textual data, which limits its use and applicability to complex analyses like sentiment analysis and context comprehension. A rigorous and robust analysis using vector-based models of Word2Vec will help tackle capturing the contextual information among which common techniques used are lexical and semantic similarity analysis. The next section of this chapter includes the ideology and working of Word2Vec models, and different similarity techniques like lexical, semantic & combined, along with measures like cosine similarity [18].

5   Word2Vec Models

Word2Vec models are neural network models for NLP-related work. These essentially represent words as embeddings. Words are represented in a continuous vector space with similar words placed closer, thereby capturing semantic relationships between words. Introduced by notable researcher Tomas Mikolov and his team from Google in 2013, Word2Vec models are based on the concept of classifying similar words based on similar contexts [19]. These models are implemented either using the CBOW (or) Skip-gram technique where the predicted words could be either context words or target words [20]. The models are trained using a shallow neural network and a single hidden layer that trains to represent words as dense vectors in a continuous vector space.

Word2Vec models are prevalently used in various NLP tasks such as information retrieval, sentiment analysis, machine translation, document clustering, and recommendation systems, among others. Information retrieval becomes challenging in our task of identifying digital competency-related keywords. To achieve this, we utilize text similarity-based techniques. Commonly used similarities are lexical and semantic analysis [21]. Frameworks like Tensorflow, PyTorch (or) Gensim with pre-trained models are available for the Word2Vec implementations.

We use the Google Gensim API 'GoogleNews-vectors-negative300.bin' to create the vector models for the Digital Competency Wordlist and each individual ECT.

5.1   Lexical Analysis

Lexical analysis, also known as scanning or tokenization, is the first stage in processing a sequence of characters that breaks down a stream of characters into meaningful units called tokens. The tokens are categorized based on the rules of the language in use and are preprocessors for further stages like syntax analysis (checking structure) and semantic analysis (meaning). The Lexer/Scanner is initialized which performs the tokenization and gives resulting meaningful units, like keywords, identifiers, operators, numbers, and punctuation marks. The process of lexical analysis works by reading input stream character by character with rules, often defined by regular expressions (sequences of characters that form a search pattern), to identify patterns, group characters into lexemes, assign a category (token type), and pass the token along with its type to the next stage [22]. Comments and whitespace are typically removed as they do not affect the program logic. Lexical analysis breaks down complex text into smaller units for easier analysis and identifies invalid tokens as errors, helping catch mistakes. Lexical analysis is used in designing compilers, interpreters, text editors, and search tools. Overall, lexical analysis plays a fundamental role in processing programming languages and natural languages by laying the groundwork for advanced analysis and understanding of the content [23].

We use lexical analysis in the processing of ECTs for generating digital competency related constructs.

5.2 Semantic Analysis

Semantic analysis extends beyond the basic syntactic and semantic analysis. It focuses on the grammatical structure of a sentence, like identifying nouns and verbs, how words relate to each other, and understanding the actual intended meaning of words and sentences, considering context, ambiguity, and implied relationships, respectively. Given the ambiguity in words with multiple meanings in specific contexts, semantic analysis helps identify the correct sense in the real world. Semantic analysis deciphers the meaning of a sentence by each word and their respective arrangements.

Semantic analysis is used in categorizing documents by topic or sentiment (positive/negative), understanding and responding to natural language queries and commands, retrieving relevant documents based on the true meaning of a search query, translating between languages, capturing accurate nuances along with the meaning, finding specific information in an unstructured text. Semantic analysis utilizes WordNet, a network of related words and concepts, to determine word meanings and relationships. Advanced semantic analysis includes ontological or knowledge base approaches, which represent structured concepts and relationships that are mapped to words and phrases of real-world entities. Given the meaning of a word is embedded by its context within a large corpus of text, retrieving the abstract meaning of the word becomes cumbersome in terms of computing and efficiency for the previous approaches. Hence vector-based representations of word models like Word2Vec & Glove, help achieve reasonable results [24].

Semantic Analysis disambiguates homonyms considering the overall sentence structure, knowledge bases, and context. Though proficient in identifying semantic meanings of words and sentences, the inherent ambiguity of the natural language and reliance on large amounts of textual data diminishes the semantic analyses' technical prowess.

We use Semantic Analysis through Word2Vec in our processing of ECTs for creating digital competency of firms.

5.3 Combined Analysis (Lexical + Semantic)

Upon consideration, a logical analysis to follow seems to be a combined analysis, lexical + semantic, to overcome the drawbacks of tokenizing the text and reading excessively into the context [25]. The middle ground approach in balancing the trade offs to achieve combined results seems beneficial. An integrated analysis approach of lexical and semantics is followed to achieve the combined analysis. It helps with surface-level tokens analysis and deciphering in-depth contextual meanings. To get a holistic meaning of the text, token/word level representations by lexical analysis and sentence/paragraph level representations by semantic analysis.

A challenging point to acknowledge is all the analysis performed is on textual data which becomes computationally heavy at the document word level. Hence to abstract and reduce the complexity, approaches like dimensionality reduction and word embeddings are used which is achieved using advanced text-mining or NLP techniques like Word2Vec, Glove, etc. [26]. Among the techniques all result in generalized vector (or) matrix format representation. The representations capture the text across dimensions that are closely aligned, which means similar words are clubbed together, and dissimilar words are detached farther apart. In the context of the next sub-section, we explore vector and matrix computation models.

5.4 Cosine Similarity: Vector (or) Matrix Computations

Text-mining implementations on ECT, inherently heavy with text, can computationally strain efficiency. Implementations such as BoWs, TF-IDF tokenize the text into chunks and add more dimensions in complexity, Vector (or) Matrix computations tackle these issues by reductions in dimension by capturing the similarity regarding specific orientation. Techniques such as Word2Vec (or) Glove give vector or matrix formats that are non-interpretable. Enhancing the interpretability of these data formats becomes challenging, which is achieved through vector (or) matrix multiplications. Cosine similarity is a standard measure that reduces the representation into quantitative and analytic interpretable. This measure is particularly used as the variable captures the quantitative alignment between texts, lexical tokens & semantic language, ECT & digital orientation wordlist, etc. Technically cosine similarity measures the distance (or) similarity between the vector representation of texts in a multidimensional space using dot product and calculate measure of cosine angle [27].

In our context, we use cosine similarity to calculate a numerical representation of the digital competency of a specific firm for a specific quarter by processing the data received from the combined analysis explained in the earlier section.

6 Importance of Digital Transformation Playbook and Automation Analysis

Earning call transcripts typically have been analyzed manually by accounting or finance analysts. Though relevant information was being captured, the cost of inaccuracy, efficiency, scalability, and monitoring the process used to be challenging. Fortunately, the advancements in technology, cost of computation & digital proficiency have enabled analysts to leverage and automate repetitive mundane tasks. Efficient, Standardized, and Productive software and systems with wide applications across various industries at differing scales like business processes, industrial operations, healthcare logistics, etc., are built and used on the design of automation [28].

Utilizing automation for inferring the digital competency of the firms from earning call transcripts is a two-step approach: integrative and iterative process. In the integrative step, we start with preprocessing data and measure the respective lexical, semantic, and combined similarities using the cosine measurement and Word2Vec Google plugin. The step ensures we obtain the digital competency of a firm for the specific quarter. To obtain the measures for all the transcripts, we use an iterative approach by standardizing the integrative step of calculating similarities.

Automating the analysis of the ECT takes a generalized process with minor tweaks over a dataset of the firms spread within folders across multiple years. Specifically, the structure of each ECT file is stored under the respective firm folder name and year. Accordingly, accessing the firm-specific ECT file under the respective folder and year must be tailored and implemented. The next step involves accessing the firm and year-specific report and calculating the vectors (or) matrices which result in a similarity score implemented using cosine multiplication and results in giving a similarity score.

The final step uses a for-loop iteration to repeat the process for all the ECTs. In this way, we calculate the lexical, semantic, and combined similarity measures. Note that the structure of storing ECT in each computation device is different, and accordingly, process and computational changes must be incorporated. The idea for this process explanation is to give a view of the steps that need to be followed, not necessarily to follow the same. Note that a major consideration for automating is having the necessary hardware resources and software compatibility to achieve the desired process outcome.

Algorithms, particularly text-mining applications, consider tokens and lexicons for analysis. Analyzing ECTs becomes cumbersome with text-mining and NLP approaches to machine requirements and the non-standardization of digital transformation practices and policies across organizations. Since machine requirements were covered previously, we now focus on the latter aspect.

To tackle standardization, a procedure must be established in this instance. We utilize the book – *The Digital Transformation Playbook* [29] for analysis. Authored by Columbia Business School professor David L. Rogers, it presents a new-age view of thinking on different domains of technology and strategy: customers, competition, data, innovation, and value. The digital transformation playbook explains how to harness customer networks, platforms, big data, rapid experimentation, and disruptive business models and entails the firm's strategic alignment, standardization, and consistency, change management, risk and resource optimization, performance measurement, competitive advantage, and the manner in which to integrate these into existing businesses and organizations. To capture different metrics among heavy textual data, we consider the frameworks and the nine-step standardized process established in the book by building upon a set of keywords across the digital, technology, and innovation of an organization. This comprehensive set of keywords can create a robust framework for capturing the digital and technological competence of the firm.

7   Alternative Approaches and Avenues for Future Research

In this chapter, we have focused on describing the process for extracting digital and IT-related information of firms at word and sentence levels using prominent text-mining and NLP techniques in practice using large-volume ECT automated analysis. Although a firm's strategic and decision-making motivation on the digital front is captured, ECTs do not capture insightful information like the firm representative's sentiment, tonality of their voice, body language and actions, nervousness, or stuttering ticks of the executives during the session.

Researchers have established that analyzing the conference calls that are recorded in audio format will help gain valuable and insightful information about the confidence/opinion of the executives about the firm's position or strategic planning and its success. On similar lines research on managers' voice tones and stock prices has also been studied [30]. Multimodality of interpreting the audiovisual content in the conference call with deep learning models should be an avenue for the research to pursue [31, 32]. Extending this research, a new stream of study can be done considering the inherent gender-based bias within the audio features. An initial study shows the female minority and acoustic modality of features lead to disproportionate results, such as a number of references, hesitations, and verbal aggression expressed during the conference calls [6, 7, 33–35].

Topic modeling is an alternative research approach to understanding earning call transcripts; given how minimal the technique has been used, future research along the lines of understanding specific trends, concerns, and topics is a favorable scope for researchers in the domain [36]. LDA is the widely used statistical approach to implement topic modeling, which was developed by DM Blei in 2003 [37]. Capturing digital competency in discrete textual data using three-level hierarchical probabilistic LDA techniques is barren ground for exploration and experimentation. Further to text-mining and NLP techniques, researchers wanting to pursue advancements in understanding ECT through topic modeling techniques need to be proficient in Bayesian statistics, Probabilistic modeling, and Machine learning. Having necessary and relevant domain knowledge is warranted.

The initial pages of the ECT contain financial information of the firm, and having access to firm-specific information over decades enables us to have a longitudinal financial dataset spread across the years. A lagged coherence model between the financial and digital aspects of the firm specified by the executives in the respective calls can be inspected. Creating robust predictive or deep learning modeling frameworks to study and forecast the outcomes of the firms will be valuable and insightful research to pursue [38].

Analyzing the directional movement of a stock price and the volatility level is an imperative study for the investors to stay invested or bail out and analysts to release their earnings estimate [39, 40]. Traditional analysis of stock prices accounts for the exogenous shocks of geopolitical events, macroeconomic conditions, and news on a firm's posture and business operations [41]. Statistical modeling has also been extensively used for forecasting using ARIMA, and AR techniques [42, 43]. Significant contributions from the stream of information systems are yet to be made by researchers employing traditional business implications, statistical approaches, and deep learning modeling.

Earning calls are presented and reported by the firm's top executive, who is likely to be the embodiment of the firm's values and ideologies. Analyzing ECT thus becomes a human-in-the-loop (HITL) system that relies on the executive's characteristics and sentiments. The executive conveys and facilitates the organizational outlook becoming an essential piece in the system. Research has shown that top executive tenures reflect the stock price movements and the stakeholder valuations. Further extending the research can examine the previous tenures and work experiences of the top executives that will impact the investment towards technology, innovation, digital, supply chain operations, market performance, and infrastructure [44–47].

Frequent disclosures of the ECTs facilitate the stakeholders having up-to-date and real-time information for the analysts, investors, and management. This makes dynamic decision-making and strategic management easier. Not to mention, market reactions in real-time stock price volatility are a consequence of these disclosures. Since C-suite management direction, vision, and sentiments are captured, it helps assess the intended versus realized outcomes. The analysts involved in the call can probe the executives about the outcomes or punitive actions. Numerous studies along with this demonstration validate the purposefulness of the ECT proffer with rich textual information for analysis.

There is a scarcity of publicly available data sources at the firm level pertaining to digital and IT constructs. Researchers are currently using proprietary sources of data or constructing novel datasets from proprietary or publicly available information. The most common proprietary datasets under study are InformationWeek dataset for firm-level data from the United States [48], Prowess for data from Indian firms [49], and the Harte Hanks dataset for data for firms from the United States or elsewhere [50], and datasets constructed using the firm's news announcements, press releases, and 10K filing reports [30, 41, 51]. ECTs can fill this critical gap and add a valuable dialogue by serving as a source of rich data in the information systems discipline, offering intriguing possibilities for research in the broad domain of the business value of IT [52–59].

On the globalization front, the overwhelming focus of scientific studies is within Western, Educated, Industrialized, Rich, and Democratic (WEIRD) domains [60]. Advancements in research have taken consideration of broader settings across inter-disciplinary disciplines applicable to the information systems domain [61–67], but most of the research studies are still centered around WEIRD contexts. Taking heed of trends is vital, considering the transformative potential within alternative settings, such as Growing, Rural, Eastern, Aspirational, and Transitional (GREAT) regions, for theory development [68, 69]. ECTs become resourceful in understanding between two perspectives by emphasizing the need for a comprehensive exploration of not only as a global phenomenon but also as an avenue to bridge the gap in understanding diverse economic and cultural contexts, ultimately enriching the broader research landscape in the field.

Additionally, ECTs can also aid with an exploration of specific contexts, such as GREAT domains. As an illustrative case, significant research has been undertaken in other domains of management within the Indian context [70–72]. India, as a context, is a noticeable gap in the information systems discipline [73]. Though there are notable exceptions [72, 74–80], exploring theory and/or data from India offers bedazzling possibilities. Considering India's potential as a fast-growing economy, it is imperative to examine such questions. Hence extracting information from ECT as a source of data to study the evolving digital and information technological landscape of India calls attention for future researchers to foreground the rich, diverse, and cultural settings offered only within the Indian subcontinent.

References

1. Allee, K.D., DeAngelis, M.D.: The structure of voluntary disclosure narratives: evidence from tone dispersion. J. Account. Res. **53**(2), 241–274 (2015)
2. Filatotchev, I., Lanzolla, G., Syrigos, E.: Impact of CEO's digital technology orientation and board characteristics on firm value: a signaling perspective. J. Manage. (2023)
3. Baginski, S.P., Hassell, J.M.: Determinants of management forecast precision. Account. Rev. **72**, 303–312 (1997)
4. Francis, J., Schipper, K., Vincent, L.: Expanded disclosures and the increased usefulness of earnings announcements. Account. Rev. **77**(3), 515–546 (2002)
5. Sonpatki, R., Kathuria, A., Sethi, S.: Earnings call transcripts as a source and resource for information systems research. In: Kathuria, A., Karhade, P.P., Zhao, K., Chaturvedi, D. (eds.) Digital Transformation in the Viral Age: 21st Workshop on e-Business, WeB 2022, Copenhagen, Denmark, December 10, 2022, Revised Selected Papers, pp. 38–63. Springer Nature Switzerland, Cham (2024). https://doi.org/10.1007/978-3-031-60003-6_4
6. Frankel, R., Mayew, W.J., Sun, Y.: Do pennies matter? Investor relations consequences of small negative earnings surprises. Rev. Acc. Stud. **15**, 220–242 (2010)
7. Brown, L.D., Call, A.C., Clement, M.B., Sharp, N.Y.: Managing the narrative: investor relations officers and corporate disclosure. J. Account. Econ. **67**(1), 58–79 (2019)
8. Pant, V.K., Sharma, R., Kundu, S.: An overview of stemming and lemmatization techniques. In: Advances in Networks, Intelligence and Computing, pp. 308–321 (2024)
9. Singh, J., Gupta, V.: Text stemming: approaches, applications, and challenges. ACM Comput. Surv. **49**(3), 1–46 (2016)
10. Kundu, S.: 31 An overview of stemming and lemmatization techniques. In: Advances in Networks, Intelligence and Computing: Proceedings of the International Conference On Networks, Intelligence and Computing (ICONIC 2023). CRC Press (2024)
11. Chin, A., Fan, Y.: Leveraging text mining to extract insights from earnings call transcripts. J. Investment Manage. **21**(1), 81–102 (2023)
12. Qader, W.A., Ameen, M.M., Ahmed, B.I.: An overview of bag of words; importance, implementation, applications, and challenges. In: International Engineering Conference (IEC). IEEE (2019)
13. Tsai, C.-F.: Bag-of-words representation in image annotation: a review. ISRN Artific. Intell. **2012**, 1–19 (2012)
14. Harman, D.: The history of IDF and its influences on IR and other fields. In: Charting a New Course: Natural Language Processing and Information Retrieval: Essays in Honour of Karen Spärck Jones, pp. 69–79. Springer (2005)
15. Chatterjee, D., Richardson, V.J., Zmud, R.W.: Examining the shareholder wealth effects of announcements of newly created CIO positions. MIS Q. **25**(1), 43 (2001)
16. Haislip, J.Z., Richardson, V.J.: The effect of CEO IT expertise on the information environment: evidence from earnings forecasts and announcements. J. Inf. Syst. **32**(2), 71–94 (2018)
17. Havakhor, T., Sabherwal, S., Sabherwal, R., Steelman, Z.: Evaluating information technology investments: insights from executives' trades. MIS Q. **46**(2), 1165–1194 (2022)
18. Church, K.W.: Word2Vec. Nat. Lang. Eng. **23**(1), 155–162 (2017)
19. Mikolov, T., Chen, K., Corrado, G., Dean, J.: Efficient estimation of word representations in vector space. arXiv:1301.3781 [cs.CL] (2013)

20. Meyer, D.: How exactly does word2vec work. Uoregon. Edu, Brocade. Com, pp. 1–18 (2016)
21. Pradhan, N., Gyanchandani, M., Wadhvani, R.: A review on text similarity technique used in ir and its application. Int. J. Comput. Appl. **120**(9), 29–34 (2015)
22. Gallagher, C., Furey, E., Curran, K.: The application of sentiment analysis and text analytics to customer experience reviews to understand what customers are really saying. Int. J. Data Warehouse. Min. **15**(4), 21–47 (2019)
23. Sarkar, D.: Text Analytics with Python, vol. 2. Springer (2016)
24. Prasetya, D.D., Wibawa, A.P., Hirashima, T.: The performance of text similarity algorithms. Int. J. Adv. Intell. Inform. **4**(1), 63–69 (2018)
25. Kuzi, S., Zhang, M., Li, C., Bendersky, M., Najork, M.: Leveraging semantic and lexical matching to improve the recall of document retrieval systems: A hybrid approach. arXiv preprint arXiv:2010.01195 (2020)
26. Vajjala, S., Majumder, B., Gupta, A.. Surana, H.: Practical Natural Language Processing: A Comprehensive Guide to Building Real-World NLP Systems. O'Reilly Media (2020)
27. Wang, J., Dong, Y.: Measurement of text similarity: a survey. Information **11**(9), 421 (2020)
28. Lewis, C., Young, S.: Fad or future? Automated analysis of financial text and its implications for corporate reporting. Account. Bus. Res. **49**(5), 587–615 (2019)
29. Rogers, D.L.: The Digital Transformation Playbook: Rethink your Business for the Digital Age. Columbia University Press (2016)
30. Haislip, J.Z., Karim, K.E., Lin, K.J., Pinsker, R.E.: The influences of CEO IT expertise and board-level technology committees on form 8-K disclosure timeliness. J. Inf. Syst. **34**(2), 167–185 (2020)
31. Baik, B., Kim, A., Kim, D.S., Yoon, S.: Managers' Vocal Delivery and Real-Time Market Reactions in Earnings Calls. Chicago Booth Research Paper, pp. 23–21 (2023)
32. Crawford Camiciottoli, B.: Earnings calls: exploring an emerging financial reporting genre. Discourse Commun. **4**(4), 343–359 (2010)
33. Sawhney, R., Aggarwal, A., Shah, R.: An empirical investigation of bias in the multimodal analysis of financial earnings calls. In: Proceedings of the 2021 conference of the North American chapter of the association for computational linguistics: human language technologies (2021)
34. Francis, B.B., Shohfi, T., Xin, D.: Gender and earnings conference calls. SSRN Electron. J. **25**, 2020 (2020)
35. Kumar, A.: Self-selection and the forecasting abilities of female equity analysts. J. Account. Res. **48**(2), 393–435 (2010)
36. Huang, A.H., Lehavy, R., Zang, A.Y., Zheng, R.: Analyst information discovery and interpretation roles: a topic modeling approach. Manage. Sci. **64**(6), 2833–2855 (2018)
37. Blei, D.M., Ng, A.Y., Jordan, M.I.: Latent dirichlet allocation. J. Mach. Learn. Res. **3**(Jan), 993–1022 (2003)
38. Al-Ali, A.G., Phaal, R., Sull, D.: Deep learning framework for measuring the digital strategy of companies from earnings calls. arXiv:2010.12418 [cs.CL] (2020)
39. Ma, Z., Bang, G., Wang, C., Liu, X.: Towards earnings call and stock price movement, in arXiv preprint arXiv:2009.01317 (2020)
40. Ma, Z., Wang, C., Bang, G., Liu, X.: Utilization of deep learning to mine insights from earning calls for stock price movement predictions. In: Proceedings of the First ACM International Conference on AI in Finance (2020)
41. Kathuria, A., Karhade, P., Jaiswal, A., Mani, D.: Stock market reactions to IT endowment at the onset of COVID-19. In: Proceedings of the International Conference on Information Systems (ICIS), vol. 5 (2023)
42. Armstrong, J.S., Evaluating forecasting methods. In: Principles of Forecasting: A Handbook for Researchers and Practitioners, pp. 443–472 (2001)

43. Wheelwright, S., Makridakis, S., Hyndman, R.J.: Forecasting: Methods and Applications. John Wiley & Sons (1998)
44. Davis, A.K., Ge, W., Matsumoto, D., Zhang, J.L.: The effect of manager-specific optimism on the tone of earnings conference calls. Rev. Acc. Stud. **20**, 639–673 (2015)
45. Dikolli, S.S., Mayew, W.J., Nanda, D.: CEO tenure and the performance-turnover relation. Rev. Acc. Stud. **19**, 281–327 (2014)
46. Rai, A., Patnayakuni, R., Seth, N.: Firm performance impacts of digitally enabled supply chain integration capabilities. MIS Q. **30**(2), 225–246 (2006)
47. Chava, S., Du, W., Paradkar, N.: More than Buzzwords? Firms' Discussions of Emerging Technologies in Earnings Conference Calls. SSRN Electron. J. (2021)
48. Saldanha, T.J., Andrade-Rojas, M.G., Kathuria, A., Khuntia, J., Krishnan, M.: How the locus of uncertainty shapes the influence of CEO long-term compensation on IT capital investments. MIS Q. **48**(2), 459–490 (2024)
49. Li, C., Peters, G.F., Richardson, V.J., Watson, M.W.: The consequences of information technology control weaknesses on management information systems: the case of Sarbanes-Oxley internal control reports. MIS Q. **36**(1), 179 (2012). https://doi.org/10.2307/41410413
50. Kathuria, A., Karhade, P.P., Ning, X., Konsynski, B.R.: Blood and water: information technology investment and control in family-owned businesses. J. Manag. Inf. Syst. **40**(1), 208–238 (2023)
51. Jing, J.: Information Acquisition from Sec Filings and Earnings Management. The Hong Kong Polytechnic University, Pao Yue-kong Library (2019)
52. Andrade, M., Saldanha, T., Khuntia, J., Kathuria, A., Boh, W.: Overcoming deficiencies for innovation in SMEs: IT for closed innovation versus IT for open innovation. In: Proceedings of the International Conference on Information Systems (ICIS), vol. 9 (2020)
53. Khuntia, J., Saldanha, T., Kathuria, A., Tanniru, M.R.: Digital service flexibility: a conceptual framework and roadmap for digital business transformation. Eur. J. Inf. Syst. **33**(1), 61–79 (2024)
54. Chaturvedi, D., Kathuria, A., Andrade, M., Saldanha, T.: Navigating the paradox of IT novelty and strategic conformity: the moderating role of industry dynamism. In: Proceedings of the International Conference on Information Systems (ICIS), vol. 14 (2023)
55. Karhade, P., Kathuria, A., Malik, O., Konsynski, B.: Digital platforms and infobesity: a research agenda. In: Garimella, A., Karhade, P., Kathuria, A., Liu, X., Xu, J., Zhao, K. (eds.) The Role of e-Business During the Time of Grand Challenges. WEB 2020. Lecture Notes in Business Information Processing, pp. 51–58. Springer, Cham (2021)
56. Ning, X., Khuntia, J., Kathuria, A., Konsynski, B.R.: Artificial Intelligence (AI) and cognitive apportionment for service flexibility. In: Xu, J.J., Zhu, B., Liu, X., Shaw, M.J., Zhang, H., Fan, M. (eds.) The Ecosystem of e-Business: Technologies, Stakeholders, and Connections: 17th Workshop on e-Business, WeB 2018, Santa Clara, CA, USA, December 12, 2018, Revised Selected Papers, pp. 182–189. Springer International Publishing, Cham (2019). https://doi.org/10.1007/978-3-030-22784-5_18
57. Barua, A., Konana, P., Whinston, A.B., Yin, F.: Assessing internet enabled business value: an exploratory investigation. MIS Q. **28**(4), 585–620 (2004)
58. Kumar, R.L.: A framework for assessing the business value of information technology infrastructures. J. Manag. Inf. Syst. **21**(2), 11–32 (2004)
59. Kohli, R., Grover, V.: Business value of IT: an essay on expanding research directions to keep up with the times. J. Assoc. Inf. Syst. **9**(1), 1 (2008)
60. Henrich, J., Heine, S.J., Norenzayan, A.: The weirdest people in the world? Behav. Brain sciences **33**(2–3), 61–83 (2010)
61. Andrade-Rojas, M.G., Kathuria, A., Konsynski, B.R.: Competitive brokerage: how information management capability and collaboration networks act as substitutes. J. Manag. Inf. Syst. **38**(3), 667–703 (2021)

62. Jha, S., Chaturvedi, D.: Systematic literature review of cloud computing research between 2010 and 2023. In: Kathuria, A., Karhade, P., Zhao, K., Chaturvedi, D. (eds.) Digital Transformation in the Viral Age. WEB 2022. Lecture Notes in Business Information Processing, Springer, Cham (2024)

63. Sachdeva, A., Kathuria, A., Karhade, P., Ray, S.: How do family businesses embark on digital transformation? a call for future is research. In: Kathuria, A., Karhade, P., Zhao, K., Chaturvedi, D. (eds.) Digital Transformation in the Viral Age. WEB 2022. Lecture Notes in Business Information Processing, Springer, Cham (2024)

64. Warudkar, H.: Digital assets and decentralized finance – emerging research opportunities for information systems. In: Kathuria, A., Karhade, P., Zhao, K., Chaturvedi, D. (eds.) Digital Transformation in the Viral Age. WEB 2022. Lecture Notes in Business Information Processing, Springer, Cham (2024)

65. Karhade, P., Kathuria, A., Dasgupta, A., Malik, O., Konsynski, B.R.: Decolonization of digital platforms: a research agenda for GREAT domains. In: Garimella, A., Karhade, P., Kathuria, A., Liu, X., Xu, J., Zhao, K. (eds.) The Role of e-Business During the Time of Grand Challenges. WEB 2020. Lecture Notes in Business Information Processing, pp. 51–58. Springer, Cham (2021)

66. Karhade, P., Kathuria, A., Malik, O., Konsynski, B.: Digital platforms and infobesity: a research agenda. In: Garimella, A., Karhade, P., Kathuria, A., Liu, X., Xu, J., Zhao, K. (eds.) The Role of e-Business during the Time of Grand Challenges: 19th Workshop on e-Business, WeB 2020, Virtual Event, December 12, 2020, Revised Selected Papers, pp. 67–74. Springer International Publishing, Cham (2021). https://doi.org/10.1007/978-3-030-79454-5_7

67. Warudkar, H.: Software as a service – a key enabler for digital transformation in organization – a multi-disciplinary information systems research agenda. In: Kathuria, A., Karhade, P.P., Zhao, K., Chaturvedi, D. (eds.) Digital Transformation in the Viral Age: 21st Workshop on e-Business, WeB 2022, Copenhagen, Denmark, December 10, 2022, Revised Selected Papers, pp. 28–37. Springer Nature Switzerland, Cham (2024). https://doi.org/10.1007/978-3-031-60003-6_3

68. Dasgupta, A., Karhade, P., Kathuria, A., Konsynski, B.: Holding space for voices that do not speak: design reform of rating systems for platforms in GREAT economies. In: Hawaii International Conference on System Sciences (2021)

69. Karhade, P., Kathuria, A.: Missing impact of ratings on platform participation in India: a call for research in GREAT domains. Commun. Assoc. Inf. Syst. **47**(1), 19 (2020)

70. Celly, N., Kathuria, A., Subramanian, V.: Overview of Indian Multinationals. Emerging Indian multinationals: Strategic players in a multipolar world (2016)

71. Khuntia, J., Kathuria, A., Saldanha, T.J., Konsynski, B.R.: Benefits of IT-enabled flexibilities for foreign versus local firms in emerging economies. J. Manag. Inf. Syst. **36**(3), 855–892 (2019)

72. Kathuria, R., Kathuria, N.N., Kathuria, A.: Mutually supportive or trade-offs: an analysis of competitive priorities in the emerging economy of India. J. High Technol. Managem. Res. **29**(2), 227–236 (2018)

73. Khuntia, J., Kathuria, A., Andrade-Rojas, M.G., Saldanha, T.J.V., Celly, N.: How foreign and domestic firms differ in leveraging it-enabled supply chain information integration in bop markets: the role of supplier and client business collaboration. J. Assoc. Inform. Syst. **22**(3), 695–738 (2021). https://doi.org/10.17705/1jais.00677

74. Capelli, P.: The India way: how india's top business leaders are revolutionizing management. NHRD Netw. J. **3**(3), 74–74 (2010). https://doi.org/10.1177/0974173920100315

75. Ning, X., Khuntia, J., Kathuria, A, Karhade, P.: Ownership and management control effects on IT investments: a study of indian family firms. In: Proceedings of the International Conference on Information Systems (ICIS), vol. 11 (2020)

76. Gupta, A.: Emergence of Indian multinationals. Technol. Exports **8**(3) (2006)
77. Pradhan, J.P., Sauvant, K.P.: Introduction: The Rise of Indian Multinational Enterprises: Revisiting Key Issues, in The rise of Indian Multinationals: Perspectives on Indian Outward Foreign Direct Investment. Palgrave Macmillan, New York (2010)
78. Kapur, D., Ramamurti, R.: India's emerging competitive advantage in services. Acad. Manag. Perspect. **15**(2), 20–32 (2001)
79. Kumar, N.: India's Global Powerhouses: How they are taking on the World. SAGE Publications Sage India, New Delhi, India (2010)
80. Nayak, A.: Indian Multinationals: The Dynamics of Explosive Growth in a Developing Country Context. Springer (2011)

Bridging the Trust Gap in Machine Learning Automation: Enhancing End-User Confidence Through Generative AI-Driven Explanations in Natural Language

Rahul Kharat and Abhinav Mathur[✉]

Indian School of Business, Hyderabad 500032, India
{Rahul_kharat,abhinav_mathur}@isb.edu

Abstract. In the evolving landscape of machine learning (ML), the explainability of complex models remains a pivotal challenge, especially in bridging the understanding between technical experts and frontline staff. This paper explores the role of Generative AI (GenAI) in demystifying the intricacies of ML explainability methods, such as Local Interpretable Model-agnostic Explanations (LIME) and SHapley Additive exPlanations (SHAP). Our investigation delves into the trust gap that often arises due to the technical nature of these methods and how GenAI can serve as a mediator in this scenario. By leveraging GenAI's capabilities in synthesizing comprehensible visualizations and intuitive explanations, we propose a framework that enhances the interpretability of ML results for non-technical audiences. This framework not only facilitates better understanding but also fosters trust and collaborative decision-making among diverse stakeholders. Our findings indicate that GenAI can significantly contribute to the democratization of ML knowledge, thereby empowering frontline staff to engage more effectively with ML outputs. This research underscores the potential of GenAI as a transformative tool in making ML more accessible and trustworthy across various sectors.

Keywords: Generative AI · ML Systems Acceptance

1 Introduction

The integration of machine learning (ML) technologies in business processes marks a significant leap in organizational capabilities, offering unprecedented opportunities for data-driven decision making and automation. However, this technological advancement is not without its challenges. One of the most critical challenges is the trust gap that exists between the technical experts who develop and understand these complex ML systems and the frontline staff who are expected to utilize or rely on them in their daily operations. This trust gap is well documented in the literature. For instance, research by Gilpin, Bau [1] (2018) highlights the difficulties non-technical staff face in interpreting ML outputs, while Caruana, Lou [2] (2015) emphasize the skepticism that arises due to a lack of understanding of the underlying mechanisms of these systems. Similarly,

© The Author(s), under exclusive license to Springer Nature Switzerland AG 2025
A. Kathuria et al. (Eds.): WeB 2023, LNBIP 525, pp. 126–138, 2025.
https://doi.org/10.1007/978-3-031-74437-2_10

Parasuraman and Riley [3] (1997), in their seminal work on the human-trust relationship in automated systems, lay the groundwork for understanding this phenomenon in the context of ML.

The complexity and often opaque nature of ML algorithms contribute significantly to this issue. Kahneman, Slovic and Tversky [4] in 1982 studied theory of cognitive biases suggests that individuals are more likely to distrust systems that they do not understand or find too complex. This is particularly relevant in the case of advanced ML models used in predictive analytics, where the decision-making process is not readily apparent to the end-user. The result is a reluctance or outright resistance to adopting these technologies, potentially hindering organizational efficiency and innovation.

Amidst these challenges, the emergence of Generative AI (GenAI) presents a new frontier for enhancing the interpretability and accessibility of ML systems. GenAI, with its capability to create intuitive and human-like content, offers a unique opportunity to make ML outputs more relatable and understandable to non-technical audiences. Strobelt, Gehrmann [5] (2018) demonstrated how communication can be enhanced by converting complex data patterns into visual narratives, while Bhatt, Xiang [6] (2020) emphasize the requirement of having explanatory communication that can accompany ML predictions, making them more transparent.

This paper also serves as an introduction to building on trust gap identifications previously identified in IS literature. This prior research identifies the emergence of trust gaps resulting from the adoption of complex IT and MIS systems [7] as well as the emergence of trust in expert knowledge. This paper also acknowledges the lack of generalized MIS and Information systems implementation [8] and explores both precedents and consequences of trust. Thus, this paper serves the purpose of demonstrating a case-based approach that enables the explanation of complicated systems in natural language leveraging Generative AI and LLMs.

The central aim of this paper is to investigate how GenAI can effectively bridge the trust gap between technical and frontline staff within organizations that employ ML technologies. We hypothesize that the enhanced interpretability and transparency provided by GenAI tools will lead to increased trust and collaboration between these two groups. To examine this hypothesis, our research will focus on the application of GenAI in making the technical aspects of ML models, particularly those explained by methods like LIME and SHAP, more comprehensible to non-technical staff. Our methodology includes both qualitative and quantitative analyses, assessing the impact of GenAI-based explainability tools in various organizational scenarios. These cases are presented in tabular format in Table 1. In summary, this paper seeks to contribute to the burgeoning field of ML and AI by providing insights into how GenAI can play a transformative role in addressing one of the most pressing challenges in this domain - the trust gap. By exploring the intersection of ML, GenAI, and organizational behavior, our research aims to offer a novel perspective on the potential of GenAI in fostering a more collaborative and trustful environment within businesses reliant on advanced technologies.

Table 1. Case Summary

Case Study	Objective	Challenges	Approach	Inferred Results
AML in Financial Risk Management	Addressing false positives in AML transactions	High rate of false positives; difficulty in interpreting complex ML models; regulatory requirements for SAR	Implementing advanced ML models (e.g., Autoencoders, OneClassSVM)	Likely reduction in false positives, but ongoing challenges in model interpretation and regulatory compliance
Corporate Recommendation Engine in CRM	Enhancing personalized financial product recommendations	Difficulty in justifying ML recommendations; computational constraints; risk of inaccurate recommendations	Development of an ML classification model for identifying client states and characteristics	Improved targeting of financial products, though challenges remain in providing justifiable rationales and managing the risk of inaccuracies
Credit Lending	Implementing ML-driven scoring models	Adherence to fair lending laws; bias in Black Box models; integrating ML scores with existing systems	Using ML models to supplement traditional scoring mechanisms	Improved system performance and potential reduction in carbon emissions, but accuracy and safety challenges persist in high-pressure environments

(continued)

Table 1. (*continued*)

Case Study	Objective	Challenges	Approach	Inferred Results
AI in Energy Industry	Enhancing safety and efficiency in energy systems	Need for accurate predictions; false positives/negatives; integration with existing systems	Using ML models for proactive control and efficiency in energy systems	Improved system performance and potential reduction in carbon emissions, but accuracy and safety challenges persist in high-pressure environments
Explainability in Model Risk Management	Ensuring compliance with SR 11- guidelines	Need for clear, understandable explanations of financial model behavior	Implementing a GenAI-based tool for model explanation generation and validation support	Ensured regulatory compliance; improved stakeholder understanding; supported robust model governance
ML in Consumer Health Corporation	Enhancing user engagement with ML-driven tools	Low user engagement due to complex algorithms; transparency issues	Integrating LLMs for data anonymization and explanation; strategic tool development	Increased user logins (from median of 2 to 10); creation of a call planning assistant; increased trust and transparency

2   The Role of Case-Based Analysis in Establishing the Trust Gap

In exploring the trust gap in ML applications, we employ case-based analysis as a methodological approach. This approach allows us to delve into real-world scenarios where the lack of explainability in ML models has tangible impacts. Through these cases, we aim to illustrate the multifaceted nature of the trust gap, showcasing how it manifests in various industries and contexts. Each case serves as an exemplar, revealing the nuances of how nontechnical stakeholders interact with complex ML systems and the challenges they face. By analyzing these cases, we intend to establish a concrete foundation for our argument that enhancing explainability through GenAI can significantly bridge this gap.

2.1 Case Study 1: Anti-Money Laundering (AML) - Trust Gap and Interpretation Challenges in Financial Risk Management

In the realm of Anti-Money Laundering (AML) within financial institutions, a critical operational challenge is the manual processing of false positives—transactions falsely flagged as probable AML cases. Industry research indicates an alarmingly high rate of these false positives, averaging around 75% and sometimes reaching as high as 98% [9]. This necessitates extensive backend operations involving multiple database checks to clear such flags. The article by Aggarwal and Raghavan [10] 2006, discusses the compliance requirements, including SAR, in the Risk Management space.

- *The Potential and Limitations of ML in AML Operations*: Advanced ML models like Autoencoders, OneClassSVM, Isolation Forest, and Restricted Boltzman Machines, with their anomaly detection capabilities, show promise in addressing this issue. However, despite their high precision, these models present a significant interpretation challenge. Their complex architectures make it difficult for non-technical staff to understand the rationale behind flagged transactions, a requirement in AML regulatory processes for Suspicious Activity Reports (SAR).
- *System Design Challenges in AML:* Black Box models, though superior in prediction, pose a challenge due to the significant impact of false predictions. The need for conservative threshold settings to mitigate risks often compromises the efficiency of these models. Furthermore, the lack of clear, interpretable rationale from methods like LIME and SHAP, which provide only approximate interpretations, further exacerbates the trust gap.

2.2 Case Study 2: Corporate Recommendation Engine – Addressing Interpretation Challenges in CRM

A global financial institution's challenge in effectively recommending financial products to its corporate clients exemplifies another aspect of the trust gap. Relationship managers handling multiple corporate accounts often struggle to provide personalized recommendations, leading to missed revenue opportunities from less focused accounts.

- *The Role of ML in Enhancing CRM:* An ML classification model was developed to identify the states and characteristics of organizations at the time of purchasing specific banking products. This corporate recommendation engine aimed to target appropriate products to clients at optimal times.
- *Interpretation and System Design Challenges:* The key challenge lies in providing justifiable rationales for these recommendations, unlike consumer-focused platforms like Netflix or Amazon. The reliance on surrogate models or methods like LIME/SHAP for interpretation results in only relative explanations, often lacking crucial interaction data due to computational constraints. This leads to additional time and effort for relationship managers to devise suitable rationales, counteracting the efficiency gains of the recommendation system. Moreover, the risk of inaccurate recommendations threatens the credibility of both the relationship manager and the institution.

2.3   Case Study 3: Credit Lending – Navigating Regulatory Compliance and Trust in ML-Driven Scoring

Major U.S. financial institutions face missed opportunities in lending to SMEs, startups, and retail customers due to the absence of alternative scoring models. The adoption of ML-driven models to supplement traditional scoring mechanisms has emerged as a solution, albeit with regulatory challenges. Harvard case study by Liu and GILLIS [11] 2020, discusses discrimination in credit lending, potential practices for mitigation, and underlying laws in the field.

- *Potential and Interpretation Challenges in ML-based Credit Lending:* While ML models can identify novel patterns and integrate alternative data for risk scoring, they must adhere to fair lending laws and avoid biases. The use of Black Box models complicates this, as their approximate interpretability challenges compliance with regulations mandating nondiscrimination in lending practices.
- *System Design Challenge in Credit Lending*: Integrating ML-driven scores into existing rule engines poses a design challenge. The model either runs parallel to or in series with the workflow, feeding alternative scores. Setting thresholds to minimize false acceptances or rejections, essential for regulatory compliance, often compromises the model's efficiency.

2.4   Case Study 4: AI-Driven Proactive Control Systems in the Energy Industry – Safety and Efficiency

The case of a large Industrial Equipment manufacturer in the energy sector highlights the potential and challenges of using AI-driven proactive control systems.

- *Potential of ML in Energy and Environment Efficiency*: ML models can predict varying operational conditions, recommending proactive actions to enhance efficiency. These insights, derived from community-connected installations, have significant potential in reducing carbon emissions and improving system performance.
- *Interpretation and System Design Challenges*: Understanding the reasons behind predictions is crucial for integrating them with existing control systems, especially in high-pressure environments where safety is paramount. The challenge lies in ensuring the accuracy of these predictions and eliminating false positives and negatives, which are crucial for the system's overall efficiency and safety.

The observations from our case studies reveal a consistent theme: the trust gap significantly impedes the effective utilization of ML models across various sectors. In scenarios like AML in financial institutions and CRM in global financial settings, we see how the complexity and lack of clarity in ML model outputs create barriers for non-technical staff. This gap not only affects operational efficiency but also raises concerns regarding regulatory compliance and risk management, as evidenced in the credit lending case. Furthermore, the AI-driven control systems in the energy industry highlight the safety implications of this trust gap. These cases collectively underscore the urgent need for explainable AI solutions that can demystify complex model outputs, fostering an environment of trust and transparency.

Bridging the Explainability Gap with Generative AI

As we transition to discussing our final case study, it's pertinent to highlight how Generative AI, particularly Large Language Models (LLMs), can play a pivotal role in mitigating the explainability problem identified in our previous cases. LLMs have shown remarkable capabilities in translating complex, technical outputs of ML models into more understandable and relatable explanations. This potential makes LLMs an invaluable tool in addressing the regulatory and compliance challenges emphasized in frameworks like SR 11-7. By utilizing LLMs for generating clear and comprehensive explanations, we can significantly reduce the trust gap, enhancing both the accessibility and credibility of ML models in critical decision making processes. The upcoming case study on model risk management in compliance with SR 11-7 will exemplify this potential, demonstrating how LLMs can effectively bridge the explainability gap in a highly regulated financial environment.

2.5   Case Study 5: Leveraging GenAI for Regulatory Compliant Explainability in Model Risk Management

A leading financial institution faced the challenge of adhering to SR 11–7 regulatory guidelines [12], which mandate rigorous model risk management, including the need for clear and comprehensive explanations of model behavior. The objective was to use an LLM to elucidate complex model outputs and decision-making processes, ensuring compliance with these regulatory standards by product necessary reports for better comprehension by front-line staff.

- *Regulatory Framework: SR 11-7 Compliance:* The Federal Reserve's SR 11-7 guidance emphasizes the importance of effective model risk management, particularly for models used in cr2itical financial decision-making [12]. It requires financial institutions to maintain robust, transparent, and well-documented model development, implementation, and use processes. This includes providing clear explanations of how models work, their limitations, and the rationale behind their outputs.
- For this particular case, a representative dataset from the Lending club [13] is used to showcase the potential of GenAI in reducing the trust gap between technical and front-line staff.
- *Approach:* The institution implemented a GenAI base tool specifically designed to interpret and explain the outputs of its financial models.
- *Model Explanation Generation:* The tool was tasked with generating user-friendly explanations for complex model outputs, translating technical jargon into comprehensible language.
- *Model Validation Support:* The tool assisted in creating documentation for model validation processes, ensuring that all aspects of the models were transparent and easily understandable, in line with SR 11-7 requirements [12].

Figure 1 is the sample output of the tool which creates auto-documentation using GenAI. The tool generates comprehensive documentation of 25–50 pages based on the use case and inputs using GenAI, which can be comprehended by both technical and non-technical staff.

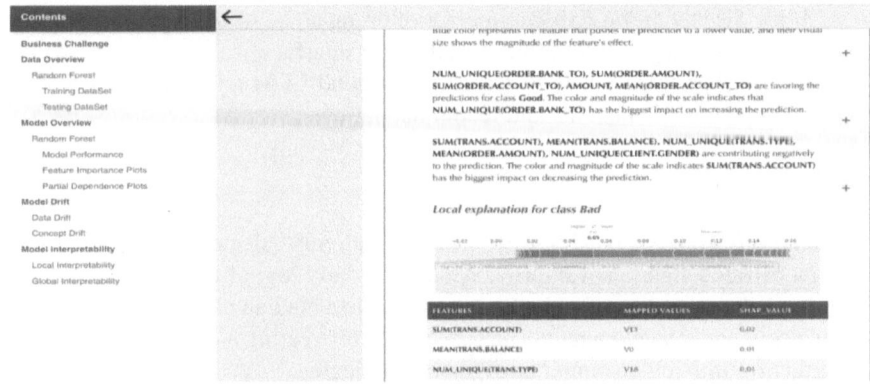

Fig. 1. Auto-documentation using GenAI

Explainability Focus: The LLM played a crucial role in:

- *Demystifying Model Outputs*: It provided clear, intuitive explanations of how various financial models arrived at their conclusions, making them accessible to non-technical stakeholders. Enhancing Documentation: It aided in producing comprehensive documentation that detailed the methodologies, assumptions, and limitations of the models, which is a key requirement of SR 11-7.
- *Results:* The deployment of the GenAI-based solution:

  - *Ensured Regulatory Compliance*: The institution met the stringent explainability requirements of SR 11-7 [12], mitigating risks associated with model misinterpretation.
  - *Improved Stakeholder Understanding*: Enhanced the overall understanding of model functionalities among both technical and non-technical staff, fostering a culture of transparency and trust.
  - *Supported Model Governance*: Assisted in maintaining a robust model governance framework, crucial for effective risk management.

2.6 Case Study 6: Enhancing User Comprehension and Trust in ML-Driven Recommendation Systems in a Consumer Health Corporation

- *Objective and Context:* A leading consumer health company developed advanced machine learning (ML) tools for marketing and commercial strategies as part of a digital transformation initiative. However, a challenge emerged when the field force exhibited low engagement with these tools due to the complexity of their underlying algorithms and variables.
- *Approach:* The company integrated Large Language Models (LLMs) to improve the transparency and comprehensibility of their ML tools. The approach involved:

  - *Data Anonymization*: Implementing NLP and tokenization techniques for data privacy and security.

- *LLM for Segmentation Explanation*: Developing an LLM to clarify the segmentation process, integrated as tooltips in the user interface.
- *LLM for CRM Data Analysis*: Creating a second LLM to synthesize CRM data, providing strategic insights and recommendations.

• Results:

- *Pilot Study Metrics*: A pilot study with 25 randomly selected field representatives demonstrated significant improvements. The daily login frequency for this group increased to a median of 10 logins, compared to a median of 2 in the control group.
- *Strategic Tool Development*: The success led to creating a call planning assistant, further optimizing customer engagement strategies.
- *Increased Trust and Transparency*: There was a notable increase in trust among the field force, attributed to a better understanding of the data and model functionalities.

This case illustrates the importance of explainable AI in enhancing user engagement with ML-driven systems. By simplifying complex AI processes, the company not only improved tool utilization but also fostered a culture of transparency and trust, essential for the successful integration of AI in business operations.

Cases 5 and 6 demonstrate the effectiveness of GenAI in translating complex model outputs into understandable language. While Case 5 focused on regulatory compliance in financial models, Case 6 leveraged GenAI to enhance user comprehension and trust in ML-driven systems, showcasing the broader applicability and impact of GenAI in various sectors. Both cases underline the crucial role of explainability in technology adoption and the successful integration of AI tools in business processes.

3   Framework for Enhancing ML Explainability and Trust Through GenAI

Figure 2 above describes a step-by-step process generalized by identifying commonalities of bridging the trust gap leveraging LLMs. The programming for the prompts involves two key understandings. The first understanding involves the operational understanding of the ML system. This involves understanding of the outcomes based on the ML recommendations & predictions and the data on which the decisions are taken. Another step is understanding the models used to generate predictions to factor in model-specific nuances along with any compliance & regulatory requirements that may be needed.

Once the discovery phases are performed, the prompts must factor in the visual representation leveraging point observations or data summary. LLM or SLM models should be carefully chosen considering model parameters, fine tuning of LLM as well as data security. The models can be fine-tuned considering feedback from stakeholders based on a POC.

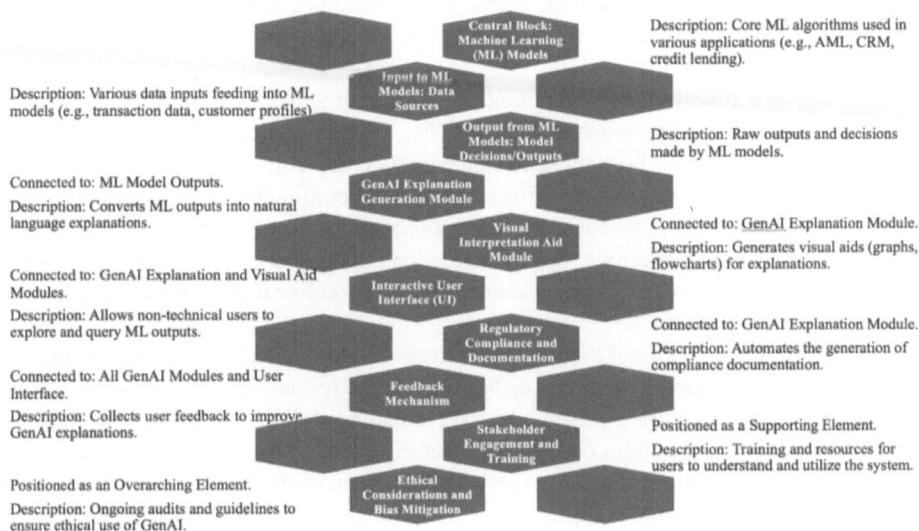

The following descriptions appear alongside the diagram:

Central Block: Machine Learning (ML) Models — Description: Core ML algorithms used in various applications (e.g., AML, CRM, credit lending).

Input to ML Models: Data Sources — Description: Various data inputs feeding into ML models (e.g., transaction data, customer profiles).

Output from ML Models: Model Decisions/Outputs — Description: Raw outputs and decisions made by ML models.

GenAI Explanation Generation Module — Connected to: ML Model Outputs. Description: Converts ML outputs into natural language explanations.

Visual Interpretation Aid Module — Connected to: GenAI Explanation Module. Description: Generates visual aids (graphs, flowcharts) for explanations.

Interactive User Interface (UI) — Connected to: GenAI Explanation and Visual Aid Modules. Description: Allows non-technical users to explore and query ML outputs.

Regulatory Compliance and Documentation — Connected to: GenAI Explanation Module. Description: Automates the generation of compliance documentation.

Feedback Mechanism — Connected to: All GenAI Modules and User Interface. Description: Collects user feedback to improve GenAI explanations.

Stakeholder Engagement and Training — Positioned as a Supporting Element. Description: Training and resources for users to understand and utilize the system.

Ethical Considerations and Bias Mitigation — Positioned as an Overarching Element. Description: Ongoing audits and guidelines to ensure ethical use of GenAI.

Fig. 2. Identifying commonalities of bridging the trust gap leveraging LLMs

4 Managerial Implications

This research highlights several critical implications for managers in organizations employing machine learning technologies:

- Enhancing Understandab'ility: Managers should prioritize initiatives that enhance the understandability of ML models. This includes investing in GenAI models like LLMs to translate complex model outputs into more accessible language.
- Fostering Collaboration: By bridging the explainability gap, managers can foster better collaboration between technical and non-technical teams, leading to more informed decision making and a culture of inclusivity.
- Regulatory Compliance: In heavily regulated industries, managers must ensure that their ML systems adhere to compliance standards. GenAI can play a crucial role in aligning model outputs with regulatory requirements, particularly in terms of transparency and explainability. Risk Management: Understanding the limitations and potential biases of ML models is essential for effective risk management. Managers should leverage GenAI to identify and mitigate these risks proactively.

5 Future Work

Future research in this field could explore several avenues. One promising area involves conducting longitudinal studies to assess the long-term impact of generative AI (GenAI) on bridging the trust gap across various industries and different country contexts. Such studies would provide a comprehensive understanding of how these technologies influence trust over time, offering valuable insights into their sustainability and effectiveness.

This is especially important given the enduring cultural and contextual differences across different environments, such as WEIRD and GREAT countries [14, 15], as borne out by previous research [16–18].

Additionally, investigating the potential of emerging GenAI technologies and their implications for enhancing machine learning (ML) model explainability is crucial. This research could delve into how these advancements contribute to more transparent and interpretable models, thereby improving stakeholders' confidence in AI systems. Understanding these dynamics is essential for developing robust AI solutions that meet industry standards and user expectations. Such confidence is necessary for humans to consider giving agency and control to AI systems and eventually realize future visions of cognitive reapportionment [19, 20].

Another important area of exploration is cross-industry comparisons. By evaluating the effectiveness of GenAI tools in different sectors, researchers can identify unique challenges and opportunities presented by these technologies in each domain. Furthermore, a focus on more human-centric approaches in the design and implementation of GenAI is needed. Emphasizing user experience and interaction can significantly enhance explainability, ensuring that AI systems are not only effective but also user-friendly and accessible. Such trust and user-centricity are critical for AI to achieve its future potential.

6 Limitations

As the paper discusses a case study-based generalization approach, the authors recognize two key limitations of this paper. The first is the lack of application across all industries and use cases. The second is the consideration of technical and regulatory architectures.

The challenge with any collection of case studies is generalization, especially when the case studies have been procured from a multitude of industries; the current corpus of case studies spans life sciences, retail, and financial services. Each of these industries has nuanced requirements for developing end-user trust for acceptance of complex machine learning-based information systems. Furthermore, this study concentrates on establishing trust from end users of the systems instead of the executive decision-makers who primarily decide and approve large-scale IT/IS/MIS investments in a firm [8]. This current approach also acknowledges the lack of primary research in pre and post-implementation of explainable AI in ML systems.

The second challenge in the current approach is the lack of acceptance of specialized regulatory and IT rules. Different industries, as well as functions across industries, have different IT technology stacks and mandatory regulatory compliances. Data compliances, especially in the consideration of sharing internal data over APIs to public LLMs, may not allow for replication of the proposed framework to be implemented.

7 Conclusion

Our investigation into the role of GenAI in enhancing the explainability of ML models has revealed a promising avenue for bridging the trust gap between technical experts and frontline staff. The case studies presented in this paper demonstrate the multifaceted challenges posed by complex ML systems across various sectors and how GenAI can effectively address these issues. By synthesizing comprehensible visualizations and intuitive explanations, GenAI tools like LLMs have the potential to democratize ML knowledge, making these advanced technologies more accessible and trustworthy. This research underscores the transformative role of GenAI in the realm of ML and AI, offering valuable insights for organizations aiming to leverage these technologies more effectively. As we advance, it is crucial to continue exploring and innovating in this space, ensuring that ML technologies are not only powerful but also understandable and reliable for all stakeholders involved.

References

1. Gilpin, L.H., Bau, D., Yuan, B.Z., Bajwa, A., Specter, M., Kagal, L.: Explaining explanations: an overview of interpretability of machine learning. In: 2018 IEEE 5th International Conference on data science and advanced analytics (DSAA). IEEE (2018)
2. Caruana, R., Lou, Y., Gehrke, J., Koch, P., Sturm, M., Elhadad, N.: Intelligible models for healthcare: predicting pneumonia risk and hospital 30-day readmission. In: Proceedings of the 21th ACM SIGKDD International Conference on Knowledge Discovery and Data Mining (2015)
3. Parasuraman, R., Riley, V.: Humans and automation: Use, misuse, disuse, abuse. Hum. Factors **39**(2), 230–253 (1997)
4. Kahneman, D., Slovic, P., Tversky, A.: Judgment Under Uncertainty: Heuristics and Biases. Cambridge, Cambridge, MA (1982)
5. Strobelt, H., Gehrmann, S., Pfister, H., Rush, A.M.: LSTMVIS: A tool for visual analysis of hidden state dynamics in recurrent neural networks. IEEE Trans. Visual Comput. Graphics **24**(1), 667–676 (2017)
6. Bhatt, U., et al.: Explainable machine learning in deployment. In: Proceedings of the 2020 Conference on Fairness, Accountability, and Transparency (2020)
7. Giddens, A.: The Consequences of Modernity (Cambridge, UK, Polity). The Consequences of Modernity 1990, Giddens (1990)
8. Ologeanu-Taddei, R., Vitari, C.: Filling gaps and re-conceptualizing trust in Information Technology. In: 28th European Conference on Information Systems (ECIS) (2020)
9. Eizenman, E.: Scotiabank's Chief Risk Officer on the State of Anti-money Laundering. McKinsey Company (2019)
10. Aggarwal, R., Raghavan, K.: Management Board Challenges Complying with Bank Secrecy Act and Anti Money Laundering Regulations. Money Laundering, Financing Terrorism and Suspicious Activities. Nova Science Publishers, New York (2006)
11. Liu, Y., Gillis, T.: Machine Learning in the Underwriting of Consumer Loans, CSP057 (2020)
12. Parkinson, C., Sinnott-Armstrong, W., Koralus, P.E., Mendelovici, A., McGeer, V., Wheatley, T.: Is morality unified? Evidence that distinct neural systems underlie moral judgments of harm, dishonesty, and disgust. J. Cogn. Neurosci. **23**(10), 3162–3180 (2011)
13. Chang, S., Kim, S.D., Kondo, G.: Predicting default risk of lending club loans. Mach. Learn. 1–5 (2015)
14. Henrich, J., Heine, S.J., Norenzayan, A.: Most people are not WEIRD. Nature **466**(7302), 29 (2010)
15. Karhade, P., Kathuria, A.: Missing impact of ratings on platform participation in India: a call for research in GREAT domains. Commun. Assoc. Inf. Syst. **47**(1), 19 (2020)
16. Muthukrishna, M., et al.: Beyond western, educated, industrial, rich, and democratic (WEIRD) psychology: measuring and mapping scales of cultural and psychological distance. Psychol. Sci. **31**(6), 678–701 (2020)

17. Masuda, T., Batdorj, B., Senzaki, S.: Culture and attention: Future directions to expand research beyond the geographical regions of WEIRD cultures. Front. Psychol. **11**, 1394 (2020)
18. Apicella, C., Norenzayan, A., Henrich, J.: Beyond WEIRD: a review of the last decade and a look ahead to the global laboratory of the future. Evol. Hum. Behav. **41**(5), 319–329 (2020)
19. Ning, X., Khuntia, J., Kathuria, A., Konsynski, B.R.: Artificial Intelligence (AI) and cognitive apportionment for service flexibility. In: Xu, J.J., Zhu, B., Liu, X., Shaw, M.J., Zhang, H., Fan, M. (eds.) The Ecosystem of e-Business: Technologies, Stakeholders, and Connections: 17th Workshop on e-Business, WeB 2018, Santa Clara, CA, USA, December 12, 2018, Revised Selected Papers, pp. 182–189. Springer International Publishing, Cham (2019). https://doi.org/10.1007/978-3-030-22784-5_18
20. Konsynski, B.R., Kathuria, A., Karhade, P.P.: Cognitive reapportionment and the art of letting Go: a theoretical framework for the allocation of decision rights. J. Manag. Inf. Syst. **41**(2), 328–340 (2024)

The Impact of Dark Side Personality on Consumer Online Brand Defending: A Study on Apple vs Android

Chen-Chia Huang[1] and Cheuk Hang Au[2]([envelope]) [ORCID]

[1] Department of Information Management, National Chung Cheng University, Chiayi, Taiwan
[2] School of Business and Law, Edith Cowan University, Perth, Australia
c.au@ecu.edu.au

Abstract. With the Internet's expansion, various online platforms have arisen, allowing people to express their views and influence electronic word-of-mouth (eWOM) for various brands. Depending on their personalities, some Internet users may express dissatisfaction or exhibit anti-brand behaviors when they receive products or services that don't meet their expectations. Not all users, however, come to the brand's defense, even if they disagree with the critics or anti-brand behaviors. Through a case study using netnography, we explored the influence of personality on online brand defense. We found that individuals seeking social recognition and self-validation are more likely to engage in online brand defense. Recognizing the impact of personality on online behavior can assist businesses and marketers in formulating strategies for fostering positive interactions with consumers.

Keywords: eWOM · brand defending · personality · social recognition

1 Introduction

The proliferation of the Internet, especially online review portals, has revolutionized consumer-brand interactions [1]. Consumers may leave comments, feedback, and reviews online, which provide valuable insights into product quality, customer service, and brand reputation [2]. For example, in 2015, American fast-food chain Wendy's enlisted a teenager to promote their chicken nuggets on Twitter, which resulted in over 3 million retweets and a significant boost in sales [3]. This demonstrates the potential of the Internet to drive consumer engagement and boost brand loyalty.

This trend has increased consumers' online brand defending, where they defend their preferred brand against criticism [4]. Consumer online behavior, including brand defense, is influenced by personality [5] and other sources like Internet feedback and comments [6]. Impulsive individuals may engage in aggressive online behavior [9], while those seeking attention may exhibit attention-seeking online behavior [1]. Understanding how personality affects online behavior is vital to foster positive customer interactions and making informed choices in internet marketing, such as endorsers' selection.

© The Author(s), under exclusive license to Springer Nature Switzerland AG 2025
A. Kathuria et al. (Eds.): WeB 2023, LNBIP 525, pp. 139–148, 2025.
https://doi.org/10.1007/978-3-031-74437-2_11

However, these traits' effects on specific consumer online brand defense behaviors are less explored. This paper presents an ongoing case study on PTT, a popular Taiwanese online community, to examine personality's influence on brand defense behavior, particularly between Apple and Android users. This study's significance lies in its potential to illuminate the role of personality in predicting and moderating attitudes toward brand defense behaviors. The results can offer valuable insights to businesses and marketers, enhancing their strategies and understanding of online brand discussion dynamics. Hence, our research question (RQ) is: *How does personality affect online brand defense behavior?*

2   Literature Review on Online Brand Defending Behavior

The Internet's growth has boosted information access and amplified brand influence on consumer behavior [2]. Certain users engage in protecting their beloved brands from perceived threats, known as consumer online brand defending [1]. Previous literature emphasizes consumers' brand defense driven by social affiliation, self-enhancement, and positive social identity maintenance. This involves mocking competitors, demonstrating loyalty, and confidently addressing criticism [4]. Additional factors influencing pro-brand behavior are group membership, positive experiences, brand trust, and identification [7]. **Table 1** lists arguments related to these behaviors and other related actions like promoting positive electronic word of mouth (eWoM).

Given online comments are more influential than offline ones [8], online brand defense carries a greater impact on eWOM and corporate reputation. By actively defending a brand online, consumers can foster positive eWOM, enhancing brand awareness and loyalty [2]. This symbiotic relationship underscores the substantial influence of online brand defense in shaping consumer perceptions and brand success [9, 10].

Table 1. Previous Arguments Around Consumers' Online Brand Defending Behavior

References	Arguments
[10]	Positive eWOM is driven by customers' desire to help the restaurant, express positive feelings, or demonstrate concern for others based on their experiences with food quality, service employees, and atmosphere
[4]	Brand defense, a unique word-of-mouth, extends WOM beyond praise and complaints. Consumers who actively counter negativity are often driven by justice or self-enhancement, challenging loyalty assumptions
[7]	Consumer-brand relationships, specifically brand trust and brand identification, significantly influence brand evangelism. Brand trust positively impacts purchase intentions and positive referrals, while brand identification influences positive and oppositional brand referrals
[9]	Self-enhancement and enjoyment are key predictors of positive eWOM behavior, while venting negative feelings and economic incentives are prominent predictors of negative eWOM behavior
[39]	When customers perceive a strong connection between the brand and their own identity, as well as a sense of belonging to a group associated with the brand, they are more likely to engage in positive WOM
[1]	Consumers' online brand defense emerges in response to product or service criticism. The research explores the catalysts, methods, and their effects on brands and stakeholders

3   Literature Review on the Role of Personality on Online Behavior

Personality's role in shaping online behavior is a topic of great interest among researchers [11]. Positive traits promote constructive interactions, fostering better consumer-brand relationships. Conversely, negative traits can lead to defensive or hostile behaviors, potentially harming brand perceptions and consumer-brand connections [12]. Among psychological personality theories, the *Dark Triad* stands out, which encompasses sub-clinical narcissism, Machiavellianism, and sub-clinical psychopathy [13]. Research suggests that individuals with high Dark Triad scores are more prone to negative online behavior, like cyberbullying and trolling [14, 15]. Table 2 outlines prior discussions on how online behaviors can be influenced by personal traits associated with the Dark Triad.

Researchers have been recently arguing regarding the nature of the Dark Triad constructs. Comprehensive measurements of these traits have shown substantial overlap, with only a few distinguishing features. However, factor analyses have not consistently supported the traditional three-factor model (narcissism, Machiavellianism, and psychopathy) [16]. Instead, a four-factor trait-based model has been proposed, including Antagonism, Agency, Impulsivity, and Emotional Stability [17]. Antagonism covers traits like callousness, arrogance, manipulativeness, cynicism, and anger. Agency includes traits related to dominance and self-assurance. Impulsivity is characterized by traits like rashness and irresponsibility, and emotional stability includes low anxiety and

Table 2. Prior research mentions personal traits according to the Dark Triad Theory.

References	Arguments
[15]	Significant correlations exist among Dark Triad traits, more prevalent in men, linked to agreeableness and honesty-humility, and tied to multiple negative psychosocial outcomes
[18]	The Dark Triad is negatively associated with life satisfaction and linked to selfish, exploitative, and aggressive outcomes
[40]	Based on the Dark Triad Theory, elevated dark tetrad traits and loneliness predict increased internet trolling. Loneliness also moderates the dark tetrad traits' impact on trolling, especially in highly Machiavellian and psychopathic individuals
[14]	There are significant positive relationships between dark personality traits and the intention to exaggerate, with moral disengagement mediating this relationship for narcissists and psychopaths
[17]	Through factor analyses, the study identifies four distinct factors (Antagonism, Agency, Impulsivity, and Emotional Stability) and discusses their implications, providing an alternative perspective to understanding the Dark Triad constructs

fearlessness. These findings suggest that psychopathy, narcissism, and Machiavellianism may not be distinct but rather various expressions of an underlying antagonistic core [16, 17].

Moreover, studies suggest that those who score highly on Dark Triad measures are more prone to criminal behavior, pose a disturbance to society, and present severe challenges for groups. These individuals generally exhibit a lack of empathy and unfriendly behavior. When their empathy is lacking and they are dissatisfied with their lives, they are unlikely to place faith in their own or others' moral character [18].

4 Research Method

We chose a netnographic case study for multiple reasons. First, case research methods are ideal for addressing "how" research questions and understanding context-specific processes [19, 20]. Second, the complexity of online brand defense, encompassing diverse dimensions, makes an objective approach challenging [21]. Therefore, a case study approach is better suited for examining such phenomena [22]. Netnography integrates methodological traditions and techniques from cultural anthropology, which can uncover insights from underrepresented online experiences in earlier research [23] and can be used with qualitative methods [24]. We selected the Taiwanese forum, PTT, known as a highly active and influential online platform in Taiwan.

The polarized brand debates on PTT over Apple and Android smartphones, featuring praise and criticism, create an ideal context to study how personal traits shape behaviour, including passionate criticism and brand-demeaning discourse. Additionally, our exploration of the Apple-Android rivalry, marked by strong personal and group identities, provides new insights into this less-studied phenomenon [19]. This unique binary conflict, integrated into our daily smartphone usage, presents an intriguing context to investigate the nature and intensity of online brand conflicts [25].

We gathered data related to the online competition between Apple and Android and how consumers defend their preferred brands. Our data sources offer unique attributes for precise motive and behavior identification, improving data collection efficiency. We analyzed relevant posts from the chosen online forum, covering discussions from February 1, 2023, to March 14, 2023. Data analysis was performed concurrently, benefiting from case research methods' flexibility [26]. Drawing from existing literature on online brand defense and the role of personality in online behavior, we established theoretical dimensions and themes [27] to guide data collection and analysis using open, axial, and selective coding [28, 29]. All authors coded separately to triangulate data interpretation and minimize bias. We also utilized visual mapping and narrative strategies to interpret the extensive collected data [22, 30]. Visual mapping helped comprehend the brand competition dynamics and highlight key themes, sentiments, and arguments emerging from the discussions. It allowed us to capture the complex nature of the brand rivalry and identify underlying trends and influences. In contrast, narrative strategies involved creating a textual overview of significant events, interactions, and choices regarding consumers' online brand defense behavior. We continued refining and integrating data, analysis, and the theoretical framework until reaching theoretical saturation [26].

5   Preliminary Findings

Our initial results indicate that five dark side traits (Antagonism, Agency, Impulsivity, Emotional Stability) can influence how individuals perceive and relate to a brand. This, in turn, can impact their affection or aversion towards the brand, shaping their brand defense behavior, which may also involve attacking another brand. We posit that these aspects are interconnected Fig. 1. The impact of personality traits on brand attacking and defending behavior. Illustrates our theoretical model based on these findings.

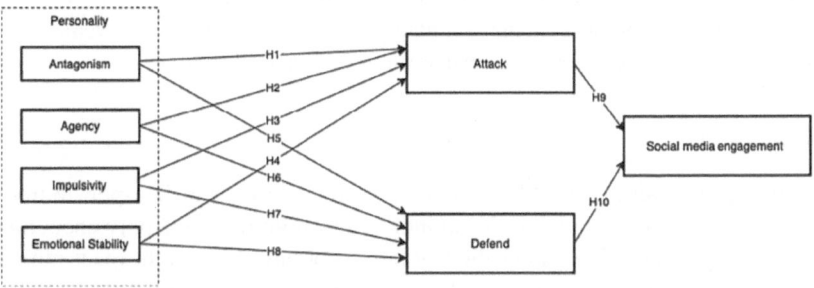

Fig. 1. The impact of personality traits on brand attacking and defending behavior.

5.1   Antagonism

The growth of digital platforms has revolutionized communication and content sharing, facilitating global connectivity and community development. Yet, they have also opened doors to antagonistic issues such as cyberbullying, misinformation, and polarization [4]. In an online article debating the merits and drawbacks of a smartphone brand, derogatory comments targeting the two smartphone ecosystems were evident.

> A: The typing experience on the iPhone is trash!
>
> B: Apple's fans are all fanboys, thinking they are superior.

Besides hostility and aggression, they disregarded opposing views with personal attacks, trying to belittle and discredit the commenter. They lacked empathy for others' perspectives and feelings, and their confrontational remarks escalated tensions, fueling online conflicts and deepening divisions within the brand's community.

5.2 Agency

We also found that people with high dominance, self-assurance, and achievement-striving traits (i.e., high agency) are more prone to promote and defend their favored brand (An et al., 2019). For instance, in an online forum dedicated to Apple's AirPods wireless headphones, individuals driven by the agency actively endorse the new products based on their personal experiences.

> C: Just got my hands on AirPods, and I'm in awe. Apple truly knows how to design products that fit perfectly into our lives. Loving the wireless freedom!
>
> D: AirPods have made my life so much easier. No more tangled wires and seamless connectivity.

Their assertiveness and confidence inspire others in the community, garnering support and admiration for the brand. This can promote positive word-of-mouth and attract new customers [10]. However, high-agency brand advocates may become overly passionate in defending the brand, resorting to aggressive tactics, like personal attacks on competitors or disregarding alternative opinions without considering their merits. These can tarnish the brand's image, alienate potential consumers, and create a negative perception among those who value respectful and open dialogue [1].

5.3 Impulsivity

Furthermore, impulsive traits like rashness, thrill-seeking, and irresponsibility could influence brand defense behavior. When individuals high in impulsivity encounter negative comments or criticism about their preferred brand, they might react impulsively without fully assessing the situation [14]. An example from a smartphone discussion forum illustrates this: a user, "UserX" (an anonymous account), displayed impulsive personality traits. When other users posted positive reviews of a new Apple product, "UserX" swiftly responded with critical comments and counterattacks (Time shown in GMT + 8).

> TitleA: "iPhone Dynamic Island Can Do." 7/25 14:08

UserX: This is too funny! Die-hard Apple fans can really support anything! 7/25 14:10

TitleB: "Apple's software ecosystem changed my life." 7/19 21:01

UserX: Another Apple-sponsored advertisement, whut u trash piece! 7/19 21:04

These reactions reveal "UserX's" emotional volatility and impatience, leading to a negative forum atmosphere and discouraging others from participating. Some users avoid interacting with "UserX" to prevent conflicts, while others criticize them directly. Consequently, many posts lose focus and turn into online arguments. Nevertheless, impulsivity can yield positive results. High impulsivity on the enthusiastic side may lead to sharing positive experiences and fervently defending one's preferred brand. This can encourage others to engage in the conversation and foster brand loyalty. The impact of impulsivity on brand defense behavior can vary based on the context and the level of self-control exercised. While impulsive reactions can contribute to conflicts and polarization, enthusiastic impulsivity can cultivate a brand community and stimulate positive WOM [7].

5.4   A Subsection Sample

Emotionally stable individuals, marked by traits like low anxiety and fearlessness, approach brand defense behaviour differently by responding to critics calmly and thoughtfully. However, emotional stability may reduce the tendency for brand attacks and defenses. In a forum discussing Apple and Android operating systems, emotionally stable users express their opinions on performance. They steer clear of personal attacks and focus on addressing concerns. They discussed rationally with logical arguments and evidence. By providing constructive feedback and solutions, they contribute positively to the brand's image.

E: Apple really nails user privacy and security, but Android could step up its game by doing more regular updates to tackle vulnerabilities.

F: Android gives you a bunch of device choices, which is cool, but they could make things smoother by tidying up the software and cutting down on fragmentation for a better overall user experience and smoother software.

Their professional demeanor earns respect in the online community, establishing credibility and reliability. Being seen as rational and trustworthy information sources, they bolster the brand's image. Emotional stability is vital in brand defense behaviour, with emotionally stable individuals embodying resilience and professionalism. Their adeptness at handling criticism calmly and offering constructive feedback fosters a positive online atmosphere and enhances brand reputation [9].

6   Discussion and Concluding Remarks

Our research is not without limitations. According to Karhade and Kathuria [31] 2020, research conducted in western, educated, industrialized, rich, and democratic (WEIRD) domains does not necessarily generalize to other more developing regions, especially those from growing, rural, eastern, aspirational, and transitional (GREAT) domains. This is borne out in multiple studies and calls for research [32–38]. Such differences were not particularly taken into consideration upon building the model. And yet, internet users' behavior can vary significantly across different countries, and we encourage future studies on consumers' online brand-defending behavior to consider the cultural aspects.

We found that individuals with traits like Antagonism, Agency, Impulsivity, and Emotional Stability are more prone to engage in negative and malicious online brand defense, encompassing both brand defense and attacks, two intermingled types of behaviors. Our insights into the role of personality have implications for online discourse management and brand reputation. For brand owners, our findings provided insights on selecting spokespersons, such as avoiding collaborations with internet celebrities with strong dark side personality traits.

In netnography, coders' interpretations of quotes can vary widely. Hence, we intend to incorporate quantitative methods for statistical validation and explore the influence of other personality traits in the future. Overall, we underscore the significance of comprehending the impact of personality on online brand defense and its relevance for online reputation management. We hope that future research can facilitate a theoretical understanding of consumer online brand defending and the creation of more efficient online brand management strategies.

Acknowledgments. This study was funded by the National Science and Technology Council of Taiwan (grant number 111-2410-H-194 -023 -MY2).

Disclosure of Interests. The authors have no competing interests to declare that are relevant to the content of this article.

References

1. Au, C.H., Ho, K.K., Law, K.M.: The bright and dark of consumers' online brand defending behaviors: exploring their enablers, realization, and impacts. J. Organ. Comput. Electron. Commer. **31**(3), 171–191 (2021)
2. See-To, E.W., Ho, K.K.: Value co-creation and purchase intention in social network sites: The role of electronic Word-of-Mouth and trust–A theoretical analysis. Comput. Hum. Behav. **31**, 182–189 (2014)
3. Ohlheiser, A.: Congrats, the most retweeted tweet ever is now a teen's plea to a brand for free nuggets. 26 Oct 2021
4. Colliander, J., Wien, A.H.: Eur. J. Market. **47**(10), 1733–1757 (2013). https://doi.org/10.1108/EJM-04-2011-0191
5. Sun, N., Rau, P.P.-L., Ma, L.: Understanding lurkers in online communities: a literature review. Comput. Hum. Behav. **38**, 110–117 (2014)
6. Zhang, K.Z., Zhao, S.J., Cheung, C.M., Lee, M.K.: Examining the influence of online reviews on consumers' decision-making: a heuristic–systematic model. Decis. Support Syst. **67**, 78–89 (2014)
7. Becerra, E.P., Badrinarayanan, V.: The influence of brand trust and brand identification on brand evangelism. J. Product Brand Manag. **22**(5/6), 371–383 (2013)

8. Rauschnabel, P.A., Kammerlander, N., Ivens, B.S.: Collaborative brand attacks in social media: exploring the antecedents, characteristics, and consequences of a new form of brand crises. J. Market. Theory Pract. **24**(4), 381–410 (2016)
9. Hu, Y., Kim, H.J.: Positive and negative eWOM motivations and hotel customers' eWOM behavior: does personality matter? Int. J. Hosp. Manag. **75**, 27–37 (2018)
10. Jeong, E., Jang, S.S.: Restaurant experiences triggering positive electronic word-of-mouth (eWOM) motivations. Int. J. Hosp. Manag. **30**(2), 356–366 (2011)
11. Sawaftah, D., Aljarah, A., Lahuerta-Otero, E.: Power brand defense up, my friend! stimulating brand defense through digital content marketing. Sustainability **13**(18), 10266 (2021)
12. Clemenz, J., Brettel, M., Moeller, T.: How the personality of a brand impacts the perception of different dimensions of quality. J. Brand Manag. **20**(1), 52–64 (2012)
13. Paulhus, D.L., Williams, K.M.: The dark triad of personality: Narcissism, Machiavellianism, and psychopathy. J. Res. Pers. **36**(6), 556–563 (2002)
14. Kapoor, P.S., Balaji, M., Maity, M., Jain, N.K.: Why consumers exaggerate in online reviews? Moral disengagement and dark personality traits. J. Retail. Consum. Serv. **60**, 102496 (2021)
15. Muris, P., Merckelbach, H., Otgaar, H., Meijer, E.: The malevolent side of human nature: A meta-analysis and critical review of the literature on the dark triad (narcissism, Machiavellianism, and psychopathy). Perspect. Psychol. Sci. **12**(2), 183–204 (2017)
16. Bader, M., Hilbig, B.E., Zettler, I., Moshagen, M.: Rethinking aversive personality: Decomposing the Dark Triad traits into their common core and unique flavors. J. Pers. **91**(5), 1084–1109 (2023)
17. Rose, L., Crowe, M.L., Sharpe, B.M., Van Til, K., Lynam, D.R., Miller, J.D.: Factor structure of the FFM ATM: antagonism, emotional stability, impulsivity, and agency. J. Pers. Assess. **105**(3), 342–354 (2023)
18. Kaufman, S.B., Yaden, D.B., Hyde, E., Tsukayama, E.: The light vs. dark triad of personality: contrasting two very different profiles of human nature. Front. Psychol. **10**, 467 (2019)
19. Benbasat, I., Goldstein, D.K., Mead, M.: The case research strategy in studies of information systems. MIS Q. **11**, 369–386 (1987)
20. Gephart, Jr, R.P.: Qualitative research and the Academy of Management Journal, vol. 10510, pp. 454–462 . Academy of Management Briarcliff Manor, NY (2004)
21. Gable, G.G.: Integrating case study and survey research methods: an example in information systems. Eur. J. Inf. Syst. **3**(2), 112–126 (1994)
22. Klein, H.K., Myers, M.D.: A set of principles for conducting and evaluating interpretive field studies in information systems. MIS Q. **23**, 67–93 (1999)
23. Langer, R., Beckman, S.C.: Sensitive research topics: Netnography revisited. J. Cetacean Res. Manag. **8**(2), 189–203 (2005)
24. O'Donohoe, S.: Netnography: Doing Ethnographic Research Online. Taylor & Francis (2010)
25. Shaw, H., Ellis, D.A., Kendrick, L.-R., Ziegler, F., Wiseman, R.: Predicting smartphone operating system from personality and individual differences. Cyberpsychol. Behav. Soc. Netw. **19**(12), 727–732 (2016)
26. Eisenhardt, K.M.: Building theories from case study research. Acad. Manag. Rev. **14**(4), 532–550 (1989)
27. Gioia, D.A., Corley, K.G., Hamilton, A.L.: Seeking qualitative rigor in inductive research: notes on the Gioia methodology. Organ. Res. Methods **16**(1), 15–31 (2013)
28. Pan, S.L., Tan, B.: Demystifying case research: a structured–pragmatic–situational (SPS) approach to conducting case studies. Inf. Organ. **21**(3), 161–176 (2011)
29. Strauss, A., Corbin, J.: Basics of Qualitative Research, vol. 15. Sage Newbury Park, CA (1990)
30. Langley, A.: Strategies for theorizing from process data. Acad. Manag. Rev. **24**(4), 691–710 (1999)

31. Karhade, P., Kathuria, A.: Missing impact of ratings on platform participation in India: a call for research in GREAT domains. Commun. Assoc. Inf. Syst. **47**(1), 19 (2020)
32. Jaiswal, A., Kathuria, A., Karhade, P.P.: Benefits of business intelligence systems and multiple national cultures during covid-19. In: Fan, S., Ilk, N., Shan, Z., Zhao, K. (eds.) From Grand Challenges to Great Solutions: Digital Transformation in the Age of COVID-19. WEB 2021. Lecture Notes in Business Information Processing. Springer, Cham (2022)
33. Jaiswal, A., Malik, O., Karhade, P., Kathuria, A.: Too many cooks spoil the broth: infobesity in multicultural firms during Covid-19. In: Proceedings of the Hawaii International Conference on System Sciences (HICSS). Maui (2022)
34. Karhade, P., Kathuria, A., Dasgupta, A., Malik, O., Konsynski, B.R.: Decolonization of digital platforms: a research agenda for GREAT domains. In: Garimella, A., Karhade, P., Kathuria, A., Liu, X., Xu, J., K. Zhao, J. (eds.) The Role of e-Business During the Time of Grand Challenges. WEB 2020. Lecture Notes in Business Information Processing, pp. 51–58. Springer, Cham (2021)
35. Khuntia, J., Kathuria, A., Saldanha, T.J., Konsynski, B.R.: Benefits of IT-enabled flexibilities for foreign versus local firms in emerging economies. J. Manag. Inf. Syst. **36**(3), 855–892 (2019)
36. Dasgupta, A., Karhade, P., Kathuria, A., Konsynski, B.: Holding space for voices that do not speak: design reform of rating systems for platforms in GREAT economies. In: Proceedings of the Hawaii International Conference on System Sciences (HICSS). Virtual (2021)
37. Khuntia, J., Kathuria, A., Andrade-Rojas, M.G., Saldanha, T., Celly, N.: How foreign and domestic firms differ in leveraging IT-enabled supply chain information integration in BOP markets: the role of supplier and client business collaboration. J. Assoc. Inf. Syst. **22**(3), 6 (2021)
38. Saldanha, T., Kathuria, A., Khuntia, J., Konsynski, B.R.: It's a dangerous business, going out your door: overcoming institutional distances through IS. In: Proceedings of the International Conference on Information Systems (ICIS). Austin (2021)
39. An, J., Do, D.K.X., Ngo, L.V., Quan, T.H.M.: Turning brand credibility into positive word-of-mouth: integrating the signaling and social identity perspectives. J. Brand Manag. **26**(2), 157–175 (2019)
40. Masui, K.: Loneliness moderates the relationship between Dark Tetrad personality traits and internet trolling. Pers. Individ. Differ. **150**, 109475 (2019)

Navigating the Storm: Business Resilience in the Age of Climate Change

Ria Sonpatki$^{(\boxtimes)}$ (iD) and Abhishek Kathuria (iD)

Indian School of Business, Hyderabad, India
{ria_sonpatki,abhishek_kathuria}@isb.edu

Abstract. The 21st century has earned the tragic sobriquet "The Century of Disasters" due to the escalating frequency, complexity, and severity of both natural and human-made calamities. Climate change, marked by an increasing frequency and severity of natural disasters, necessitates a paradigm shift for businesses operations, urging a transition from reactive to proactive and resilient strategies. Research in this area has become crucial, offering organizations vital insights to better prepare for and mitigate the impacts of future disasters. This chapter delves into the multifaceted impact of natural disasters on businesses, exploring how different disciplines are rising to meet these unique challenges. Key findings emphasize the need for flexible supply chains, robust disaster preparedness, and innovative financing mechanisms to mitigate risks and ensure business continuity. As the business landscape becomes increasingly shaped by the realities of disaster risk, it is clear that an interdisciplinary approach is essential. This chapter offers insights from the convergence of literature from Operations Management, Finance, Marketing, and Information Systems. Together, these findings offer a comprehensive framework for understanding and mitigating the complex challenges that disasters present. Pertinently, this chapter explores the burgeoning field of IS in disaster management, highlighting its critical role in saving lives, protecting assets, and building more resilient communities. While this discourse demonstrates the growing importance of IS in disaster management, a number of critical questions remain unanswered. These pave the way for future research opportunities, which are presented at the conclusion of this chapter.

Keywords: Disaster Resilience · Interdisciplinary Approach · Information Systems (IS)

1 Introduction

The 21st century has earned the tragic sobriquet "The Century of Disasters" [1], due to the escalating frequency, complexity, and severity of both natural and human-made calamities [2]. Various factors are driving this surge, including growing vulnerabilities in infrastructure, rapid population growth and urbanization, climate change, and shifting social dynamics [3]. When disasters strike, they wreak havoc on civil and technical infrastructure, causing loss of life [4], disrupting social and economic stability, and inflicting environmental damage.

© The Author(s), under exclusive license to Springer Nature Switzerland AG 2025
A. Kathuria et al. (Eds.): WeB 2023, LNBIP 525, pp. 149–167, 2025.
https://doi.org/10.1007/978-3-031-74437-2_12

Businesses, once secure in a relatively predictable environment, now confront extraordinary obstacles as extreme weather events increasingly disrupt operations, fracture supply chains [2], and reshape financial markets [5]. This evolving landscape demands a significant shift in how organizations approach risk management, pushing them to adopt proactive strategies rather than relying solely on reactive measures. Research in this area has become crucial, offering organizations vital insights to better prepare for and mitigate the impacts of future disasters.

This chapter delves into the multifaceted impact of natural disasters on businesses, exploring how different disciplines are rising to meet these unique difficulties. From Operations Management grappling with disrupted supply chains and debris management [6] to Finance navigating volatile markets and evolving risk profiles [7], each area has witnessed a surge in research dedicated to understanding and mitigating the diverse impacts of disasters. Marketing, once solely focused on consumer desires, now grapples with the ethical implications of promoting sustainability amidst a climate crisis [8], while Information Systems emerge as a critical tool for coordinating relief efforts and enhancing organizational resilience through real-time data and predictive analytics [9].

As the business landscape becomes increasingly shaped by the realities of disaster risk, it is clear that an interdisciplinary approach is essential. The convergence of insights from Operations Management, Finance, Marketing, and Information Systems offers a comprehensive framework for understanding and mitigating the complex difficulties that disasters present. This chapter will illuminate the pivotal role each discipline plays in fostering resilience and adaptability, ultimately equipping businesses with the tools they need to navigate an era marked by uncertainty and change. In Table 1, we summarize the theme of each section of this chapter.

2 Research on Climate Change in Strategy

The devastating impact of natural disasters on businesses is undeniable. Disasters cause widespread disruption, crippling operations, decimating meticulously constructed supply chains, and ultimately inflicting significant financial losses. A study by Oetzel and Oh [10] in 2021 revealed the staggering economic toll disasters can take on businesses, emphasizing the urgent need for effective risk management strategies. This need is further amplified by the escalating threat of climate change, with projections from the National Oceanic and Atmospheric Administration (NOAA) in 2016 indicating a concerning increase in the frequency and severity of extreme weather events. This confluence of factors places immense pressure on firms to not only react effectively to the immediate aftermath of a disaster but also to proactively prepare for such events, weaving resilience into the very fabric of their operations.

While the immediate aftermath of a disaster often necessitates a focus on recovery, some organizations recognize the opportunity to strategically reshape their image and mitigate potential reputational damage. This strategic response goes beyond mere crisis communication; it leverages the disaster as a catalyst for demonstrating corporate social responsibility and solidifying stakeholder trust. Muller and Kräussl [11] study in 2011 of corporate philanthropic disaster response (CRDR) following Hurricane Katrina offers compelling evidence of this phenomenon. Their analysis of U.S. Fortune 500 companies

Table 1. Thematic Outline

	Response to Disasters	Proactive Disaster Preparedness
Strategy	Minimize reputational damage through social responsibility initiatives	Invest in preparedness based on lessons learned from past disasters. Integrate disaster preparedness into CSR
Operations	Develop resilient supply chains. Implement efficient debris management systems	Invest in supply chain capacity to minimize response time. Develop flexible frameworks for collaboration with relief organizations
Finance	Adjust financial models to account for disaster risks	Incorporate climate-related scenarios in stress tests. Incentivize sustainable practices through regulatory updates
Marketing	Leverage emotional marketing to encourage donations and prosocial behavior	Promote sustainability as a core brand value. Use choice architecture to nudge consumers towards eco-friendly choices.
IS	Utilize IS for real-time data collection, communication, and coordination	Leverage IS for proactive risk mitigation and predictive analytics. Integrate smart technologies for long-term resilience

revealed a correlation between charitable donations made in response to the disaster and improved stock performance. Interestingly, this positive correlation was particularly pronounced for firms with a pre-existing track record of social responsibility, suggesting that CRDR can be a powerful tool for signaling genuine commitment to stakeholders and mitigating financial losses associated with reputational damage. By employing an event study methodology, utilizing cumulative abnormal returns and data from the Kinder, Lydenberg, and Domini (KLD) database, Muller and Kräussl [11] provide a nuanced understanding of the complex interplay between disaster response, public perception, and market performance.

However, effectively responding to disasters represents only one side of the equation. Proactive disaster preparedness is paramount for minimizing losses and ensuring business continuity in the face of unforeseen events. This proactive stance is increasingly recognized as a critical component of a robust organizational risk management strategy, as highlighted by Aggarwal, Posen and Workiewicz [12] in 2017. Moreover, focusing on preparedness is not merely a precautionary measure but rather a strategic decision that firms undertake to enhance resilience and maintain a competitive edge in an increasingly volatile world.

The importance of experience, perception, and organizational learning in shaping disaster preparedness is a key area of research. While prior experience with disasters can serve as a powerful motivator for preparedness, as evidenced by studies from Dahlhamer and D'Souza [13] in 1997 and Lampel, Shamsie and Shapira [14] in 2009, the translation of experience into concrete action is not always straightforward. Oetzel and Oh [10], 2021 emphasizes the crucial role of managers in this process. Acting as filters, managers shape how information about past events is processed and interpreted within their organizations, as noted by Christianson, Farkas [15] in 2009. This subjective judgment, often influenced by managerial perceptions of disaster risk, significantly influences the extent to which organizations invest in preparedness measures. This finding is echoed in the work of [16–19], all emphasizing the pivotal role of managerial perception in shaping organizational preparedness.

However, Oetzel and Oh [20] 2013 study cautions against assuming that experiencing a disaster automatically guarantees effective learning or subsequent preparedness. Organizations with similar location-specific experiences can exhibit vastly different responses, underscoring the complex interplay of managerial interpretation and organizational learning processes. This is vividly illustrated by the case of a repeatedly destroyed structure in Mississippi [21], where reconstruction continued despite its known vulnerability to hurricanes.

Recognizing the complexity of disaster preparedness, Oetzel and Oh [10] conducted two insightful surveys in 2021, targeting top managers in disaster-prone locations. By assessing the relationship between preparedness and factors such as organizational experience, managerial threat perceptions, and willingness to learn from others, the study provides valuable insights into the drivers and barriers to effective disaster preparedness. The research design, encompassing an international sample and a focused study of firms in New York City and Miami, provides a rich understanding of the diverse factors shaping preparedness across different contexts.

Research scholars offer insights for managers grappling with strategic decisions in the face of adverse events. Wenzel, Stanske and Lieberman [22], in 2020, provided four major strategies that managers can consider during turbulent times.

1. **Retrenchment**: This common strategic response to crises is defined as implementing reductions in various areas, including costs, assets, products, product lines, and overhead [23, 24]. While retrenchment can foster focus and transparency in the short term, its long-term impact is more complex [25, 26]. Prolonged periods of retrenchment can risk depleting valuable resources, capabilities, and even organizational culture, potentially leading to underperformance when compared to firms that prioritize growth or innovation strategies [27]. This risk is amplified when considering that retrenchment can erode synergy effects, hindering economies of scale and scope [28]. Therefore, while retrenchment may provide a temporary lifeline, managers must carefully consider its long-term implications, finding a balance between necessary cuts and the preservation of core competencies while maintaining a forward-looking vision for renewal [29].

2. **Perseverance**: This approach centers on maintaining existing business activities despite the challenging environment [30]. Instead of scaling back operations, perseverance emphasizes sustaining the status quo and minimizing the negative impact of crisis. This approach, often perceived as passive, can be surprisingly effective, particularly in situations characterized by high uncertainty. Frequent strategic shifts during turbulent times can be detrimental, giving a competitive advantage to those firms that persevere and maintain strategic consistency [31]. This advantage highlights

by Chakrabarti [32] lies in the ability to leverage existing strengths and resources as a more effective survival strategy, particularly when radical renewal during crises can amplify negative impacts. It's important to note that perseverance does not equate to inaction [22]. Perseverance, contingent on the availability of slack resources, offers a viable strategic response, especially in the medium term. By diligently managing resources, leveraging existing strengths, and adapting decision-making to navigate challenging circumstances, firms can weather the storm and emerge well-positioned for future success.

3. **Innovation**: This approach seizes new opportunities amidst disruption. Crises often dismantle existing paradigms, relaxing constraints on decision-making and creating opportunities for exploring previously unconsidered or unfeasible strategies [33–35]. This potential for strategic renewal through innovation is highlighted by Reymen, Andries [36] 2015 study, where increased environmental uncertainty spurred ventures to explore new markets and business models.

4. **Exit**: Wenzel, Stanske and Lieberman [22] highlights exist as the discontinuation of a firm's business activities represents a final strategic response to a crisis [37, 38]. While often perceived as a last resort or a consequence of fatalistic managerial judgments, a strategic exit can be a deliberate and even advantageous choice [39]. Factors such as firm vulnerability, the nature of the crisis, and the strength of external institutions all contribute to the decision to exit [20, 39]. It is crucial to understand that while not without costs [40], a strategic exit can pave the way for renewal by freeing up resources for new ventures [41, 42], demonstrating that it does not signify a definitive end.

3 Research on Climate Change in Operations

Natural disasters inflict severe disruptions on firms, often with long-term consequences for their operations and recovery. These disruptions go far beyond immediate physical damage, creating a cascade of challenges, including inventory loss [43], supply chain interruptions [44], halted production, and, ultimately, significant financial losses. The devastating earthquake and tsunami that struck Japan in March 2011 offer a stark illustration of the magnitude of such events. This disaster directly impacted over 27,000 businesses, crippling their production, warehousing, and retail facilities [45]. The long-lasting effects were evident a year later with 22% of these businesses still shuttered, demonstrating the prolonged and arduous recovery process [46].

Beyond the immediate devastation, the 2011 Japan earthquake and tsunami exposed the fragility and interconnectedness of global supply chains. The subsequent floods in Thailand that same year forced the closure of nearly 1,000 manufacturing factories, sending ripples of disruption throughout global markets [47]. These closures disrupted the intricate network of suppliers and manufacturers, leading to production halts, order delays, and significant drops in pipeline inventory worldwide. Japanese and Thai businesses, deeply embedded in these global supply chains, were particularly hard-hit [45].

This crisis sparked extensive research in Operations, aiming to enhance supply chain resilience. Scholars began analyzing the dynamics of supply chain disruptions [48], particularly in scenarios where multiple suppliers faced sudden closures. These analyses revealed a reluctance among suppliers to relocate production to alternate facilities, even when facing significant disruptions [45]. Scholars identified this reluctance, that would often stem from relocation costs and demand uncertainties, thereby highlighting the need for robust preparedness strategies.

The 2011 events highlighted the critical need for robust supply chain preparedness as a cornerstone of organizational resilience [49]. Strategic investments in supply chain capacity emerged as crucial for minimizing response times, reducing costs, and mitigating human losses during future crises [50, 51]. However, despite the evident benefits, supply chain preparedness often receives inadequate attention and resources [50, 52]. This underinvestment is partly attributed to the limited empirical evidence demonstrating the tangible benefits of preparedness initiatives and the interconnected nature of supply chains [50].

This lack of preparedness is particularly evident in the often-chaotic aftermath of disasters, where a critical bottleneck often emerges: debris management. The sheer volume of debris generated — vegetation, construction waste, municipal waste, and even hazardous materials can be staggering often equivalent to multiple years worth of regular waste. For instance, Hurricane Katrina in 2005 generated an estimated 100 million cubic yards of debris [53]. This debris not only poses environmental hazards but also physically impedes critical search-and-rescue and relief distribution efforts.

Recognizing the urgency of efficient debris management, researchers have increasingly focused on developing effective debris clearance strategies that account for the inherent uncertainty of disasters. Çelik, Ergun and Keskinocak [54] in 2015 highlights prioritizing roads for clearance is important to restore vital supply routes and enable timely delivery of aid. This task, however, presents a complex operational challenge. Fluctuating demand for resources, unpredictable debris levels, and evolving damage assessments make it difficult to create static clearance plans.

To address this complexity, researchers have turned to advanced modeling techniques from the field of Operations. For instance, the stochastic debris clearance problem (SDCP), incorporates uncertainty and dynamic decision-making into the clearance process, allowing for adjustments as consitions on the ground change [55]. Such models, often employing system dynamics, help planners evaluate trade-offs between pre-positioning inventory and investing in disaster management capabilities [52].

Another research area focuses on specific investment elements within the supply chain, such as framework agreements for relief organizations [52, 56]. For example, studies have investigated the value of quantity flexibility contracts, which guarantee relief organizations a minimum quantity of supplies in exchange for reserved capacity and guaranteed delivery terms. Stochastic programming models are frequently used to assess the associated costs and benefits of these contracts under unpredictable demand conditions [57].

However, the unpredictable nature of disasters poses significant challenges for preparedness efforts. Jahre and Jahre [58] in 2019 on page.13, captured this challenge aptly: "Unpredictable demand makes it impossible to plan and prepare for everything. It is simply too risky (items can be in the wrong place, and/or expire) and costly as disasters occur at other places and other times than predicted." This inherent uncertainty necessitates a nuanced approach to preparedness, balancing the need for readiness with the risks of overinvestment.

Despite these challenges, Operations Research has emerged as a valuable tool for navigating the complexities of disaster preparedness. Researchers have developed models focusing on sudden-onset emergencies that simulate the relief response from humanitarian organizations across various settings [59]. These models track the flow of resources, information, and personnel from the initial disaster impact to the delivery of aid, providing valuable insights into potential bottlenecks and areas for optimization.

4   Research on Climate Change in Finance

The rising tide of natural disasters, increasing in both frequency and severity, poses a significant threat to the global economy. This impact is particularly pronounced on businesses, creating ripple effects that disrupt markets and redefine the financial realm. Researchers have called attention to the multifaceted nature of these events, highlighting how they not only stifle economic growth and disrupt supply chains but also send shockwaves through financial markets, labor mobility, and the stability of the banking system [60–63]. Understanding these far-reaching implications is crucial, as the ability of companies to weather these storms directly influences their value, access to capital, and, ultimately, their survival.

One of the most immediate impacts of natural disasters on businesses is the surge in financial uncertainty and risk. This heightened risk profile makes it more expensive for firms to secure loans, limiting their access to critical funding and potentially hindering their ability to recover [63]. This financial strain can drastically alter a company's structure, impacting debt levels and increasing borrowing costs. The uncertainty also spills over into the realm of valuation, challenging traditional models like CAPM and discounted cash flow analysis, as Huang, Kerstein and Wang [64] in 2018 highlights in their research on the impact of extreme weather events on firm valuation.

Beyond individual firms, natural disasters reverberate throughout the entire financial ecosystem, with the banking sector particularly susceptible. Garmaise and Moskowitz [65] 2009 analysis of the 1994 Northridge earthquake in California provides as an example, demonstrating a significant decline in commercial real estate loans following the disaster. This highlights the profound impact these events can have on credit markets. Research shows that banks adapt their lending practices in response, often reallocating funds to disaster-stricken areas while maintaining lending levels in unaffected regions [66, 67]. This reallocation, while intended to support recovery, can inadvertently impact economic activity and capital availability for businesses across the board. Interestingly, smaller banks emerge as crucial players in this landscape, often stepping in to ensure continued access to credit after disasters and bolstering overall economic resilience [68].

While these findings suggest that firms are actively adapting, there is a growing consensus that individual actions may not be enough to address the systemic risks posed by natural disasters, highlighting the need for updated financial regulations. This need is further underscored by the crucial role banks play in post-disaster recovery, as businesses often rely heavily on bank financing to rebuild [69–71]. While Cortés [69] found that lenders play a vital role in helping firms restore their balance sheets after natural disasters, and Koetter, Noth and Rehbein [71] 2020 demonstrated that firms experiencing losses from extreme weather are more likely to require bank credit, their analyses also revealed that these firms are not necessarily more likely to be credit constrained. This delicate balance between reliance on bank financing and the potential strain on the financial system emphasizes the need for robust regulatory frameworks to mitigate systemic risks. These regulatory changes are crucial in a financial domain struggling with heightened uncertainty. Natural disasters, by influencing lending practices and overall economic stability, directly impact investment decisions and risk assessment strategies.

This volatile environment, characterized by disaster-induced shifts in financial stability, significantly impacts investment decisions. Studies by Alok, Kumar and Wermers [72] and Krueger, Winkler and Schumann [73] in 2020 independently highlight how climate-related events fuel risk aversion among fund managers, potentially impacting investment returns. This aversion is driven in part by the realization that companies exposed to extreme weather often experience greater volatility in earnings and cash flows, making traditional investment analysis more complex [64]. Further complicating matters is the finding by Kong, Lin [74] 2021 that analysts may overestimate the negative impacts of certain disasters, particularly salient events like earthquakes. This complex interplay of factors underscores the challenges of accurately assessing and pricing risk for informed investment decisions in an era increasingly defined by natural disasters.

The impact of these events is far from uniform, varying significantly across industries. Akter, Roy and Aktar [75] 2023 sheds light on how disasters involving casualties can create opportunities for market manipulation due to information gaps and emotional responses. However, factors like community resilience, company location, and disaster preparedness can mitigate these risks. Research suggests that companies incurring losses due to extreme weather often increase investments in fixed assets, either for rebuilding or adapting to future climate risks [70]. Interestingly, the study also reveals that older managers may be less inclined to adopt climate-friendly practices, potentially due to a preference for established technologies [70].

Faced with these evolving challenges, businesses are adopting a range of strategies to mitigate the financial risks posed by natural disasters. While insurance payouts and government aid are essential, they often prove insufficient to cover the full extent of losses, especially for large-scale events [63]. This has led to a growing recognition of the importance of proactive measures, with companies increasingly integrating disaster preparedness into their Corporate Social Responsibility (CSR) initiatives. This proactive approach not only strengthens resilience but also resonates with investors, who are more likely to favor companies demonstrating a commitment to sustainability and risk mitigation. This suggests that proactive CSR can enhance company value and potentially reduce the cost of capital.

The financial risks associated with climate change and natural disasters necessitate a reassessment of traditional risk management practices and call for updated financial regulations. The emergence of "climate risk" as a distinct category has spurred research into modeling and assessing these new threats. Financial institutions are increasingly incorporating climate-related scenarios into their stress testing frameworks and integrating climate data into their investment analyses. This shift reflects a growing understanding that climate change is not a distant threat, but a present reality with significant financial implications. Proposals for stress testing financial institutions against climate-related risks are gaining traction, along with calls for regulatory frameworks that incentivize sustainable practices. Ongoing research is exploring the potential for new regulations to mitigate the systemic risks associated with climate change and natural disasters, ensuring financial stability in an increasingly volatile world.

5 Research on Climate Change in Marketing

The specter of climate change hangs heavy over the 21st century, presenting significant challenges and unexpected opportunities for marketers. As climate-related disasters escalate in frequency and intensity, understanding their profound impact on consumer behavior becomes not just important, but crucial for developing effective and ethical marketing strategies. This section provides research on the intricate relationship between disasters and consumerism, exploring how these events influence perceptions, decision-making processes, and, ultimately, engagement with sustainable products and prosocial behaviors.

One of the most significant impacts of climate change is the heightened awareness and concern among consumers, transforming the very landscape of the market. No longer a niche interest, sustainability is now a core value for a growing segment of the population. Consumers, driven by a sense of urgency to mitigate their environmental impact, are actively seeking eco-friendly alternatives. This shift is evident in a study by McKinsey & Company [76], which found that over half of consumers globally expressed a willingness to prioritize sustainable products (e.g., energy-efficient appliances, environmentally friendly packaging) as a means to combat climate change [77]. This presents a significant market opportunity for companies offering sustainable solutions. However, as scholars like Bollinger and Gillingham [78] in 2012 emphasize, successfully capitalizing on this shift requires a deeper understanding of the factors that drive the adoption of such products. To achieve widespread adoption of sustainable solutions in the face of climate change, marketers must move beyond simply providing options and delve deeper into the psychological, social, and economic barriers that hinder consumer adoption, as highlighted by the work of Bollinger and Gillingham [78] 2012.

Mass media plays a pivotal role in shaping public perception and influencing consumer behavior, especially in the context of disasters. News outlets and scientific publications, often using "climate change" and "global warming" interchangeably, wield significant power in framing these issues [79]. The way information is presented—the language, the images—profoundly affects how individuals perceive the severity of climate change and its potential consequences, ultimately influencing consumption choices and actions. This dynamic is evident in Chen, Ghosh [80] in 2019 highlights how media coverage of climate change directly influences consumer behavior. This influence manifests in various ways: shaping risk perception, influencing purchasing decisions, and even encouraging pro-environmental behaviors like reducing carbon footprints.

Taking this understanding of media influence a step further, researchers are employing neuroscientific methods to delve deeper into the psychological mechanisms underlying consumer responses to disaster-related information. Cerf, Greenleaf [81] 2015's pioneering work using single-neuron analysis explores how fear, a powerful emotion often triggered by disaster-related stimuli, can influence behavior. This research sheds light on consumers' capacity to consciously regulate their emotions in response to persuasive messaging—a finding with significant implications for designing effective public service announcements and social marketing campaigns. For instance, a compelling study comparing reactions to a fear-inducing video of a spider versus a video of Al Gore discussing climate change (interspersed with footage of Hurricane Katrina's aftermath) found that individuals could voluntarily increase their fear levels when motivated by a goal. This suggests that framing climate change messages in a way that highlights personal relevance and agency could be effective in promoting pro-environmental behavior.

Beyond media influence, Researchers have explored to understand how choice architecture—the careful design of decision-making environments—affects donation behavior in the wake of disasters is crucial for marketers and policymakers. Research by Evangelidis and Levav [82] in 2013 demonstrates that the presence of "decoy" options within a choice set can significantly influence donation behavior. Specifically, when presented with a donation appeal alongside options strategically designed to highlight the donation's value, individuals were less likely to prioritize the sheer number of people affected by a disaster. This counterintuitive finding has significant implications for fundraising efforts, highlighting the importance of carefully crafting choice architecture to nudge individuals towards prosocial behaviors.

Furthermore, marketing itself can be a powerful tool for driving prosocial behavior following a disaster. Hung and Wyer Jr [83] 2009's research revealed that advertisements designed to evoke empathy and encourage perspective-taking (e.g., featuring compelling imagery of disaster victims) were significantly more effective in eliciting donations than those focused solely on factual information. This highlights the power of emotionally resonant marketing in driving prosocial action. By crafting appeals that connect with individuals on a deeper emotional level, marketers can tap into a wellspring of compassion and inspire contributions to disaster relief efforts.

6   Research on Climate Change in Information Systems

In the face of natural disasters, access to accurate and timely information is paramount. It empowers individuals, communities, and organizations to make informed decisions, coordinate relief efforts, and ultimately save lives. With the rise of technological systems, firms are able to harness the power of information like never before, particularly through Information Systems (IS). These systems have emerged as invaluable tools for disaster management, going beyond immediate response to encompass mitigation, preparedness, and long-term resilience [84].

This represents a paradigm shift in disaster management techniques—moving beyond reactive responses to embracing proactive mitigation, preparedness, and long-term resilience [2]. IS with its ability to collect, analyze, and disseminate vast amounts of data, is proving to be an invaluable tool in this transformation. The following section explores the burgeoning field of IS in disaster management, highlighting its critical role in saving lives, protecting assets, and building more resilient communities.

While IS plays a critical role in coordinating immediate disaster response and recovery efforts, its potential extends far beyond these immediate concerns. Research increasingly focuses on leveraging IS for proactive risk mitigation. By analyzing historical disaster data, IS can identify potential vulnerabilities in infrastructure or geographical areas prone to specific hazards. For instance, geographical information systems (GIS) can model flood zones, aiding authorities in planning evacuation routes and strategically allocating resources for maximum impact [85, 86].

The true power of IS lies in its ability to integrate disparate systems and organizations, creating a seamless flow of communication and coordination between government agencies, relief organizations, and citizens. This interconnectedness is especially crucial during emergencies, where real-time information is paramount. Picture a scenario where mobile apps, fueled by IS, provide citizens with real-time updates on the disaster situation, guiding them to nearby shelters or connecting them with aid. This level of interconnectedness empowers individuals and communities, equipping them to make informed decisions during chaotic times.

Recognizing this critical link between IS and effective disaster management, a growing body of research explores how businesses can leverage these systems not only to survive disasters but also to maintain operational continuity. Disasters often disrupt supply chains, damage critical infrastructure, and cripple communication networks, posing significant challenges for businesses [87]. IS can mitigate these disruptions by providing real-time data on the evolving situation, empowering data-driven decision-making regarding resource allocation, evacuation procedures, and the activation of business continuity plans.

This shift from reactive to proactive disaster management is further fueled by research focused on developing sophisticated models using machine learning algorithms. These models, trained on historical disaster data, can predict future resource demands, allowing businesses to anticipate needs and allocate resources proactively. Imagine a business leveraging such predictive models to ensure the timely delivery of aid to disaster-stricken areas, minimizing losses and potentially saving lives. This proactive approach, enabled by integrating predictive models with existing IS infrastructure, transforms disaster management from a reactive scramble to a strategic and resilient discipline.

The COVID-19 pandemic served as a stark reminder of the critical need for robust, technology-enabled disaster management (DM) [88]. The pandemic exposed the vulnerability of many national health departments worldwide that initially lacked the IT systems to effectively track cases and coordinate responses. This experience underscores the importance of continuous improvement in DM, incorporating lessons learned from past incidents and embracing innovative technologies to build a resilient framework capable of safeguarding communities.

This constant evolution of technology-driven disaster management (TDM) has led to several important trends studied by Researchers. 4 specific TDM that Abbasi et al. 2024 mentions are as follows:

1. **Smart Technologies and Resilience**: The convergence of AI with technologies like the Internet of Things (IoT), robots, image/speech recognition, UAVs, mobile sensors/wearables, and advanced platforms is revolutionizing disaster management [89]. These smart technologies enhance resilience, providing the ability to effectively

absorb, adapt to, and recover from disruptive events [90]. From improved risk assessment and resource allocation to enhanced situational awareness during emergencies, smart technologies are transforming every stage of disaster management [91].

2. **Digital Humanitarianism**: Harnessing the power of digital technologies, data, and online platforms, digital humanitarianism is redefining disaster response and humanitarian aid [92]. Social media and mobile apps are being leveraged to collect and disseminate critical information, coordinate relief efforts, facilitate remote participation, and deliver aid directly to affected communities. While challenges remain, such as addressing potential dehumanization, algorithmic bias, and privacy concerns, the potential of digital humanitarianism to streamline aid and empower communities during crises is undeniable [93].

3. **Integrated Decision-Support Agility**: Enhancing situational awareness and responsiveness during disasters relies on seamless information sharing and collaboration. Integrated decision-support agility, achieved through enterprise-wide and cross-organizational data sharing and systems integration, provides a comprehensive view of the situation, enabling informed decision-making. While challenges exist in aligning organizational capabilities and ensuring consistent cross-organization management strategies, this interconnected approach is crucial for effective and coordinated disaster response [94].

4. **AI-Enabled Early Warning Systems**: Predicting and preparing for natural disasters is becoming increasingly sophisticated with the emergence of AI-enabled early warning systems [95]. These systems utilize machine learning to forecast natural disaster-related phenomena such as intensifying storms, pandemics, earthquakes, and flooding, providing valuable lead time for proactive response measures. As disasters increase in complexity, these intelligent systems will become indispensable in providing timely warnings and enabling effective mitigation strategies [96].

This diverse application of TDM highlights the need for continued research and development to meet the challenges of an increasingly disaster-prone world. A central challenge lies in understanding the interconnectedness of decisions made across different stages of disaster risk management (DRM) – mitigation, preparedness, response, and recovery [97]. Evaluating the impact of strategic decisions across these stages is crucial for developing informed risk management policies and optimizing resource allocation.

Comprehensive decision support systems for disaster management require information systems capable of seamlessly integrating diverse data sources. This includes information on hazards and vulnerabilities, organizational capabilities, and logistical resources. Such integrated systems would enable the development of sophisticated analytical frameworks, enabling informed decision-making and ultimately, saving lives. The integration of predictive and prescriptive models, fueled by real-time data, holds immense potential for transforming disaster management from a reactive to a proactive and resilient discipline, capable of meeting the challenges of an uncertain future. Ultimately, by providing timely insights, coordinating resources, and enabling proactive responses, IS is proving to be an indispensable tool for businesses and communities striving to not only weather the storm but emerge stronger in the face of increasingly frequent and severe disasters.

7 Future Research Areas

While the advances discussed in this chapter demonstrate the growing importance of IS in disaster management, a number of critical questions remain unanswered, paving the way for future research opportunities [98]. The debate between centralized and decentralized IT infrastructure takes on a heightened urgency in disaster-prone contexts. Traditionally, firms have favored centralized data centers for their cost-effectiveness and ease of management. However, this approach becomes a critical vulnerability during disasters. If a localized data center is damaged, vital data becomes inaccessible, crippling business continuity for other branches and operations.

Future research can investigate the viability of hybrid approaches, combining the strengths of both centralized and decentralized systems. For instance, leveraging cloud computing for data redundancy and accessibility [99–102], while maintaining essential local backups, could offer a more resilient solution. However, this necessitates exploring strategies to mitigate the risk of internet outages during disasters, which could disrupt cloud access. This area of research could explore:

- Optimal data distribution strategies: Determining which data sets are critical for local operations and which can be securely stored in the cloud.
- Offline functionality and data synchronization: Developing applications and systems that can operate offline and synchronize data when connectivity is restored.
- Edge computing for disaster scenarios: Exploring how edge computing, which brings computation and data storage closer to the user, can ensure business continuity even when central systems are unavailable.

Beyond the immediate disruption caused by disasters, there is a need to systematically assess their long-term impact on IT infrastructure. This includes quantifying downtime, data loss, and the costs associated with recovery. Armed with this data, researchers can develop more effective mitigation strategies, including:

- Designing resilient IT infrastructure: This involves exploring the trade-offs between cloud-based, hybrid, and edge computing models, considering factors like cost, security, and accessibility in disaster scenarios.
- Leveraging "Power to the Edge" technologies: Investigating how technologies like fog computing, which distributes computing resources across a network, can empower decentralized organizations to operate effectively during disasters, even when central systems are down.
- Optimizing mobile applications for disaster response: Developing mobile apps that provide critical information, facilitate communication, and enable decision-making in offline or low-bandwidth environments.

While technological advancements in IS hold immense potential for disaster response and building resilient communities, it is crucial to acknowledge the stark disparities in their impact across different socioeconomic contexts. The effects of climate-related disasters, for instance, vary significantly between WEIRD (Western, Educated, Industrialized, Rich and Democratic) and GREAT (Growing, Rural, Eastern, Aspirational, Transitional) nations [103–105]. This disparity stems largely from the difference in technological infrastructure.

WEIRD nations, with their advanced technology and robust infrastructure, often possess greater resilience in the face of disruptions. Conversely, GREAT regions, characterized by high population density and limited resources, face unique challenges [106]. The lack of robust technological infrastructure in these areas can lead to more severe and prolonged disruptions in the aftermath of a disaster.

Furthermore, as our reliance on digital platforms grows, so too does vulnerability to climate-induced disruptions. This raises critical questions about the role of technology in both exacerbating and mitigating risks. On one hand, technologies like AI and hybrid organizational models offer promising avenues for enhancing resilience. For example, if an organization with multiple offices experiences flooding in one location, business continuity can be maintained through remote work arrangements or automation. On the other hand, our growing dependence on digital platforms also introduces vulnerabilities [107–110]. The recent Crowdstrike outage, which disrupted airline systems globally, underscores how interconnected and fragile our technological systems can be.

This duality is even more pronounced in the context of climate change. Events like extreme weather can trigger cascading failures in critical infrastructure, amplifying the impact on daily life. For instance, in India, a failure of the Unified Payments Interface (UPI) due to a climate-related event could halt transactions nationwide, while the collapse of a food delivery platform could disrupt access to essential goods. Given the heavy reliance on technology for business operations, supply chains, and consumer services [111], the potential for IT infrastructure failure during climate events is a significant concern. Future research must therefore explore strategies to bridge the digital divide and ensure that technological advancements contribute to equitable and resilient societies in the face of climate change.

References

1. Achenbach, J.: The Century of Disasters. Slate, vol. 13. The Slate Group (2011)
2. Altay, N., Ramirez, A.: Impact of disasters on firms in different sectors: implications for supply chains. J. Supply Chain Manag. **46**(4), 59–80 (2010)
3. Abbasi, A., Dillon, R., Rao, H.R., Liu Sheng, O.R.: Preparedness and response in the century of disasters: overview of information systems research frontiers. Inform. Syst. Res. **35**(2), 460–468 (2024)
4. Chou, C.-H., Zahedi, F.M., Zhao, H.: Ontology-based evaluation of natural disaster management websites. MIS Q. **38**(4), 997–1016 (2014)
5. Gourieroux, C., Monfort, A., Mouabbi, S., Renne, J.-P.: Disastrous defaults. Rev. Finan. **25**(6), 1727–1772 (2021)
6. Paciarotti, C., Valiakhmetova, I.: Evaluating disaster operations management: an outcome-process integrated approach. Prod. Oper. Manag. **30**(2), 543–562 (2021)
7. Gillman, M., Kejak, M., Pakoš, M.: Learning about rare disasters: implications for consumption and asset prices. Rev. Finan. **19**(3), 1053–1104 (2015)
8. Lockwood, M.: The political sustainability of climate policy: the case of the UK climate change act. Glob. Environ. Chang. **23**(5), 1339–1348 (2013)
9. Liu, Y., Li, X., Zheng, Z.: Smart natural disaster relief: assisting victims with artificial intelligence in lending. Inf. Syst. Res. **35**(2), 489–504 (2024)
10. Oetzel, J., Oh, C.H.: A storm is brewing: antecedents of disaster preparation in risk prone locations. Strateg. Manag. J. **42**(8), 1545–1570 (2021)

11. Muller, A., Kräussl, R.: Doing good deeds in times of need: a strategic perspective on corporate disaster donations. Strateg. Manag. J. **32**(9), 911–929 (2011)
12. Aggarwal, V.A., Posen, H.E., Workiewicz, M.: Adaptive capacity to technological change: a microfoundational approach. Strateg. Manag. J. **38**(6), 1212–1231 (2017)
13. Dahlhamer, J.M., D'Souza, M.J.: Determinants of business-disaster preparedness in two US metropolitan areas. Int. J. Mass Emerg. Disasters **15**(2), 265–281 (1997)
14. Lampel, J., Shamsie, J., Shapira, Z.: Experiencing the improbable: rare events and organizational learning. Organ. Sci. **20**(5), 835–845 (2009)
15. Christianson, M.K., Farkas, M.T., Sutcliffe, K.M., Weick, K.E.: Learning through rare events: significant interruptions at the Baltimore & Ohio Railroad Museum. Organ. Sci. **20**(5), 846–860 (2009)
16. Haimes, Y.Y.: On the complex definition of risk: a systems-based approach. Risk Anal.: an Int. J. **29**(12), 1647–1654 (2009)
17. Miceli, R., Sotgiu, I., Settanni, M.: Disaster preparedness and perception of flood risk: a study in an alpine valley in Italy. J. Environ. Psychol. **28**(2), 164–173 (2008)
18. Slovic, P. The Perception of Risk (London-Sterling, Va: Earthscan) (2000)
19. Wachinger, G., Renn, O., Begg, C., Kuhlicke, C.: The risk perception paradox—implications for governance and communication of natural hazards. Risk Anal. **33**(6), 1049–1065 (2013)
20. Oetzel, J.M., Oh, C.H.: Learning to carry the cat by the tail: firm experience, disasters, and multinational subsidiary entry and expansion. Organ. Sci. **25**(3), 732–756 (2014)
21. Lewis, T.: Why people dont learn from natural disasters (2013)
22. Wenzel, M., Stanske, S., Lieberman, M.B.: Strategic responses to crisis. Strateg. Manag. J. **41**(7/18), 3161 (2020)
23. Bruton, G.D., Ahlstrom, D., Wan, J.C.: Turnaround in east asian firms: evidence from ethnic overseas Chinese communities. Strateg. Manag. J. **24**(6), 519–540 (2003)
24. Pearce, J.A., II., Robbins, K.: Toward improved theory and research on business turnaround. J. Manage. **19**(3), 613–636 (1993)
25. Benner, M.J., Zenger, T.: The lemons problem in markets for strategy. Strategy Sci. **1**(2), 71–89 (2016)
26. Gartenberg, C.: Do parents matter? Effects of lender affiliation through the mortgage boom and bust. Manage. Sci. **60**(11), 2776–2793 (2014)
27. Ndofor, H.A., Vanevenhoven, J., Barker, V.L., III.: Software firm turnarounds in the 1990s: an analysis of reversing decline in a growing, dynamic industry. Strateg. Manag. J. **34**(9), 1123–1133 (2013)
28. Barker, K., Haimes, Y.Y.: Assessing uncertainty in extreme events: applications to risk-based decision making in interdependent infrastructure sectors. Reliab. Eng. Syst. Saf. **94**(4), 819–829 (2009)
29. de Figueiredo, R.J.P., Feldman, E.R., Rawley, Evan: The costs of refocusing: evidence from hedge fund closures during the financial crisis. Strateg. Manag. J. **40**(8), 1268–1290 (2019)
30. Wenzel, M.: Path dependence and the stabilization of strategic premises: how the funeral industry buries itself. Bus. Res. **8**, 265–299 (2015)
31. Pacheco-de-Almeida, G.: Erosion, time compression, and self-displacement of leaders in hypercompetitive environments. Strateg. Manag. J. **31**(13), 1498–1526 (2010)
32. Chakrabarti, A.: Organizational adaptation in an economic shock: the role of growth reconfiguration. Strateg. Manag. J. **36**(11), 1717–1738 (2015)
33. Bryson, J.M.: A perspective on planning and crises in the public sector. Strateg. Manag. J. **2**(2), 181–196 (1981)
34. Rosenbloom, R.S.: Leadership, capabilities, and technological change: the transformation of NCR in the electronic era. Strateg. Manag. J. **21**(10–11), 1083–1103 (2000)

35. Roy, R., Lampert, C.M., Stoyneva, I.: When dinosaurs fly: the role of firm capabilities in the 'avianization' of incumbents during disruptive technological change. Strateg. Entrep. J. **12**(2), 261–284 (2018)

36. Reymen, I.M., Andries, P., Berends, H., Mauer, R., Stephan, U., Van Burg, E.: Understanding dynamics of strategic decision making in venture creation: a process study of effectuation and causation. Strateg. Entrep. J. **9**(4), 351–379 (2015)

37. Argyres, N., Bigelow, L., Nickerson, J.A.: Dominant designs, innovation shocks, and the follower's dilemma. Strateg. Manag. J. **36**(2), 216–234 (2015)

38. Burgelman, R.A.: A process model of strategic business exit: Implications for an evolutionary perspective on strategy. Strateg. Manag. J. **17**(S1), 193–214 (1996)

39. Dai, L., Eden, L., Beamish, P.W.: Caught in the crossfire: dimensions of vulnerability and foreign multinationals' exit from war-afflicted countries. Strateg. Manag. J. **38**(7), 1478–1498 (2017)

40. Moulton, W.N., Thomas, H.: Bankruptcy as a deliberate strategy: theoretical considerations and empirical evidence. Strateg. Manag. J. **14**(2), 125–135 (1993)

41. Carnahan, S.: Blocked but not tackled: who founds new firms when rivals dissolve? Strateg. Manag. J. **38**(11), 2189–2212 (2017)

42. Ren, C.R., Hu, Y., Cui, T.H.: Responses to rival exit: Product variety, market expansion, and preexisting market structure. Strateg. Manag. J. **40**(2), 253–276 (2019)

43. Zhang, Y., Richter, A.R., Shanthikumar, J.G., Shen, Z.J.M.: Dynamic inventory relocation in disaster relief. Prod. Oper. Manag. **31**(3), 1052–1070 (2022)

44. Stumpf, J., Besiou, M., Wakolbinger, T.: Supply chain preparedness: how operational settings, product and disaster characteristics affect humanitarian responses. Prod. Oper. Manag. **32**(8), 2491–2509 (2023)

45. MacKenzie, C.A., Barker, K., Santos, J.R.: Modeling a severe supply chain disruption and post-disaster decision making with application to the Japanese earthquake and Tsunami. IIE Trans. **46**(12), 1243–1260 (2014)

46. Yomiuri, D.: One year after the disaster: 20% of disaster-hit businesses still closed (2012)

47. Nakata, H., Ripples from Thai floods splash Japan. Japan Times (2011)

48. Hendricks, K.B., Singhal, V.R.: The effect of demand–supply mismatches on firm risk. Prod. Oper. Manag. **23**(12), 2137–2151 (2014)

49. Hendricks, K.B., Jacobs, B.W., Singhal, V.R.: Stock market reaction to supply chain disruptions from the 2011 Great East Japan Earthquake. Manuf. Serv. Oper. Manag. **22**(4), 683–699 (2020)

50. Jahre, M., Kembro, J., Rezvanian, T., Ergun, O., Håpnes, S.J., Berling, P.: Integrating supply chains for emergencies and ongoing operations in UNHCR. J. Oper. Manag. **45**, 57–72 (2016)

51. Lewin, R., Besiou, M., Lamarche, J.-B., Cahill, S., Guerrero-Garcia, S.: Delivering in a moving world… looking to our supply chains to meet the increasing scale, cost and complexity of humanitarian needs. J. Humanitarian Logistics Supp. Chain Manag. **8**(4), 518–532 (2018)

52. Kunz, N., Reiner, G., Gold, S.: Investing in disaster management capabilities versus prepositioning inventory: a new approach to disaster preparedness. Int. J. Prod. Econ. **157**, 261–272 (2014)

53. Luther, L.: Managing disaster debris: Overview of regulatory requirements, agency roles, and selected challenges. Congressional Research Service, Library of Congress (2008)

54. Çelik, M., Ergun, Ö., Keskinocak, P.: The post-disaster debris clearance problem under incomplete information. Oper. Res. **63**(1), 65–85 (2015)

55. Besiou, M., Pedraza-Martinez, A.J., Van Wassenhove, L.N.: Vehicle supply chains in humanitarian operations: decentralization, operational mix, and earmarked funding. Prod. Oper. Manag. **23**(11), 1950–1965 (2014)

56. Rodríguez-Espíndola, O., Albores, P., Brewster, C.: Disaster preparedness in humanitarian logistics: a collaborative approach for resource management in floods. Eur. J. Oper. Res. **264**(3), 978–993 (2018)
57. Balcik, B., Ak, D.: Supplier selection for framework agreements in humanitarian relief. Prod. Oper. Manag. **23**(6), 1028–1041 (2014)
58. Jahre, M., Jahre, M.: Logistics preparedness and response: a case of strategic change. In: Villa, S., Urrea, G., Castañeda, J.A., Larsen, E.R. (eds.) Decision-making in humanitarian operations, pp. 3–29. Springer, Cham (2019). https://doi.org/10.1007/978-3-319-91509-8_1
59. Balcik, B., Beamon, B.M.: Facility location in humanitarian relief. Int. J. Logist. **11**(2), 101–121 (2008)
60. Noy, I.: The macroeconomic consequences of disasters. J. Dev. Econ. **88**(2), 221–231 (2009)
61. Cavallo, E., Noy, I.: Natural disasters and the economy—a survey. Int. Rev. Environ. Resour. Econ. **5**(1), 63–102 (2011)
62. Kirchberger, M.: Natural disasters and labor markets. J. Dev. Econ. **125**, 40–58 (2017)
63. Schüwer, U., Lambert, C., Noth, F.: How do banks react to catastrophic events? Evidence from Hurricane Katrina. Rev. Finan. **23**(1), 75–116 (2019)
64. Huang, H.H., Kerstein, J., Wang, C.: The impact of climate risk on firm performance and financing choices: an international comparison. J. Int. Bus. Stud. **49**, 633–656 (2018)
65. Garmaise, M.J., Moskowitz, T.J.: Catastrophic risk and credit markets. J. Financ. **64**(2), 657–707 (2009)
66. Chavaz, M.: Dis-integrating credit markets: diversification, securitization, and lending in a recovery (2016)
67. Cortés, K.R., Strahan, P.E.: Tracing out capital flows: how financially integrated banks respond to natural disasters. J. Financ. Econ. **125**(1), 182–199 (2017)
68. Berger, A.N., Bouwman, C.H., Kim, D.: Small bank comparative advantages in alleviating financial constraints and providing liquidity insurance over time. Rev/ Financ. Stud. **30**(10), 3416–3454 (2017)
69. Cortés, K.R.: Rebuilding after disaster strikes: How local lenders aid in the recovery (2014)
70. Benincasa, E., Betz, F., Gattini, L.: How do firms cope with losses from extreme weather events? J. Corp. Finan. **84**, 102508 (2024)
71. Koetter, M., Noth, F., Rehbein, O.: Borrowers under water! Rare disasters, regional banks, and recovery lending. J. Financ. Intermediation **43**, 100811 (2020)
72. Alok, S., Kumar, N., Wermers, R.: Do fund managers misestimate climatic disaster risk. Rev. Financ. Stud. **33**(3), 1146–1183 (2020)
73. Krueger, S., Winkler, J., Schumann, R.L.: Residential taxable value recovery in coastal Mississippi after Hurricane Katrina. In: Local Disaster Management, pp. 80–101. Routledge (2020)
74. Kong, D., Lin, Z., Wang, Y., Xiang, J.: Natural disasters and analysts' earnings forecasts. J. Corp. Finan. **66**, 101860 (2021)
75. Akter, R., Roy, T., Aktar, R.: The challenges of women in post-disaster health management: a study in Khulna District. Int. J. Disaster Risk Manage. **5**(1), 51–66 (2023)
76. Frey, S., Am, J.B., Noble, S.: Consumers Care About Sustainability—and Back It Up with Their Wallets. McKinsey & Company (2023)
77. Bonini, S.M., Oppenheim, J.M.: Helping 'green'products grow. McKinsey Q. **3**(2), 1–8 (2008)
78. Bollinger, B., Gillingham, K.: Peer effects in the diffusion of solar photovoltaic panels. Mark. Sci. **31**(6), 900–912 (2012)
79. Yanovitzky, I., Stryker, J.: Mass media, social norms, and health promotion efforts: a longitudinal study of media effects on youth binge drinking. Commun. Res. **28**(2), 208–239 (2001)

80. Chen, Y., Ghosh, M., Liu, Y., Zhao, L.: Media coverage of climate change and sustainable product consumption: evidence from the hybrid vehicle market. J. Mark. Res. **56**(6), 995–1011 (2019)
81. Cerf, M., Greenleaf, E., Meyvis, T., Morwitz, V.G.: Using single-neuron recording in marketing: opportunities, challenges, and an application to fear enhancement in communications. J. Mark. Res. **52**(4), 530–545 (2015)
82. Evangelidis, I., Levav, J.: Prominence versus dominance: how relationships between alternatives drive decision strategy and choice. J. Mark. Res. **50**(6), 753–766 (2013)
83. Hung, I.W., Wyer, R.S., Jr.: Differences in perspective and the influence of charitable appeals: when imagining oneself as the victim is not beneficial. J. Mark. Res. **46**(3), 421–434 (2009)
84. Park, I., Sharman, R., Rao, H.R.: Disaster experience and hospital information systems: an examination of perceived information assurance, risk, resilience, and his usefulness. MIS Q. **39**, 317–344 (2015)
85. Al-Ankary, K.: An incremental approach for establishing a geographical information system in a developing country: Saudi Arabia. Int. J. Geogr. Inform. Syst. **5**(1), 85–98 (1991)
86. Sternad Zabukovšek, S., Tominc, P., Bobek, S., Štrukelj, T.: Spatial exploration of economic data—insight into attitudes of students towards interdisciplinary knowledge. ISPRS Int. J. Geo-Inform. **9**(7), 421 (2020)
87. Jacobs, B.W., Singhal, V.R.: The effect of the Rana Plaza disaster on shareholder wealth of retailers: implications for sourcing strategies and supply chain governance. J. Oper. Manag. **49**, 52–66 (2017)
88. Security, H., National Preparedness Goal (2015)
89. Yang, C., Hu, Z., Zhou, S.X.: Multilocation newsvendor problem: centralization and inventory pooling. Manage. Sci. **67**(1), 185–200 (2021)
90. Francis, R., Bekera, B.: A metric and frameworks for resilience analysis of engineered and infrastructure systems. Reliab. Eng. Syst. Saf. **121**, 90–103 (2014)
91. Cañavera-Herrera, J.S., Tang, J., Nochta, T., Schooling, J.M.: On the relation between 'resilience' and 'smartness': a critical review. Int. J. Disaster Risk Reduction **75**, 102970 (2022)
92. Kumar, A., Joshi, S., Sharma, M., Vishvakarma, N.: Digital humanitarianism and crisis management: an empirical study of antecedents and consequences. J. Humanitarian Logistics Supply Chain Manage. **12**(4), 570–593 (2022)
93. Devidal, P.: 'Back to basics' with a digital twist: humanitarian principles and dilemmas in the digital age (2023)
94. Oktari, R.S., Munadi, K., Idroes, R., Sofyan, H.: Knowledge management practices in disaster management: Systematic review. Int. J. Disaster Risk Reduct. **51**, 101881 (2020)
95. Yabe, T., Rao, P.S.C., Ukkusuri, S.V., Cutter, S.L.: Toward data-driven, dynamical complex systems approaches to disaster resilience. Proc. Natl. Acad. Sci. **119**(8), e2111997119 (2022)
96. Wever, M., Shah, M., O'Leary, N.: Designing early warning systems for detecting systemic risk: a case study and discussion. Futures **136**, 102882 (2022)
97. Suarez, D., Gomez, C., Medaglia, A.L., Akhavan-Tabatabaei, R., Grajales, S.: Integrated decision support for disaster risk management: aiding preparedness and response decisions in wildfire management. Inform. Syst. Res. **35**(2), 609–628 (2024)
98. Kathuria, A., Sonpatki, R., Andrade, M., Saldanha, T.: Apocalypse now (or later?): climate change and non-implementation of IT applications. In: Proceedings of the International Conference on Information Systems (ICIS) (2024)
99. Kathuria, A., Mann, A., Khuntia, J., Saldanha, T.J., Kauffman, R.J.: A strategic value appropriation path for cloud computing. J. Manag. Inf. Syst. **35**(3), 740–775 (2018)

100. Jha, S., Chaturvedi, D.: Systematic literature review of cloud computing research between 2010 and 2023. In: Kathuria, A., Karhade, P.P., Zhao, K., Chaturvedi, D. (eds.) Digital Transformation in the Viral Age: 21st Workshop on e-Business, WeB 2022, Copenhagen, Denmark, December 10, 2022, Revised Selected Papers, pp. 64 88. Springer Nature Switzerland, Cham (2024). https://doi.org/10.1007/978-3-031-60003-6_5

101. Jha, S., Kathuria, A.: How firm age and size influence value creation from cloud computing. In: Proceedings of the International Conference on Information Systems (ICIS). Hyderabad (2023)

102. Mann, A., Kathuria, A., Khuntia, J., Saldanha, T.: Cloud-integration and business flexibility: the mediating role of cloud functional capabilities. In" Proceedings of the Americas Conference on Information Systems (AMCIS). San Diego (2016)

103. Karhade, P., Kathuria, A.: Missing impact of ratings on platform participation in India: a call for research in GREAT domains. Commun. Assoc. Inf. Syst. 47(1), 19 (2020)

104. Karhade, P., Kathuria, A., Dasgupta, A., Malik, O., Konsynski, B.R.: Decolonization of digital platforms: a research agenda for GREAT domains. In: Garimella, A., Karhade, P., Kathuria, A., Liu, X., Xu, J., Zhao, K. (eds.) The Role of e-Business During the Time of Grand Challenges. WEB 2020. Lecture Notes in Business Information Processing, pp. 51–58. Springer, Cham (2021)

105. Henrich, J., Heine, S.J., Norenzayan, A.: The weirdest people in the world? Behav. Brain Sci. 33(2–3), 61–83 (2010)

106. Dasgupta, A., Karhade, P., Kathuria, A., Konsynski, B.: Holding space for voices that do not speak: design reform of rating systems for platforms in GREAT economies. In: Proceedings of the Hawaii International Conference on System Sciences (HICCS). Virtual (2021)

107. Kathuria, A., Karhade, P.P., Konsynski, B.R.: In the realm of hungry ghosts: multi-level theory for supplier participation on digital platforms. J. Manag. Inf. Syst. 37(2), 396–430 (2020)

108. Karhade, P., Kathuria, A., Konsynski, B.: When choice matters: assortment and participation for performance on digital platforms. In: Proceedings of the Hawaii International Conference on System Sciences (HICCS). Virtual (2021)

109. Karhade, P., Kathuria, A., Malik, O., Konsynski, B.: Digital platforms and infobesity: a research agenda. In: Garimella, A., Karhade, P., Kathuria, A., Liu, X., Xu, J., Zhao, K. (eds.) The Role of e-Business during the Time of Grand Challenges: 19th Workshop on e-Business, WeB 2020, Virtual Event, December 12, 2020, Revised Selected Papers, pp. 67–74. Springer International Publishing, Cham (2021). https://doi.org/10.1007/978-3-030-79454-5_7

110. Fu, X., Avenyo, E., Ghauri, P.: Digital platforms and development: a survey of the literature. Innov. Dev. 11(2–3), 303–321 (2021)

111. Khuntia, J., Kathuria, A., Andrade Rojas, M.G.. Saldanha, T.: Supply chain information integration and firm performance: evidence from India. In: Proceedings of the Americas Conference on Information Systems (AMCIS). Boston (2017)

ESG Risk Assessment Tool for Indian Small and Medium Enterprises

Asha Prasuna$^{(\boxtimes)}$ ⓘ and S. N. V. Siva Kumar ⓘ

Department of Economics, K J Somaiya Institute of Management, Somaiya Vidyavihar University [SVU], Vidyavihar [E], Mumbai 400077, India
{ashasivakumar,sivakumar}@somaiya.edu

Abstract. Small and Medium Enterprises [SMEs] have been contributing 30.27 percent to the gross domestic product and 49% to exports of India. There have been many success stories of Indian SMEs that have become global entities. Business entities are increasingly becoming conscious about protecting the environment, addressing social factors, and adhering to governance (ESG). ESG score has an impact on SMEs' financial performance, stock price movement, risk profile, and liquidity. Various financial and database service providers have been computing ESG scores based on the published data that quantify the ESG components. The current research aims to analyze ESG risks of listed Indian SME companies that will enhance the knowledge of ESG risks for all stakeholders. The objective of the research is to propose a web/mobile-based tool that can assess the impacts of ESG risks on the financial performance of Indian SMEs.

Keywords: Risk management · computer Software tools · environment · social · governance

1 Introduction

1.1 Introduction to Information Systems iS Research in India

Research in India on Information Systems (IS) has evolved over the decades. Much work has examined the adoption and impacts of information technology (IT) in the past. This research has shown that the use of Information Systems in business enhances efficiency in processes, cost reductions, manpower management, and reporting and regulatory compliance. For example, Bhagwat and Sharma [1] conducted an exploratory study on Management Information Systems in small and medium enterprises (SMEs) in India. Dincer and Dincer [2] in 2016 carried out a literature review on the use of Technology Information Systems in Indian SMEs. Significant work currently focuses on the application of innovative IT and the role of artificial intelligence (AI) and machine learning (ML). For example, Kulkarni, Joseph and Patil [3] 2023 studied the role of artificial Intelligence in sustainability reporting by leveraging ESG theory into action. An exciting new context is the implementation of environmental, social, and governance (ESG) practices that were laid down under Sustainable Development Goals and information systems. For example, Nulkar [4] 2019 elaborated on the concepts, methodologies, and tools for environmentally sustainable practices for SMEs.

© The Author(s), under exclusive license to Springer Nature Switzerland AG 2025
A. Kathuria et al. (Eds.): WeB 2023, LNBIP 525, pp. 168–181, 2025.
https://doi.org/10.1007/978-3-031-74437-2_13

A fundamental concern is that the majority of IS theories have been developed in the context of Western countries – which are categorized together in the framework of western, educated, industrialized, rich, and democratic (WEIRD) countries [5]. Applicability of these theories to growing, rural, Eastern, aspirational, and transitional (GREAT) domains [6] that have significant differences in terms of population and economic output is questionable [6–8]. Hence, special attention is required while developing theories with an implicit assumption of replication of WEIRD theories for GREAT nations. Researchers need to incorporate the plurality of the GREAT nations to reflect the applicability of the theories. Other areas in management have expended significant research in the Indian context [9–11]. Barring a few exceptions [11–18], there is less research in IS that uses India as a context for theory or data. Since India is the fastest-growing major economy and largest democracy, there is a recent trend of increasing IS research in India [10, 11, 19–27] and calls for such research [15, 28–32]. These are good beginnings, indeed.

1.2   Introduction to SMEs in India

Economic liberalization reforms initiated in 1991 resulted in the rise of SMEs, with many entrepreneurs venturing into this domain. The policy thrust in the last decade also enhanced the vibrant growth of SMEs in India. The emergence of the internet, digital payments systems, and other innovative technologies implementation led to the increase in SMEs in IT and non-IT services, pharmaceuticals, auto components, health care, and textile domains. Some of the Indian SMEs produced superior products and services that the global players recognized. Classification of the MSMEs and definitions as per law[1] is provided in Appendix 1.

Financing, technical and other support required to create an efficient system for the Indian SMEs, the government of India had initiated various schemes using the technology platforms right from registration [UDYAM portal] 2 to supply of funds, certification, tax payments, and dissemination of information processes.

With a thrust on providing and enhancing the Indian SME ecosystem, the government of India has undertaken various initiatives. In terms of policy support, the establishment of a Credit Guarantee Trust for Micro and Small Enterprises is being implemented to provide collateral-free credit to MSMEs. The Cluster Development Program aims to provide common facility centers in terms of infrastructure development, marketing hubs, and facilities to host exhibition centers by various associations. Schemes for skill development and training, technological upgradation, incentives for MSME sustainable Zero Defect [ZED][2], incubators funding, improve IPR culture for SME products and services were among the major initiatives that supported the growth in SME sector.

Indian SME success stories in the recent past include Arvind Eyecare, Jain Irrigation, Desicrew, and Waste Ventures India. SMEs had to adapt to the COVID-19 challenges in terms of handling demand dips, liquidity crunch, and production lags. With the support of government relief and various programs like cluster-based approach, skill development

---

[1] https://msme.gov.in/faqs/q1-what-definition-msme.

[2] http://www.zed.msme.gov.in/.

schemes, MSME Sambandh portal, Sampark platform, Udayam for registrations helped the sector to cope with the challenges and bounce back.

Recent data indicate that there are 6.33 crore units of SMEs among which 96% are proprietary units, spread across urban 49% and rural 51%. This sector provides employment to the tune of 11.10 crore people, mostly in the unorganized sector. Emerging sectors in SMEs include automotive, biotech, chemicals, electronics, food and agriculture, industrial manufacturing, pharma, renewable energy, textile continue to be resilient and bouncing back with all the relief and support programs. SMEs in India contribute significantly in terms of employment and exports and support large industries as well as contribute to the GDP. The policy initiatives aimed at strengthening the entrepreneurial mindset have resulted in vibrant growth and performance of the SME sector. Data published in the SME Annual Report 2022–23[3] that were classified, consisting of 36,75,597 enterprises registered under the Manufacturing category and 94,18,101 enterprises registered under the Service sector as of 2023. Recent data indicate that there are 6.33 crore units of SMEs among which 96% are proprietary units, spread across urban 49% and rural 51%. This sector provides employment to the tune of 11.10 crore people, mostly in the unorganized sector. India hosts a remarkable 63 million micro, small, and medium enterprises, which collectively employ approximately 110 million individuals and contribute to nearly one-third of the country's gross domestic product (GDP).

1.3   Significance of Government Schemes for Indian SME's

Advances in technology and innovations the government of India has undertaken various IT and ICT-based schemes to support small and medium-sized enterprises, which have a substantial influence on employment, international trade, and innovation, all of which are critical to India's economic growth. The MySME mobile app[4] provides entrepreneurs to apply for various government funding schemes and can track the status of their applications. The Direct Benefit Transfer [DBT] scheme helps to transfer funds to various inter-governmental bodies in terms of cash, kind or composite of both is operational for seven schemes. Digital Payment System [DPS] consisted of 97.67% in terms of value and 88.64% in numbers that occurred during 2022–23 among the MSME Ministry and its attached agencies to fasten the fund transfers and ensure to reach to the respective SME entrepreneurs.

MSME Sampark is another portal that aligns the job seekers and providers, which the aspirants of both sides have used. Statistics reported indicate that as of 2023, job seeker registrations were 4,80,511, resumes were 49,415, and recruiters were 6469. Job offers were made to 33,593 job seekers. Creation of Harmonious Application of Modern Processes for Increasing the Output and National Strength [CHAMPION], which was based on ICT, was started on 01–06-2020 to support SMEs' handholding, dissemination of information, and providing new business opportunities. 53 central public sector enterprises [CPSEs] and 58 banks, including 19 private sector banks, handle the credit issues and resolve grievances of SMEs by appointing nodal officers [Annual Report 2022–23].

---

[3] https://msme.gov.in/sites/default/files/msmeannualreport2022-23english.pdf.

[4] https://my.msme.gov.in/MyMsme/Reg/welcome.htm.

1.4 Select Review of Literature

Empirical research in the Indian context, specifically on sustainability and ESG frame-work for SMEs, is in a nascent stage. Due to availability of data and for large enterprises, there have been many research papers examining the impact of ESG on firm performance Maji and Lohia [33] [2023]. Lunawat and Lunawat [34] [2022] examined ESG impact firm performance in Indian context sustainability reporting practices and their impact on stock price performance. Shikha, Tuteja and Dhingra [35] [2022] examined sec-toral differences in ESG practices in Indian context. Other studies include ESG and its impacts on firms' financial performance that include Clark, Feiner and Viehs [36] [2015], Domanović [37] [2022], Eccles, Ioannou and Serafeim [38] [2014], Ferrell, Liang and Renneboog [39] [2016], Sachdeva, Kathuria [27] [2015], Fulton, Kahn and Sharples [40] [2012], Ge, Xiao [41] [2022], Henisz, Koller and Nuttall [42] [2019], and Lee, Marshall [43] [2015]. Sharma, Panday and Dangwal [44] [2020] studied the determinants of ESG disclosures for Indian companies.

Increased attention for conducting research and to the implementation of technolog-ical innovations and AI, tools call for integration of SME ESG domain specific research along with the IS tools and applicability that can provide opportunities for IT sector players and also enhance business productivity and performance.

1.5 Research Gaps

In recent past, there has been academic research in analyzing the impact of ESG scores on the financial performance of the business entities like asset management companies, banks, listed companies and logistics and manufacturing companies. Based on select literature review, on the credit risk rating front, the existing rating agencies provide the rating reports that are required for the SME when applying for a loan from a bank or financial institution. These rating agencies currently assess only credit risk based on the risks like business, financial, management, client base, etc. This rating has an impact on the company share price performance as well as the interest cost. Top rated companies tend to have an advantage of lower borrowing cost from the funding agencies or banks.

Recent focus on sustainable business and Business Responsibility and Sustainable Reporting [BRSR] regulations in force, all listed companies are required to comply with the ESG mandate. The existing rating agencies provide only credit ratings, and just recently, they started computing and publishing the ESG ratings. CRISIL floated a 100% subsidiary that provides ESG rating which got the regulator RBI approval.

One observation on these ratings is that these ESG ratings do not segregate the companies into manufacturing and services SMEs where the factors and components to compute ESG score need specific attention and differential weightage. Further, in the services sector, segregation of IT services and non-IT services needs to be carried out as the components for capturing ESG effects are different for both sets of companies.

Our current research focuses on creating ESG scores separately for Indian SME man-ufacturing and services sector companies, which is a novelty and a specific contribution to the existing research. Also, it proposes that in credit appraisal, banks, and financial institutions must consider both credit risk and ESG risk. This will provide incentives to SMEs in terms of complying with ESG norms. The proportion can be 75:25 or 70:30 based on the loan portfolio of the respective lending institution.

1.6 Research Questions

We ask the following four research questions.

1. Are the published ESG scores relevant to be used for Indian SME companies' ESG risk assessment?
2. What is the need for having separate ESG scores for Indian manufacturing and services SMEs?
3. Can we use innovative technology-based AI tools to measure the ESG risks of Indian SMEs?
4. How do we carry out the impact analysis of ESG on the financial performance of SMEs?

1.7 Objectives

Thus, our research objectives are as below.

1. To critically analyze existing ESG scores provided by select agencies.
2. To propose ESG components for constructing the Index for Manufacturing and Services sector SME companies separately
3. To create a web-based mobile tool to compute the ESG scores and Reports.
4. Propose a model to study the impact of ESG rating on financial performance of SMEs.

2   Proposed ESG Model for SMEs

The ESG risk score tool is developed considering different categories of risks namely, environment, social and governance. Within each of these risks the sub-factors are identified, giving weightage, and quantified using company-specific disclosures. The scoring model will have weights to all the attributes and comes out with an eight-point scale as per the Basel-III Norms. This tool helps SME internally for use and tracking the ESG score over a period. Once this model is estimated to capture the initial information and analyze to get insights into the performance of SMEs on ESG front. Over regular intervals, the performance of SMEs and associated risks can be monitored, and reports generated that provide insights about the business performance and corrective actions needed.

2.1 Specification of SME ESG Risk Assessment Model

Equations (1), (2) and (3) provide an analytical expression for each composite risk score. Equations (4), (5) and (6) specify these direct and indirect links to risk factors. The model equations in matrix form in eq. (7) and (8) contain the analytical solution for the structural equations in our model.

2.2 Specification 1 of the SEM

The composite Environment risk index is constructed from 10 sub-components, with parameter φ_i being the weight of each sub-factor towards the composite as:

$$Env = \sum_{i=1}^{10} \varphi_i Env_i \tag{1}$$

Composite Social index is constructed from 10 sub-components with parameter τ_i being weight of each sub-factor towards the Social composite as:

$$Soc = \sum_{i=1}^{10} \tau_i Soc_i \tag{2}$$

Composite Governance index is constructed from 10 sub-components with parameter μ_i composite as:

$$Gov = \sum_{i=1}^{10} \mu_i Gov_i \tag{3}$$

Then risk is modeled as a latent factor from the above three composite factors representing ESG factors.

Specification 2

The SEM model equations to derive the direct effect can be explained as follows:

$$K_1 + A.K_1 + E.K_1 = Env.R \tag{4}$$

$$AK_2 + K_2 + B.K_2 = Soc.R \tag{5}$$

$$CK_3 + B.K_3 + K_3 = Gov.R \tag{6}$$

$$\begin{bmatrix} 1 & A & E \\ A & 1 & B \\ C & B & 1 \end{bmatrix} \begin{bmatrix} K_1 \\ K_2 \\ K_3 \end{bmatrix} = \begin{bmatrix} Env.R \\ Soc.R \\ Gov.R \end{bmatrix} \tag{7}$$

Solution

$$\begin{bmatrix} K_1 \\ K_2 \\ K_3 \end{bmatrix} = \begin{bmatrix} 1 & A & E \\ A & 1 & B \\ C & B & 1 \end{bmatrix}^{-1} \begin{bmatrix} Env.R \\ Soc.R \\ Gov.R \end{bmatrix} \tag{8}$$

2.3 Research Methodology

The study employs both secondary and primary data analysis. Secondary data of the SMEs are collected from the annual reports of the respective companies. Panel data estimation models are being used to test the hypothesis.

Primary data are being collected from the below mentioned sample size of listed Indian SMEs. The above proposed model is being used to prepare a survey questionnaire to collect primary data from the respondents. The responses are being analyzed using PLS-SEM software.

Sample size details are mentioned below:

- As of March 2024, BSE has 483 companies listed on this platform with a total market capitalization ₹1,36,314.21.
- The NSE Emerge has around 397 companies listed as of early 2024 with a combined market capitalization of over ₹1 lakh Crore.
- Compiled published data for 351 SMEs is being used for analysis.

2.4 ESG Components

As a part of sustainability, the ESG components are drawn for all listed SMEs and grouped into three categories. Weights are given separately for manufacturing and services companies (IT and Non-IT) based on the criticality of the sub-factor instead of using the same weights for both sectors.

The questionnaire was prepared on a Likert scale of 1–5, and respondents were requested to fill in the details. Once data is collected using the above-mentioned SEM model the ESG risks were computed.

The sub-components of each of the factors in the scoring model are specified in the table below. Environment analysis has sub-components of GHG SCOPE 1, 2, and 3, water policy, air quality, waste management, industry type, energy efficiency, biodiversity, and environmental fines.

Social risk measures are constructed using sub-components, including the gender pay gap, human rights policy, business ethics policy, child labor policy, and others specified in the table below.

Governance sub-components include a diversity of women on Board, anti-bribery policy, and whistle-blower policy, to name a few. Questions to capture these components are expected to provide initial inputs. Then, at specified intervals, the data will be collected to capture improvements in the respective components. Impact and sensitivity analysis is also performed to check which component has positive or negative impacts.

Weights are assigned considering the differences among Manufacturing, IT, and non-IT services. The maximum score is computed to be used as a benchmark for ESG. The actual score will be compared with the maximum score to arrive at a composite score. ESG scores can be found in Table 1.

Table 1. ESG SCORING MODEL FOR SMEs

Parameters	Evaluated Score	Score
1. Environmental Analysis		MAX
GHG SCOPE1 Energy Used [DIRECT EMMISSIONS]		
GHG SCOPE 2 Energy Purchased [INDIRECT EMISSIONS]		
GHG SCOPE 3 [OTHER EMMISSIONS]		
WATER POLICY		
AIR QUALITY		
INDUSTRY TYPE		
WASTE MANAGEMENT		
ENERGY EFFICIENCY		
BIODIVERSITY		
ENVIRONMENTAL FINES		
2. Social Analysis		MAX
Employee turnover% of women in workforce		
PWD		
GENDER PAY GAP		
Hours spent on training		
Employee benefits policies		
Quality assurance policies		
Human rights policies		
Child Labor policies		
Health and safety policies		
Business ethics policies		
3. Governance Analysis		MAX
% of non-executive directors		
Diversity% of women on Board		
% of female executives		
Audit Committee – % of independent directors		
Compensation committee - % of independent directors		
CSR activity linked to ESG		
Executive compensation linked to ESG		
No of years auditor employed		
Whistle blower policy		

(*continued*)

Table 1. (*continued*)

Parameters	Evaluated Score	Score
Anti bribery policy		
Score range	SME evaluation	
90 to 100	1	
80 to 89	2	
70 to 79	3	
60 to 69	4	
50 to 59	5	
40 to 49	6	
30 to 39	7	
<30	8	

Source: Author compilation.

3   Model Architecture

At its core, this web application provides users with the ability to design comprehensive risk models by creating the desired number of input fields necessary for evaluation. These input fields serve as the building blocks of the model, capturing the essential data elements required for accurate analysis. Moreover, the software offers unique features like section assignment, which allows users to categorize and evaluate each risk and performance variable based on different sections. This promotes a structured and systematic assessment of SME risk, enabling a more holistic understanding.

To enhance usability, the software grants users the capability to label fields, providing context and clarity to the risk scoring and evaluation process. Additionally, users can set fixed ranges for the fields, facilitating precise benchmarking and comparison across different risks. Furthermore, users have the flexibility to enable or disable each field as needed, allowing them to focus on the most relevant factors during the evaluation. Behind the scenes, the software utilizes the robust Python Django framework for its backend implementation. Known for its reliability and scalability, Django ensures efficient data processing and handles complex calculations seamlessly, enabling users to interact with the application smoothly.

Complementing the backend, the application's frontend is developed using React, a cutting-edge JavaScript library recognized for its responsive and user-friendly design. The front-end interface ensures a seamless and intuitive experience for users, facilitating efficient model creation and evaluation.

In addition to its modeling capabilities, this web application fosters collaboration with third parties. It allows external entities to fill in the inputs for the created models, encouraging broader participation and diverse perspectives. Furthermore, the software handles the login/signup flow, ensuring secure access to the platform. It also manages the distribution flow of model input requests, facilitating the seamless sharing and dissemination of risk assessment models among stakeholders.

4   Strengths

Segregation of ESG computation for manufacturing and services at first level and then further services sector is disaggregated as IT and Non-IT services sector. This is expected to enhance the specification of components in each E, S, and G that have more relevance, and hence, the quality of computation of scores will be more realistic. Secondly our analysis is based on both secondary data on ESG scores and financial performance and also reconfirmed with the primary survey of ESG practices among select SMEs. Third, strength of our research is preparing a static and dynamic model for ESG score computation that captures the contemporary issues and challenges of data validation and verification for sensitivity and impact analysis.

5   Limitations

The proposed ESG model is specifically designed for Indian SMEs, taking into account the unique economic, regulatory, and cultural factors of the Indian business environment. This tailored approach, while beneficial for Indian SMEs, might not be easily generalizable to SMEs in other countries with different market dynamics, regulatory frameworks, and socio-economic conditions. Collecting the longitudinal data for impact analysis of the same sample is time consuming and incur lot of costs.

6   Conclusions

As this research is work-in-progress, the survey data and estimated Structural Equation Model are still being prepared. However, the authors conducted a pilot study, and results indicated the expected impacts. This proposed model aimed at capturing the Environment, Social and governance (ESG) scores from the published data of listed SMEs in India. Once the input data are captured, based on the allocated weights, the scores for components of ESG separately will be computed by the algorithm. Aggregate ESG score also gets computed in the second stage. Based on the computed score, the rating scorecard will be created as output. Reports can be generated that will help the SMEs to take corrective action where necessary.

Acknowledgments. The initial part of the study received funding from the seed grant of SIRAC, Somaiya Vidyavihar University, Mumbai.

Disclosure of Interests. The authors have no competing interests.

Appendix 1 – Website Links

- Arabesque S-Ray - https://www.arabesque.com/s-ray/
- Bloomberg - https://www.bloomberg.com/professional
- CDP [Carbon Disclosure Project] - https://www.cdp.net/
- Ceres - https://www.ceres.org/

- DJSI [Dow Jones Sustainability Indices] - https://www.spglobal.com/esg/csa/indices/djsi-index-family
- EcoVadis - https://www.ecovadis.com/
- FTSE Russell - https://www.ftserussell.com/
- GRESB [Global ESG Benchmark for Real Assets] - https://gresb.com/
- ISS ESG [Institutional Shareholder Services] - https://www.issgovernance.com/esg/
- ISS-oekom - https://www.iss-oekom.com/
- KPMG - https://home.kpmg/
- Moody's ESG Solutions - https://www.moodys.com/esg-solutions
- MSCI [formerly Morgan Stanley Capital International] - https://www.msci.com/
- Oekom Research - https://www.oekom-research.com/
- PwC - https://www.pwc.com/
- RepRisk - https://www.reprisk.com/
- RobecoSAM - https://www.robecosam.com/
- SASB [Sustainability Accounting Standards Board] - https://www.sasb.org/
- Sustainalytics - https://www.sustainalytics.com/
- Trucost [part of S&P Global] - https://www.trucost.com/
- Vigeo Eiris - https://vigeo-eiris.com/
- World Economic Forum - https://www.weforum.org/

Appendix 2 – Indian SME Classification

In accordance with Indian legislation, SMEs are categorized according to their capital expenditure in Equipment, as well as their yearly turnover. The MSMED Act, 2006, which underwent amendments in 2018 and 2020, establishes the legal structure for categorizing SMEs in India.

   As per the revised classification, effective from July 1, 2020, the definition of SMEs is as follows:

1. Micro Enterprises:
   a. Manufacturing and Service Companies:

      - Investment in equipment - $< ₹1$ Crore
      - Annual revenue: $< ₹5$ crores

2. Small Enterprises:
   a. Manufacturing Company:

      - Investment in Equipment: $₹1$ Crores $< x < ₹10$ Crores
      - Annual revenue: $₹5$ Crores $< x < ₹50$ Crores

   b. Service Company:

      - Investment in Equipment: $₹1$ Crores $< x < ₹10$ Crores
      - Annual revenue: $₹5$ Crores $< x < ₹50$ Crores

3. Medium Company:
   a. Manufacturing Company:

- Investment in Equipment: ₹10 Crores < x < ₹50 Crores
- Annual revenue: ₹50 Crores < x < ₹250 Crores

b. Service Company:

- Investment in Equipment: ₹10 Crores < x < ₹50 Crores
- Annual revenue: ₹50 Crores < x < ₹250 Crores

The categorization is determined by considering both the investment and annual turnover requirements. To be classified under a specific category, an organization must meet both the investment and annual turnover standards.

This categorization aids the government in devising focused policies, programs, and endeavors to bolster and foster the expansion of small and medium-sized enterprises [SMEs] in India. SMEs can take advantage of several perks, including priority sector lending, tax rebates, and faster access to loans and technological improvements, depending on their size and type of operations.

References

1. Bhagwat, R., Sharma, M.K.: Management of information system in Indian SMEs: an exploratory study. Int. J. Enterp. Network Manag. **1**(1), 99–125 (2006)
2. Dincer, B., Dincer, C.: Literature review on the use of technology and information systems in SMEs. Int. J. Acad. Res. Bus. Soc. Sci. **6**(12), 678–684 (2016)
3. Kulkarni, A., Joseph, S., Patil, K.: Role of artificial intelligence in sustainability reporting by leveraging ESG theory into action. In: 2023 international Conference on Advancement in Computation & computer technologies (InCACCT). IEEE (2023)
4. Nulkar, G.: Environmental sustainability practices for SMEs. In: Paul, A.K., Bhattacharyya, D.K., Anand, S. (eds.) Green Initiatives for Business Sustainability and Value Creation, pp. 1–20. IGI Global (2018). https://doi.org/10.4018/978-1-5225-2662-9.ch001
5. Henrich, J., Heine, S.J., Norenzayan, A.: The weirdest people in the world? Behav. Brain Sci. **33**(2–3), 61–83 (2010)
6. Karhade, P., Kathuria, A.: Missing impact of ratings on platform participation in India: a call for research in GREAT domains. Commun. Assoc. Inf. Syst. **47**(1), 19 (2020)
7. Dasgupta, A., Karhade, P., Kathuria, A., Konsynski, B.: Holding space for voices that do not speak: design reform of rating systems for platforms in GREAT economies. In: Proceedings of the Hawaii International Conference on System Sciences (HICCS). Virtual (2021)
8. Karhade, P., Kathuria, A., Dasgupta, A., Malik, O., Konsynski, B.R.: Decolonization of digital platforms: a research agenda for GREAT domains. In: Garimella, A., Karhade, P., Kathuria, A., Liu, X., Xu, J., Zhao, K. (eds.) The Role of e-Business during the Time of Grand Challenges: 19th Workshop on e-Business, WeB 2020, Virtual Event, December 12, 2020, Revised Selected Papers, pp. 51–58. Springer International Publishing, Cham (2021). https://doi.org/10.1007/978-3-030-79454-5_5
9. Celly, N., Kathuria, A., Subramanian, V.: Overview of Indian multinationals. Emerging Indian multinationals: Strategic players in a multipolar world, pp. 54–101 (2016)
10. Khuntia, J., Kathuria, A., Saldanha, T.J., Konsynski, B.R.: Benefits of IT-enabled flexibilities for foreign versus local firms in emerging economies. J. Manag. Inf. Syst. **36**(3), 855–892 (2019)
11. Kathuria, R., Kathuria, N.N., Kathuria, A.: Mutually supportive or trade-offs: an analysis of competitive priorities in the emerging economy of India. J. High Technol. Managem. Res. **29**(2), 227–236 (2018)

12. Cappelli, P.: The India way: How India's Top Business Leaders are Revolutionizing Management. Harvard Business Press (2010)
13. Ning, X., Khuntia, J., Kathuria, A., Karhade. P.: Ownership and management control effects on IT investments: a study of Indian family firms. In: Proceedings of the International Conference on Information Systems (ICIS). Virtual (2020)
14. Gupta, A.: Emergence of Indian multinationals. Technol. Exports **8**(3), 1–12 (2006)
15. Pradhan, J.P., Sauvant, K.P.: Introduction: the rise of Indian multinational enterprises: Revisiting key issues. In: The rise of Indian multinationals: Perspectives on Indian outward foreign direct investment, pp. 1–23. Springer (2010)
16. Kapur, D., Ramamurti, R.: India's emerging competitive advantage in services. Acad. Manag. Perspect. **15**(2), 20–32 (2001)
17. Kumar, A.: Self-selection and the forecasting abilities of female equity analysts. J. Account. Res. **48**(2), 393–435 (2010)
18. Nayak, A.: Indian Multinationals: The Dynamics of Explosive Growth in a Developing Country Context. Springer (2011)
19. Karhade, P., Kathuria, A., Konsynski, B.: When choice matters: assortment and participation for performance on digital platforms. In: Proceedings of the Hawaii International Conference on System Sciences (HICCS). Virtual (2021)
20. Kathuria, A., Karhade, P.P., Konsynski, B.R.: In the realm of hungry ghosts: multi-level theory for supplier participation on digital platforms. J. Manag. Inf. Syst. **37**(2), 396–430 (2020)
21. Khuntia, J., Kathuria, A., Andrade-Rojas, M.G., Saldanha, T., Celly, N.: How foreign and domestic firms differ in leveraging IT-enabled supply chain information integration in BOP markets: the role of supplier and client business collaboration. J. Assoc. Inf. Syst. **22**(3), 6 (2021)
22. Khuntia, J., Saldanha, T., Kathuria, A., Tanniru, M.R.: Digital service flexibility: a conceptual framework and roadmap for digital business transformation. Eur. J. Inform. Syst. **33**(1), 61–79 (2022)
23. Jha, S., Kathuria, A.: How firm age and size influence value creation from cloud computing. In: Proceedings of the International Conference on Information Systems (ICIS). Hyderabad (2023)
24. Kathuria, A., Mann, A., Khuntia, J., Saldanha, T.J., Kauffman, R.J.: A strategic value appropriation path for cloud computing. J. Manag. Inf. Syst. **35**(3), 740–775 (2018)
25. Mann, A., Kathuria, A., Khuntia, J., Saldanha, T.: Cloud-integration and business flexibility: the mediating role of cloud functional capabilities. In: Proceedings of the Americas Conference on Information Systems (AMCIS). San Diego (2016)
26. Jha, S., Chaturvedi, D.: Systematic literature review of cloud computing research between 2010 and 2023. In: Kathuria, A., Karhade, P.P., Zhao, K., Chaturvedi, D. (eds.) Digital Transformation in the Viral Age: 21st Workshop on e-Business, WeB 2022, Copenhagen, Denmark, December 10, 2022, Revised Selected Papers, pp. 64–88. Springer Nature Switzerland, Cham (2024). https://doi.org/10.1007/978-3-031-60003-6_5
27. Sachdeva, A., Kathuria, A., Karhade, P., Ray, S.: How do family businesses embark on digital transformation? a call for future IS research. In: Kathuria, A., Karhade, P.P., Zhao, K., Chaturvedi, D. (eds.) Digital Transformation in the Viral Age: 21st Workshop on e-Business, WeB 2022, Copenhagen, Denmark, December 10, 2022, Revised Selected Papers, pp. 99–118. Springer Nature Switzerland, Cham (2024). https://doi.org/10.1007/978-3-031-60003-6_7
28. Sonpatki, R., Kathuria, A., Sethi, S.: Earnings call transcripts as a source and resource for information systems research. In: Kathuria, A., Karhade, P.P., Zhao, K., Chaturvedi, D. (eds.) Digital Transformation in the Viral Age: 21st Workshop on e-Business, WeB 2022, Copenhagen, Denmark, December 10, 2022, Revised Selected Papers, pp. 38–63. Springer Nature Switzerland, Cham (2024). https://doi.org/10.1007/978-3-031-60003-6_4

29. Andrade-Rojas, M.G., Kathuria, A., Lee, H.-H.: Multilevel synergy of information technology for operational integration: competition networks and operating performance. Product. Operat. Manag. **33**(5), 1116–1141 (2024). https://doi.org/10.1177/10591478241239005

30. Chaturvedi, D., Karhade, P., Kathuria, A., Rai, A., Naik, N.: IT and the Dual Bottom-Line Objective of Rational Social Enterprises. In: Proceedings of the European Conference on Information Systems (ECIS) (2024)

31. Saldanha, T., Kathuria, A., Khuntia, J., Konsynski, B.R.: It's a dangerous business, going out your door: overcoming institutional distances through IS. In: Proceedings of the International Conference on Information Systems (ICIS). Austin (2021)

32. Malik, O., Karhade, P.P., Kathuria, A.: How technology use drives infobesity: an in-depth look at ERP systems. In: Proceedings of the Pacific Asia Conference on Information Systems (PACIS). Virtual (2021)

33. Maji, S.G., Lohia, P.: Environmental, social and governance (ESG) performance and firm performance in India. Soc. Bus. Rev. **18**(1), 175–194 (2023)

34. Lunawat, A., Lunawat, Di.: Do environmental, social, and governance performance impact firm performance? Evidence from Indian firms. Indonesian J. Sustain. Account. Manag. **6**(1), 133–146 (2022). https://doi.org/10.28992/ijsam.v6i1.519

35. Shikha, P., Tuteja, R., Dhingra, S.: Examining the sectoral differences in ESG practices of select companies in india: a comparative testing based on scores. Manage. Accountant J. **57**(8), 73–79 (2022)

36. Clark, G.L., Feiner, A., Viehs, M.: From the stockholder to the stakeholder: How sustainability can drive financial outperformance. SSRN 2508281 (2015)

37. Domanović, V.: The relationship between ESG and financial performance indicators in the public sector: empirical evidence from the Republic of Serbia. Manage.: J. Sustain. Bus. Manage. Solutions Emerg. Econ. **27**(1), 69–80 (2022)

38. Eccles, R.G., Ioannou, I., Serafeim, G.: The impact of corporate sustainability on organizational processes and performance. Manage. Sci. **60**(11), 2835–2857 (2014)

39. Ferrell, A., Liang, H., Renneboog, L.: Socially responsible firms. J. Financ. Econ. **122**(3), 585–606 (2016)

40. Fulton, M., Kahn, B., Sharples, C.: Sustainable investing: Establishing long-term value and performance. SSRN 2222740 (2012)

41. Ge, G., Xiao, X., Li, Z., Dai, Q.: Does ESG performance promote high-quality development of enterprises in China? The mediating role of innovation input. Sustainability **14**(7), 3843 (2022)

42. Henisz, W., Koller, T., Nuttall, R.: Five ways that ESG creates value. McKinsey Q. **4**, 1–12 (2019)

43. Maiso Fontecha, L.: Women on boards. ERA Forum **14**(3), 315–318 (2013). https://doi.org/10.1007/s12027-013-0318-8

44. Sharma, P., Panday, P., Dangwal, R.: Determinants of environmental, social and corporate governance (ESG) disclosure: a study of Indian companies. Int. J. Discl. Gov. **17**(4), 208–217 (2020)

Author Index

© The Editor(s) (if applicable) and The Author(s), under exclusive license
to Springer Nature Switzerland AG 2025
A. Kathuria et al. (Eds.): WeB 2023, LNBIP 525, p. 183, 2025.
https://doi.org/10.1007/978-3-031-74437-2